D0681281

PHRASEBOOK & DICTIONARY

Acknowledgments

Editors Robyn Loughnane, Jodie Martire, Branislava Vladisavljevic, Tracy Whitmey
Production Support Chris Love
Language Writers Anthony Garnaut, Tim Lu
Cover Researcher Naomi Parker

Thanks

James Hardy, Angela Tinson

Published by Lonely Planet Publications Pty Ltd

ABN 36 005 607 983

9th Edition – October 2015
ISBN 978 1 74321 607 1
Text © Lonely Planet 2015
Cover Image Chinese New Year celebrations, Singapore
Maurizio Rellini/4Corners

Printed in China   10 9 8 7 6 5 4 3 2 1

Contact lonelyplanet.com/contact

MIX
Paper from
responsible sources
FSC™ C021741

Look out for the following icons throughout the book:

'Shortcut' Phrase
Easy to remember alternative to the full phrase

Q&A Pair
'Question-and-answer' pair – we suggest a response to the question asked

Look For
Phrases you may see on signs, menus etc

Listen For
Phrases you may hear from officials, locals etc

Language Tip
An insight into the foreign language

Culture Tip
An insight into the local culture

How to read the phrases:

- Coloured words and phrases throughout the book are phonetic guides to help you pronounce the foreign language.
- Lists of phrases with tinted background are options you can choose to complete the phrase above them.

These abbreviations will help you choose the right words and phrases in this book:

a	adjective	n	noun	sg	singular
inf	informal	pl	plural	v	verb
lit	literal	pol	polite		

Contents

PAGE
6

About Mandarin

Learn about Mandarin, build your own sentences and pronounce words correctly.

Introduction 6
Top Phrases 8
Pronunciation 10
Grammar 18

PAGE
31

Travel Phrases

Ready-made phrases for every situation – buy a ticket, book a hotel and much more.

Basics 31

Understanding 32
Numbers & Amounts 34
Time & Dates 38

Practical 43

Transport 44
Border Crossing 61
Directions 63
Accommodation 66
Shopping 78
Communications 88
Money & Banking 94
Business 97

PAGE 199 🍴 **Menu Decoder**
Dishes and ingredients explained –
order with confidence and try new foods.

PAGE 209 📖 **Two-Way Dictionary**
Quick reference vocabulary guide –
3500 words to help you communicate.

INTRO # Mandarin
普通话 Pǔtōnghuà

Who speaks Mandarin?

OFFICIAL LANGUAGE
MAINLAND CHINA
TAIWAN
SINGAPORE

WIDELY UNDERSTOOD
HONG KONG
MACAU
MALAYSIA

Why Bother

With more than one billion speakers worldwide, Mandarin is the most widely spoken language on the planet. How can you miss the chance to communicate with one in seven people on Earth?

Distinctive Sounds

In Mandarin you can change the meaning of a word by raising and lowering the pitch level (tone) on certain syllables. Mandarin has four tones (high, high-rising, high-falling and low falling-rising), plus a fifth, neutral tone.

840 million
Mandarin speakers
in China

one billion
Mandarin speakers
worldwide

Pinyin

Pinyin was officially adopted in 1958 as a way of writing Chinese using the Roman alphabet. Today in Chinese cities you'll see it everywhere: on maps, road and shop signs and in brand names.

Chinese Script

Many of the basic Chinese characters are pictographs (highly stylised pictures of what they represent), but most have a 'meaning' element and a 'sound' element. Each character represents a syllable, and most words consist of two characters.

Chinglish

'Chinglish' (Chinese English) provides many entertaining mistranslations – eg a 'Keep Quiet' notice might instead read 'the subliminal of thought has started while the noisy has stopped'.

Language Family

The term 'Mandarin' refers to one of the seven Chinese dialect groups and is more accurately called Modern Standard Chinese or Pǔtōnghuà 普通话 (literally 'the common dialect'). Close relatives in the Sino-Tibetan family are the other six dialects: Gan, Hakka, Min, Wu, Xiang and Yue.

Must-Know Grammar

Mandarin doesn't have direct equivalents of 'yes' and 'no' used in isolation. Instead, to answer the question affirmatively, repeat the verb used in the question (eg shì 是 – 'be'). For a negative answer, add bù 不 (not) before the verb.

Donations to English

Quite a few – for example, *gung-ho, Japan, ketchup, kung fu, silk, t'ai chi, tea* …

5 **Phrases** to Learn Before You Go

1 **Where would you go for yum cha?**
哪里的早茶好？ Nǎlǐ de zǎochá hǎo?

When in China, make sure you find the right place for what has to be the signature dining experience in Chinatowns the world over.

2 **Please bring a knife and fork.**
请拿一副刀叉来。 Qǐng ná yī fù dāochā lái.

Don't be afraid to ask for cutlery at a restaurant if you haven't quite mastered the art of eating with chopsticks.

3 **Can I get a discount (for the room)?**
这（房间）能打折吗？ Zhè (fángjiān) néng dǎzhé ma?

In China, always bargain for a hotel room – discounts of 10% to 50% off the rack rate are the norm, available by simply asking at reception.

4 **I'd like to hire a bicycle.**
我想租一辆自行车。 Wǒ xiǎng zū yīliàng zìxíngchē.

Bikes are a great option for getting around Chinese cities and tourist sites. They can also be invaluable for exploring the countryside.

5 **Can you write that in Pinyin for me?**
请用拼音写。 Qǐng yòng Pīnyīn xiě.

If you find Chinese script intimidating, Pinyin (the official system for writing Mandarin in the Roman alphabet) is your next best option.

10 Phrases to Sound Like a Local

| Great! | 真棒! | Zhēnbàng! |

| Hey! | 喂! | Wèi! |

| It's OK. | 还行。 | Háixíng. |

| Just a minute. | 等一下。 | Děngyīxià. |

| Maybe. | 有可能。 | Yǒu kěnéng. |

| No problem. | 没事。 | Méishì. |

| No way! | 不可能! | Bù kěnéng! |

| Sure, whatever. | 行,行,行。 | Xíng, xíng, xíng. |

| That's enough! | 够了,够了! | Gòule, gòule! |

| Just joking. | 开玩笑。 | Kāiwánxiào. |

ABOUT MANDARIN

Pronunciation

For speakers of English, the sounds of Mandarin are quite easy to produce, as many of them have equivalents in English. One aspect of the language that may prove a little challenging is the use of tones. In Mandarin you can change the meaning of a word by altering the pitch level (tone) at which it is spoken. See **tones** on page 13 for an explanation of how this works.

The Pinyin System

Pinyin was officially adopted by the Chinese in 1958 as a way of writing Chinese using the Roman alphabet. It provided access to a common language in a vast country with countless dialects, and so played an important role in communication and development. Today in Chinese cities you'll see Pinyin everywhere: on maps, road signs, shop signs and in brand names. Nevertheless, many Chinese can't read Pinyin and its use is very limited in rural areas, so this book includes the Chinese script characters as well.

Pinyin is back by popular demand in this new edition of the Mandarin phrasebook. You'll find it an easy system to use once you've learnt the rules on how to pronounce letters. For example, Pinyin c is pronounced like the 'ts' in 'cats' and Pinyin q is pronounced like the 'ch' in 'cheese'.

For information on the Chinese names of the Roman alphabet letters – useful if, for example, you need to spell out your name on check-in – see the box on page 16.

Mandarin Beijing-style

The pronunciation given in this book is based on 'Beijingese', the dialect of Mandarin spoken in the capital. This is because Modern Standard Chinese is based on the Beijing dialect. You'll be understood throughout China as all Chinese have broad exposure to the official language.

One feature of standard Mandarin that's a reflection of a peculiarly Beijing pronunciation is the addition of an 'r' sound at the end of many words. This 'r' sound is represented in this phrasebook by the character 儿. You won't normally hear this 'r' in other parts of China. Also be aware that outside the capital the sibilant (hissing) sounds 's' and 'z' may not match the patterns of the Beijing standard. Generally speaking, the greater the distance from the capital the more you should expect to hear different pronunciations.

Vowel Sounds

Mandarin vowels are straightforward and you'll notice that there's quite a lot of overlap with English vowel sounds. Be aware that in Pinyin vowels are often pronounced differently depending on the other letters surrounding them, as shown in the table below.

~ PINYIN ~	~ ENGLISH SOUND ~	~ MANDARIN EXAMPLE ~
a (an, ang)	father (fun, sung)	fà (fàn, fǎng)
e (en, eng)	her (broken, Deng)	gě (mèn, fēng)
i (in, ing)	peel (pin, ping)	pí (pǐn, píng)
i (after z, c, or s)	girl	zǐ
i (after zh, ch, sh or r)	like the r in Grrr!	shí
o (ong)	more (Jung)	bó (tóng)
u	tool	shù
ü (and u or un after j, q, x or y)	similar to 'new' pronounced with rounded lips	lǚ (qù, yùn)

Vowel/Consonant Combinations

Mandarin has quite a few diphthongs (vowel sound combinations) and vowel and consonant combinations – when the letters i and u occur before other vowels, they are pronounced 'y' and 'w' respectively. Again, you'll notice that most of these have counterparts in English.

~ PINYIN ~	~ ENGLISH SOUND ~	~ MANDARIN EXAMPLE ~
ai	aisle	zài
ao	now	báo
ei	pay	bèi
ia	yard	jiā
ian	yen	tiān
iang	young	xiǎng
iao	loud	xiǎo
ie	yes	xié
iong	Jung	xiōngdì
iu	yolk	qiú
ou	low	lóu
ua	wah!	guā
uai	why	kuài
uan	one	chuān
uan (after j, q, x or y)	went	yuān
uang	swung	kuàng
ue	you wet	yuè
ui	way	tuǐ
uo	war	huǒ

Consonant Sounds

The consonants should be quite easy for you to get your tongue around, as they'll all be familiar from English.

~ PINYIN ~	~ ENGLISH SOUND ~	~ MANDARIN EXAMPLE ~
b	bit	bāng
c	cats	cè
ch	true	chū
d	dog	dì
f	fun	fēng
g	go	gān
h	hot	hǎi
j	jump	jùn
k	kid	kě
l	lip	lín
m	map	mín
n	no	néng
ng	sing	máng
p	pig	pèi
q	churn	qū
r	run	rì
s	sip	sī
sh	shop	shǎo
t	top	tú
w	win	wàng
y	you	yǒu
x	sheet	xiá
z	lads	zì
zh	gem	zhāo

Tones

Many words in Mandarin appear to have the same basic pronunciation. What distinguishes these 'homophones' is their tonal quality – the raising and lowering of pitch on certain syllables. Mandarin is usually described as having four tones, (numbered first through to fourth), plus a fifth, neutral tone.

Apart from the unmarked neutral tone, Pinyin uses diacritics (symbols) to indicate each tone, appearing above the vowels as shown below.

1ST – HIGH TONE	2ND – HIGH RISING TONE	3RD – LOW FALLING-RISING TONE	4TH – HIGH FALLING TONE
ā	á	ǎ	à

The following table shows how one 'word' ma can have five different meanings which are distinguished by tone only.

~ TONE ~	~ EXAMPLE ~	~ MEANING ~
1st – high	mā	mother
2nd – high rising	má	hemp
3rd – low falling-rising	mǎ	horse
4th – high falling	mà	scold
neutral	ma	question marker

Tones in Mandarin allow for some amusing tone-based tongue twisters. This one uses the example words given above:

Mother rides a horse. The horse is slow. Mother scolds the horse.

妈妈骑马, 马慢, 妈妈骂马。
(lit: mother ride horse, horse slow, mother scold horse)
Māma qí mǎ, mǎ màn, māma mà mǎ.

Bear in mind that tones are not absolute in pitch but are relative to your natural vocal range. So don't feel inhibited – just experiment with the contours of your natural voice. English speakers do this anyway to a small extent. When you pronounce 'What?' you're getting close to a Mandarin high rising tone and when you say 'Damn!' you're approximating a high falling tone.

There's no need to feel daunted by this 'foreign' system. There's nothing obscure or mysterious about tones – over half of the world's languages use them. You might have mixed success in getting your meaning across to start with, but remember that patient repetition is all it takes to learn. Even if your tones are slightly off, the meaning you wish to convey will often be clear from the context. Failing that, you can always point to the word or phrase you're aiming for in this phrasebook.

Tonal Variations

In spoken Mandarin, tones can sometimes vary with context. The most common change occurs when there are two low falling-rising (3rd) tones in sequence – the first one changes to something more like a high rising (2nd) tone, for example:

at least	起码	qǐ mǎ is pronounced as qí mǎ

Another common change occurs when the word bù 不 'no/not' is followed by another high falling tone – in that case it's pronounced as a high rising tone, for example:

incorrect	不对	bù duì is pronounced as bú duì

The common character yī 一 'one' has a couple of tonal variations. It has a high tone when used in isolation, a high rising tone when followed by a high falling tone (as in 一会儿 yīhuìr 'a little while' which is pronounced as yíhuìr), and a high falling tone when followed by any other tone (see the examples on the following page).

ordinary	一般	yībān is pronounced as yìbān
together	一同	yītóng is pronounced as yìtóng
a little	一点儿	yīdiǎnr is pronounced as yìdiǎnr

In our coloured pronunciation guides throughout the book we show the unmodified version of these tones – the ones mentioned first in the examples above – which is the correct style for written Pinyin.

LANGUAGE TIP

Spelling

Most Chinese are familiar with the Latin alphabet through their knowledge of Pinyin and English. If you want to spell out your name in hotels etc, you should follow the Chinese pronunciation of the alphabet in the chart below as you probably won't be understood if you say the letters as in English. Latin letters can be represented with characters denoting the sounds.

A	诶	ēi	N	恩	ēn
B	必	bì	O	呕	ǒ
C	西	xī	P	披	pī
D	弟	dì	Q	酷	kù
E	衣	yī	R	耳	ěr
F	艾付	àifù	S	艾斯	àisī
G	记	jì	T	踢	tī
H	爱耻	àichǐ	U	忧	yōu
I	挨	āi	V	维	wéi
J	宅	zhái	W	大波留	dàbōliù
K	开	kāi	X	埃克斯	āikèsī
L	饿罗	èluó	Y	歪	wāi
M	饿母	èmǔ	Z	再得	zàide

Writing System

Chinese is often described as a language of pictographs. Many of the basic Chinese characters are in fact highly stylised pictures of what they represent, but the majority are compounds of a 'meaning' element and a 'sound' element. Each Chinese character represents a spoken syllable, and most words are comprised of two separate characters.

The bulkiest Chinese dictionaries have some 100,000 characters, but to be able to read a newspaper you 'only' need to know a few thousand. Theoretically, all Chinese dialects use the same writing system and people from all over China should be able to read and understand the characters in the words and phrases in this book. In practice, however, Cantonese adds about 3000 specialised characters and many dialects don't have a written form at all. Note that in this book we've used simplified Chinese characters, along with Pinyin (the official system of writing Chinese using the Roman alphabet) in the pronunciation guides. Simplified Chinese is used in mainland China and has been adopted by Singapore, Malaysia and other Southeast Asian countries (whereas traditional Chinese characters are used in Taiwan, Hong Kong and Macau).

ABOUT MANDARIN PRONUNCIATION

ABOUT MANDARIN

Grammar

This chapter is designed to explain the main grammatical structures you need in order to make your own sentences. Look under each heading for information on functions which these grammatical categories express in a sentence. For example, demonstratives are used for giving instructions, so you'll need them to tell the taxi driver where your hotel is.

Adjectives

Describing People/Things • Comparing People/Things

As in English, words that describe or modify nouns, ie adjectives, come before the noun. Usually, the particle de 的 is placed between an adjective consisting of more than one syllable and the noun.

a big strawberry　　　　很大的草莓
　　　　　　　　　　　　　(lit: very big de strawberry)
　　　　　　　　　　　　　hěn dà de cǎoméi

To compare one thing to another, you insert the word bǐ 比 'compare' between the two objects you wish to compare. The object being compared comes before this term of comparison (which plays the same role as the word 'than' in English).

China is bigger than Australia.	中国比澳大利亚大。(lit: China compare Australia big) Zhōngguó bǐ Àodàlìyà dà.
This one's better than that one.	这个比那个好。(lit: this-one compare that-one good) Zhège bǐ nàge hǎo.

Articles

Naming People/Things

One thing that you won't have to bother about when putting together a Mandarin sentence are the equivalents for the English articles 'a/an' and 'the': Mandarin has no articles at all. In Mandarin the context indicates whether something indefinite (corresponding to 'a/an') or definite (corresponding to 'the') is meant.

Be

Describing People/Things • Making Statements

Although Mandarin has an equivalent of the English verb 'to be', shì 是, it's not used in quite the same way as in English. The verb shì is only ever used with a noun, as in this sentence:

I'm a doctor.	我是医生。(lit: I am doctor) Wǒ shì yīshēng.

The verb shì is dropped altogether with adjectives – a Mandarin speaker says literally 'I thirsty' not 'I am thirsty'. (The particle le 了 indicates a change of state, ie 'I was not thirsty but I am thirsty now'.)

I'm thirsty.	我渴了。(lit: I thirsty-le) Wǒ kěle.

Classifiers/Counters

Counting People/Things

In Mandarin, when you talk about quantities of any noun, it's important to put a classifier or 'measure word' between the number and the noun. This concept is not entirely alien to English. We talk about 'two pairs of pants', 'two bunches of bananas', 'two sheets of paper' etc. The system is a bit more highly developed in Mandarin and classifiers must be used every time numbers are used with a noun. Different classifiers are used for different kinds of objects, taking into account their shape, or a general category (based on Chinese logic) to which they belong. The full list of classifiers is too long to give here but these are the most common ones:

– COMMON CLASSIFIERS/COUNTERS –

generic classifier	个	ge
big things (mountains, buildings, etc)	座	zuò
chairs, knives, teapots, tools or implements with handles	把	bǎ
drinking receptacles (cups, glasses etc)	杯	bēi
flat things (tickets, stamps etc)	张	zhāng
flowers (the blossoms, not the plants)	朵	duǒ
long things (fish, snakes, rivers etc)	条	tiáo
nondescript animals (dogs, cats etc)	只	zhī
people	位	wèi
trees	棵	kē
vehicles	辆	liàng

Don't be intimidated by this system. The good news is that you can get by just using the 'generic' (all-purpose) classifier ge 个. It may not be strictly correct, and you may find people gently correcting you, but you'll be understood.

Classifiers are used with the demonstrative pronouns 'this' (zhè 这) and 'that' (nà 那) and between pronouns and nouns (see also **demonstratives**).

this week	这个星期 (lit: this-ge week)	
	zhège xīngqī	
that woman	那位女士 (lit: that-wèi woman)	
	nàwèi nǚshì	

Conjunctions

Asking Questions • Making Statements

To connect two words or phrases, place a joining word (or conjunction) between the two elements. The most common conjunctions are 'and' hé 和 and 'or' háishì 还是.

I like rice and noodles.	我喜欢米饭和面条。
	(lit: I like rice and noodle)
	Wǒ xǐhuān mǐfàn hé miàntiáo.
Are you American or English?	你是美国人还是英国人?
	(lit: you are America person or England person)
	Nǐ shì Měiguó rén háishì Yīngguó rén?

Demonstratives

Giving Instructions • Indicating Location • Pointing Things Out

To point things out in Mandarin you can use the following expressions (known as demonstrative pronouns).

that	那	nà
this	这	zhè

The demonstratives can be combined with the generic classifier ge to give the following expressions:

that one	那个	nàge
this one	这个	zhège

Have

Possessing

To say that you have something in Mandarin, you use the word yǒu 有.

I have a ticket.	我有票。(lit: I have ticket)
	Wǒ yǒu piào.

To say that you don't have something, just place the particle méi 没 'not' before yǒu.

I don't have a ticket.	我没有票。(lit: I not-have ticket)
	Wǒ méiyǒu piào.

Imperatives

Giving Instructions

To express a command in Mandarin you place emphasis on the verb. A positive command is formed by just stating the verb in a commanding tone:

Leave!	滚！(lit: roll (away))
	Gǔn!

A negative command is formed by putting 'not want' bùyào 不要 (sometimes abbreviated to bié 别) before a verb. There's also a polite form of a negative command – akin to saying 'needn't' in English. In this case 'not need' bùyòng 不用 is placed before the verb. This has an abbreviated form béng 甭.

not want	不要 bùyào
not want **(abbreviated form)**	别 bié
not need	不用 bùyòng
not need **(abbreviated form)**	甭 béng
Don't shout!	不要喊！ (lit: not-want shout) Bùyào hǎn!
No need for formalities!	不用客气！ (lit: not-need politeness) Bùyòng kèqi!

Need

Making Statements

The verb 'need' is expressed by the compound word xūyào 需要, which includes the word yào 要 'to want'.

I need to go to the toilet.	我需要上厕所。 (lit: I need mount toilet) Wǒ xūyào shàng cèsuǒ.

As with all negatives, to say you don't need something, just place bù 不 'not' before xūyào.

I don't need money.	我不需要钱。 (lit: I not-need money) Wǒ bù xūyào qián.

Negatives

Negating

To form negative sentences in Mandarin, you place the particle bù 不 'not' before the verb or adjective that you wish to negate. (Note that when bù appears before a word with the same tone, it changes to a rising tone.)

I'm not hungry.	我不饿。(lit: I not hungry) Wǒ bù è.
It's not OK.	不行。(lit: not passable) Bù xíng.

The particle méi 没 is used instead of bù to make a negative of 'have' and also when the sentence refers to past events. Here méi can be thought of as the equivalent of the English 'haven't'.

I haven't eaten lunch.	我没吃午饭。(lit: I méi eat lunch) Wǒ méi chī wǔfàn.

Nouns

Naming People/Things

Nouns are usually compounds made up of two words (characters). Nouns have only one fixed form and they don't show gender (masculine, feminine etc) or number (singular or plural).

lunch/lunches	午饭 (lit: noon-rice) wǔfàn

Particles

Doing Things • Making Statements

Mandarin makes use of a number of particles. These are 'function words' which don't necessarily have a definable meaning of their own but serve a grammatical function in a sentence.

The particle le 了, for example, when attached to a verb indicates that an action has been completed.

Personal Pronouns

Making Statements • Naming People/Things

Pronouns in Mandarin don't change their form according to whether they are the subject (performer of the action, eg 'I') or object (undergoer of the action, eg 'me') of a sentence. Note that whilst 'he/him', 'she/her' and 'it' are represented by different characters they are pronounced in exactly the same way.

~ PERSONAL PRONOUNS ~

I/me	我	wǒ
you sg	你	nǐ
he/him	他	
she/her	她	tā
it	它	
we/us	我们	wǒmen
you pl	你们	nǐmen
they/them	他们	tāmen

You'll notice that plural pronouns are formed with the simple addition of men 们 to the singular forms.

Possessives

Possessing

To show possession, simply add de 的 to a personal pronoun, then follow it with the object or person that's possessed.

my passport	我的护照 (lit: I-de passport)
	wǒde hùzhào
your child	你的孩子 (lit: you-de child)
	nǐde háizi

ABOUT MANDARIN

GRAMMAR

~ POSSESSIVE PRONOUNS ~

my/mine	我的	wǒde
your(s) sg	你的	nǐde
his/her(s)/its	他的/她的/它的	tāde
our(s)	我们的	wǒmende
your(s) pl	你们的	nǐmende
their(s)	他们的	tāmende

Prepositions

Giving Instructions • Indicating Location/Time •
Pointing Things Out

A time relationship between a noun and another word in the
sentence is reflected by the use of prepositions of time.

I watched TV before eating.	我吃饭前看了电视。 (lit: I ate-rice before (that I) watch-le television) Wǒ chī fàn qián kànle diànshì.

~ PREPOSITIONS ~

after	后	hòu
before	前	qián
until	到	dào

Location is indicated by the word zài 在, which literally means
'is located'. The word zài is used with almost all prepositions
of place (words such as 'opposite' or 'behind' which indicate a
spatial relationship). Note that zài comes before, but not necessarily next to, the preposition in the sentence.

The bank is opposite the hotel.	银行在酒店对面。 (lit: bank is-located hotel opposite) Yínháng zài jiǔdiàn duìmiàn.

You're sitting behind me.	你坐在我的后边。
	(lit: you sit is-located my behind)
	Nǐ zuò zài wǒde hòubian.

Questions

Asking Questions • Answering Questions • Negating

The most common way of forming questions in Mandarin is simply to put the particle ma 吗 at the end of a statement.

He's going to see the Great Wall.	他要去长城。
	(lit: he going Great-Wall)
	Tā yào qù Chángchéng.
Is he going to see the Great Wall?	他要去长城吗?
	(lit: he going Great-Wall ma)
	Tā yào qù Chángchéng ma?

~ QUESTION WORDS ~

who	谁	shéi/shuí
which	哪个	nǎge
what	什么	shénme
where	哪儿	nǎr
how	怎么	zènme
when	什么时候	shénme shíhòu

Mandarin doesn't have words that correspond directly to 'yes' and 'no' when used in isolation. To answer a question in the affirmative, you simply repeat the verb used in the question. To answer a question in the negative, place the negative particle bù 不 'not' before the repeated verb. The particle ma 吗 is a question marker (see above for an explanation).

Are you hungry?	你饿吗?
	(lit: you hungry ma)
	Nǐ è ma?

| **Yes.** | 饿。(lit: hungry)
È. |
| **No.** | 不饿。(lit: not hungry)
Bù è. |

You're likely to hear the word duì 对 as an equivalent to 'yes' as well. It literally means 'correct'. In the negative, this becomes bù duì 不对 ('not correct').

Are you leaving tomorrow?	你明天走吗? (lit: you tomorrow leave ma) Nǐ míngtiān zǒu ma?
Yes, I am.	对,明天走。 (lit: correct tomorrow leave) Duì, míngtiān zǒu.
No, I'm leaving today.	不(对),我今天走。 (lit: not (correct) I today leave) Bù (duì), wǒ jīntiān zǒu.

Verbs

Doing Things • Expressing Past/Future Actions

Mandarin verbs have fixed forms – they don't change form according to who or what the subject (the person or thing performing the action of the verb) is, as they do in English, eg 'I am' vs 'you are' etc. Only one form of each verb exists, so there's no need to memorise long lists of varying verb forms as you may have had to do when learning other languages. To see how this works, look at the following table for the verb chī 吃 'eat'.

~ PRESENT TENSE ~

I eat a meal.	我吃饭。 Wǒ chī fàn.	We eat a meal.	我们吃饭。 Wǒmen chī fàn.
You eat a meal. sg	你吃饭。 Nǐ chī fàn.	You eat a meal. pl	你们吃饭。 Nǐmen chī fàn.
He/She eats a meal.	他/她/它吃饭。 Tā chī fàn.	They eat a meal.	他们吃饭。 Tāmen chī fàn.

Not only do Mandarin verbs not change according to who or what is performing the action of the verb, but they also remain fixed regardless of when the action took place, ie they don't change according to tense. The time something takes place can be, instead, conveyed by the use of adverbs of time (words that modify a verb and indicate time). So to talk about things in the past, present or future, you place an adverb of time – such as 'a while ago' (yǐqián 以前), 'last year' (qùnián 去年), 'now' (xiànzài 现在), 'tomorrow' (míngtiān 明天) or '(this) morning' (zǎoshàng 早上) – before the verb to specify when the action took place.

Tomorrow I'm going to Beijing.	我明天去北京。 (lit: I tomorrow go Beijing) Wǒ míngtiān qù Běijīng.
Now she lives in Beijing.	她现在住在北京。 (lit: she now live in Beijing) Tā xiànzài zhù zài Běijīng.
In the morning I didn't eat anything.	我早上什么也没吃。 (lit: I morning anything not eat) Wǒ zǎoshàng shénme yě méi chī.

Past Tense Alternative Forms

The particle le 了 can be added to a verb to indicate that an action has been completed. In many cases this is just like the past tense in English.

He has gone to Shanghai.	他去了上海。 (lit: he go-le Shanghai) Tā qùle Shànghǎi.

For things that have happened some time in the unspecified past, the particle guò 过 is used.

He's been to Taiwan.	他去过台湾。 (lit: he go-guò Taiwan) Tā qùguò Táiwān.

Future Tense Alternative Forms

The verb yào 要 'want', when placed before a verb, can be used to indicate the future. For less certain future actions, it can be replaced with xiǎng 想 'feel like' or dǎsuàn 打算 'plan to'.

I'm going to Hong Kong.	我要去香港。 (lit: I want go Hong-Kong) Wǒ yào qù Xiānggǎng.
I feel like going to Hong Kong.	我想去香港。 (lit: I feel-like go Hong-Kong) Wǒ xiǎng qù Xiānggǎng.
I'm planning to go to Hong Kong.	我打算去香港。 (lit: I plan-to go Hong-Kong) Wǒ dǎsuàn qù Xiānggǎng.

Want

Making Statements

The equivalent of 'to want' in Mandarin is the verb xiǎng 想. To say you don't want something, just place the negative particle bù 不 'not' before xiǎng.

I want to eat.	我想吃。(lit: I want eat) Wǒ xiǎng chī.
I don't want to eat.	我不想吃。(lit: I not want eat) Wǒ bù xiǎng chī.

Word Order

Making Statements

Word order of basic sentences in Mandarin is the same as in English, ie subject–verb–object.

I eat a meal.	我吃饭。(lit: I eat rice) Wǒ chī fàn.

Basics

Understanding

KEY PHRASES

Do you speak English?	你会说英文吗?	Nǐ huìshuō Yīngwén ma?
I don't understand.	我不明白。	Wǒ bù míngbai.
What does ... mean?	……是什么意思?	... shì shénme yìsi?

Q Do you speak English?
你会说英文吗?
Nǐ huìshuō Yīngwén ma?

Q Does anyone speak English?
有谁会说英文吗?
Yǒu shéi huìshuō Yīngwén ma?

A I speak a little.
我会说一点。
Wǒ huìshuō yīdiǎn.

Q Do you understand?
你明白吗?
Nǐ míngbai ma?

A I understand.
明白。
Míngbai.

A I don't understand.
我不明白。
Wǒ bù míngbai.

Could you write that in Pinyin for me?
请用拼音写。
Qǐng yòng Pīnyīn xiě.

Could you write that down for me in Chinese characters?
请用中文写下来。
Qǐng yòng Zhōngwén xiěxiàlái.

Please point to the phrase in this book.
请指出书上的范句。
Qǐng zhǐchū shūshàng de fànjù.

BASICS

UNDERSTANDING

LANGUAGE TIP

Tones & Tongue Twisters

Mandarin is a tonal language (see **pronunciation**, page 13). While this can be a challenge for the foreign visitor to China, it's also a source of mirth for locals who happen upon outsiders. For example, foreign diplomats (wàijiāoguān 外交官) often introduce themselves in Mandarin as wāijiāoguǎn 歪胶管 (lit: 'rubber U-bend pipes').

Fortunately, not only foreigners have trouble with Mandarin pronunciation. Southerners, particularly Cantonese speakers, are notorious in Beijing for getting their sibilants (the sounds 's', 'sh' and 'z') mixed up. Practice with tongue twisters, such as this one:

四十四只石狮子是死的。 sìshísì zhī shíshīzi shì sǐde
Forty-four stone lions
are dead.

What does ... mean?	……是什么意思？ ... shì shénme yìsi?
How do you pronounce this?	怎么念这个？ Zěnme niàn zhège?
How do you write ...?	怎么写...？ Zěnme xiě ……?
Could you please repeat that?	请你再说一遍？ Qǐng nǐ zài shuō yībiàn?
Could you please write it down?	请你写下来？ Qǐng nǐ xiěxiàlái?
Could you please speak more slowly?	请你慢一点说？ Qǐng nǐ màn yīdiǎn shuō?
✂ **Slowly, please.**	请慢点。　　Qǐng màndiǎn.

Numbers & Amounts

KEY PHRASES

How much?	多少?	Duōshǎo?
a few	一些	yìxiē
many	许多	xǔduō

Cardinal Numbers

Numbers in Mandarin are easy to learn. Multiples of 10 are made by stating the multiple followed by 10 – so 20 is literally 'two ten'. Two is a tricky number, generally pronounced èr unless it's joined with a classifier, in which case it will be pronounced liǎng (see **classifiers/counters**, page 20).

0	零	líng
1	一	yī
2	二/两	èr/liǎng
3	三	sān
4	四	sì
5	五	wǔ
6	六	liù
7	七	qī
8	八	bā
9	九	jiǔ
10	十	shí
11	十一	shíyī
12	十二	shí'èr
13	十三	shísān

14	十四	shísì
15	十五	shíwǔ
16	十六	shíliù
17	十七	shíqī
18	十八	shíbā
19	十九	shíjiǔ
20	二十	èrshí
21	二十一	èrshíyī
22	二十二	èrshí'èr
30	三十	sānshí
40	四十	sìshí
50	五十	wǔshí
60	六十	liùshí
70	七十	qīshí
80	八十	bāshí
90	九十	jiǔshí
100	一百	yībǎi
101	一百零一	yībǎi língyī
103	一百零三	yībǎi língsān
113	一百一十三	yībǎi yīshísān
122	一百二十二	yībǎi èrshí'èr
200	两百	liǎngbǎi
1000	一千	yīqiān
10,000	一万	yīwàn
1,000,000	一百万	yībǎiwàn
100,000,000	一亿	yīyì

Ordinal Numbers

1st	第一	dìyī
2nd	第二	dì'èr
3rd	第三	dìsān
4th	第四	dìsì
5th	第五	dìwǔ

Fractions

a quarter	四分之一	sìfēnzhīyī
a third	三分之一	sānfēnzhīyī
a half	一半	yíbàn
three-quarters	四分之三	sìfēnzhīsān
all	所有	suǒyǒu
none	没有	méiyǒu

Classifiers/Counters

The following are the most commonly used classifiers or 'counters', used when counting things (see also **grammar**, page 20).

generic classifier	个	gè
flat things (tickets, stamps etc)	张	zhāng
long things (fish, snakes, rivers etc)	条	tiáo
people	位	wèi
nondescript animals (dogs, chickens etc)	只	zhī
big things (buildings, mountains, etc)	座	zuò

Amounts

China uses a complete set of words for imperial weights and measures. In mainland China (though not in Hong Kong or Taiwan) these have all been recast in metric mould, so that foreign visitors are, at most, required to multiply by two to yield a standard international metric measure.

How much?	多少?
	Duōshǎo?

How many?	几个?
	Jǐge?

Please give me ...	请给我⋯⋯
	Qǐng gěi wǒ ...

(50) grams	(50)克	(wǔshí) kè
one Chinese ounce (50 grams)	1两	yīliǎng
one *jīn* (about 0.6kg)	1斤	yījīn
(two) *jīn*	(两)斤	(liǎng) jīn
a kilo	1公斤	yìgōngjīn
(two) kilos	(两)公斤	(liǎng) gōngjīn
a few	一些	yìxiē
less	少一点	shǎoyìdiǎn
a little	一小块	yīxiǎokuài
a lot	好多	hǎoduō
many	许多	xǔduō
more	多一些	duōyìxiē
some	一些	yìxiē

BASICS

TIME & DATES

Time & Dates

What time is it?	现在几点钟?	Xiànzài jǐdiǎn zhōng?
At what time?	什么时候?	Shénme shíhòu?
What date is it?	今天几号?	Jīntiān jǐhào?

Telling the Time

Telling the time in Mandarin is simple. To express a time on the hour, simply give the hour followed by diǎn 点 'point' and zhōng 钟 'clock'. For all other times, give the hour followed by diǎn 点 and then the number of minutes past the hour followed by the word fēn 分 'minutes'. For example, the literal translation of 'quarter past 10' is '10 points 15 minutes'.

Q What time is it?	现在几点钟?	Xiànzài jǐdiǎn zhōng?
A It's (10) o'clock.	(十)点钟。	(Shí)diǎn zhōng.
Five past (10).	(十)点零五分。	(Shí)diǎn língwǔfēn.
Quarter past (10).	(十)点十五分。	(Shí)diǎn shíwǔfēn.
Half past (10).	(十)点三十分。	(Shí)diǎn sānshífēn.
Twenty to (11).	(十)点四十分。	(Shí)diǎn sìshífēn.
Quarter to (11).	(十)点四十五分。	(Shí)diǎn sìshíwǔfēn.
am	早上	zǎoshàng
pm	晚上	wǎnshàng

Q **At what time (does it start)?**	什么时候 （开始）？	Shénme shíhòu (kāishǐ)?
A **(It starts) At 10.**	十点钟 （开始）。	Shídiǎn zhōng (kāishǐ).
A **It starts at (9:57pm).**	（晚上9点57分) 开始。	(Wǎnshàng jiǔdiǎn wǔshíqīfēn) kāishǐ.

Time during the day is divided up slightly differently in Mandarin than it is in English. In China, meals are considered so important that parts of the day are defined as falling before or after meals.

afternoon	下午	xiàwǔ
dawn (before breakfast)	黎明	límíng
day	白天	báitiān
early morning (after breakfast)	早上	zǎoshàng
evening (after dinner)	晚上	wǎnshàng
late morning (before lunch)	上午	shàngwǔ
midday (lunch & siesta time)	中午	zhōngwǔ
night (sleep time)	深夜	shēnyè
sunrise	日出	rìchū
sunset	日落	rìluò

The Calendar

The days of the week follow a simple pattern in Mandarin. The word 'week' (xīngqī 星期) comes first, followed by numbers one to six (starting with Monday). Sunday is the 'day of heaven' – the day of worship in the Western world, from which the seven-day week was introduced.

BASICS   TIME & DATES

Monday	星期一	xīngqī yī
Tuesday	星期二	xīngqī èr
Wednesday	星期三	xīngqī sān
Thursday	星期四	xīngqī sì
Friday	星期五	xīngqī wǔ
Saturday	星期六	xīngqī liù
Sunday	星期天	xīngqī tiān

As with the days of the week, the months in Mandarin follow a system of pure logic. The word 'month' (yuè 月) is prefaced with the numbers one to twelve starting with January. The Western-style calendar was only imported in China some 200 years ago and, as this new calendar was felt to be foreign enough, further complicated linguistic terms were thought best avoided.

January	一月	yīyuè
February	二月	èryuè
March	三月	sānyuè
April	四月	sìyuè
May	五月	wǔyuè
June	六月	liùyuè
July	七月	qīyuè
August	八月	bāyuè
September	九月	jiǔyuè
October	十月	shíyuè
November	十一月	shíyīyuè
December	十二月	shí'èryuè

| Q What date is it? | 今天几号？ | Jīntiān jǐhào? |
| A It's (18 October). | （十月十八号）。 | (Shíyuè shíbā hào). |

spring	春天	chūntiān
summer	夏天	xiàtiān
autumn	秋天	qiūtiān
winter	冬天	dōngtiān

Present

now	现在	xiànzài
today	今天	jīntiān
this morning (after breakfast)	这个早上	zhège zǎoshàng
this morning (before lunch)	这个上午	zhège shàngwǔ
this afternoon	这个下午	zhège xiàwǔ
tonight	今天晚上	jīntiān wǎnshàng
this week	这个星期	zhège xīngqī
this month	这个月	zhège yuè
this year	今年	jīnnián

Past

(three days) ago	(三天) 以前	(sāntiān) yǐqián
day before yesterday	前天	qiántiān
yesterday morning (after breakfast)	昨天早上	zuótiān zǎoshàng
yesterday morning (before lunch)	昨天上午	zuótiān shàngwǔ
yesterday afternoon	昨天下午	zuótiān xiàwǔ
yesterday evening (after dinner)	昨天晚上	zuótiān wǎnshàng

last night	昨天晚上	zuótiān wǎnshàng
last week	上个星期	shàngge xīngqī
last month	上个月	shàngge yuè
last year	去年	qùnián
since (May)	从(五月)以来	cóng (wǔyuè) yǐlái

Future

in (six days)	(六天)以后	(liùtiān) yǐhòu
day after tomorrow	后天	hòutiān
tomorrow morning (after breakfast)	明天早上	míngtiān zǎoshàng
tomorrow morning (before lunch)	明天上午	míngtiān shàngwǔ
tomorrow afternoon	明天下午	míngtiān xiàwǔ
tomorrow evening (after dinner)	明天晚上	míngtiān wǎnshàng
next week	下个星期	xiàge xīngqī
next month	下个月	xiàge yuè
next year	明年	míngnián
until (June)	到(六月)为止	dào (liùyuè) wéizhǐ

Practical

Transport

KEY PHRASES

When's the next bus?	下一趟车 几点走?	Xià yītàng chē jǐdiǎn zǒu?
A ticket to ...	一张到…… 的票。	Yìzhāng dào ... de piào.
Can you tell me when we get to ...?	到了…… 请叫我, 好吗?	Dàole ... qǐng jiào wǒ, hǎoma?
Please take me to this address.	请带我到 这个地址。	Qǐng dàiwǒ dào zhège dìzhǐ.
I'd like to hire a self-drive car.	我想租 一辆轿车。	Wǒ xiǎng zū yīliàng jiàochē.

Getting Around

Which ... goes to (Hangzhou)?	到(杭州) 坐什么……? Dào (Hángzhōu) zuò shénme ... ?
Is this the ... to (Hangzhou)?	这个……到 (杭州)去吗? Zhège ... dào (Hángzhōu) qù ma?

boat	船	chuán
bus	车	chē
plane	飞机	fēijī
train	火车	huǒchē

When's the first (bus)?	首班(车)几点走? Shǒubān (chē) jǐdiǎn zǒu?
When's the last (bus)?	末班(车)几点走? Mòbān (chē) jǐdiǎn zǒu?
When's the next (bus)?	下一趟(车)几点走? Xià yītàng (chē) jǐdiǎn zǒu?
What time does it leave?	几点钟出发? Jǐdiǎnzhōng chūfā?
What time does it get to (Hangzhou)?	几点钟到(杭州)? Jǐdiǎnzhōng dào (Hángzhōu)?
How long will it be delayed?	推迟多久? Tuīchí duōjiǔ?
Is this seat free?	这儿有人吗? Zhèr yǒurén ma?
✂ **Is it free?**	有人? Yǒurén?
That's my seat.	那是我的座。 Nà shì wǒde zuò.
Can you tell me when we get to (Hangzhou)?	到了(杭州)请叫我, 好吗? Dàole (Hángzhōu) qǐng jiào wǒ, hǎoma?
I want to get off here.	我想这儿下车。 Wǒ xiǎng zhèr xiàchē.
How long do we stop here?	在这里停多久? Zài zhèlǐ tíng duōjiǔ?
Are you waiting for more people?	还等人吗? Háiděng rén ma?
Can you take us around the city, please?	请带我到城里转一圈。 Qǐng dàiwǒ dào chénglǐ zhuàn yī quān.
How many people can ride on this?	车上能坐多少人? Chēshàng néngzuò duōshǎo rén?

Buying Tickets

On Chinese trains there are no classes, instead the options are: hard seat (yìngzuò 硬座) or soft seat (ruǎnzuò 软座) and hard sleeper (yìngwò 硬卧) or soft sleeper (ruǎnwò 软卧). Classes do exist on long-distance boat services in China.

Where do I buy a ticket?	哪里买票？	
	Nǎli mǎi piào?	
Do I need to book?	要先订票吗？	
	Yào xiān dìngpiào ma?	
A ... ticket to (Dalian).	一张到(大连)的……票。	
	Yìzhāng dào (Dàlián) de ... piào.	

1st-class	头等	tóuděng
2nd-class	二等	èrděng
3rd-class	三等	sānděng
child's	儿童	értóng
one-way	单程	dānchéng
return	来回	láihuí
student	学生	xuéshēng

I want to travel by ... train.	我想坐……	
	Wǒxiǎng zuò ...	

direct	直达车	zhídá chē
express	特快车	tèkuài chē
fast	快车	kuài chē
local	普通车	pǔtōng chē
slow	慢车	màn chē

I'd like a hard-seat ticket.	我想买硬座票。	
	Wǒ xiǎng mǎi yìngzuò piào.	
I'd like a soft-seat ticket.	我想买软座票。	
	Wǒ xiǎng mǎi ruǎnzuò piào.	

Buying a Ticket

 ### What time is the next ...?
下一趟……几点走?
Xià yītàng ... jǐdiǎn zǒu?

 boat
船
chuán

bus
车
chē

train
火车
huǒchē

 ### One ... ticket, please.
一张到的……票。
Yīzhāng dào de ... piào.

 one-way
单程
dānchéng

 return
来回
láihuí

 ### I'd like a/an ... seat.
我想要……的座位。
Wǒ xiǎngyào ... de zuòwèi.

aisle
靠走廊
kào zǒuláng

  window
靠窗户
kào chuānghu

 ### Which platform does it depart from?
这列火车从几号站台出发?
Zhèliè huǒchē cóng jǐhào zhàntái chūfā?

CULTURE TIP

Buying Tickets

Buying tickets in China can be something of a nightmare for foreigners as seemingly interminable queues snake towards small ticket windows. The etiquette of not pushing or cutting in simply doesn't apply. One approach to overcoming these difficulties might be to find someone who wants to practise their English to help you, and cut to the front of the queue on your behalf. Ask around with these phrases:

Do you speak English?	你会说英文吗?
	Nǐ huìshuō Yīngwén ma?
Does anyone speak English?	有谁会说英文吗?
	Yǒu shéi huìshuō Yīngwén ma?

Even better, you could bring a slip of paper, prepared in advance, with your ticket details written down in Mandarin script to post through the ticket window. Use these phrases to help devise your message:

Could you write down the ticket details in Chinese characters for me?	请帮我用中文写车票的详细情况。
	Qǐng bāngwǒ yòng zhōngwén xiě chēpiào de xiángxì qíngkuàng.
Could you write down (Dalian) in Chinese characters?	请帮我用中文写下(大连)。
	Qǐng bāngwǒ yòng zhōngwén xiěxià (Dàlián).

With this in hand, you should be assured of obtaining your ticket to ride as long as you can fight your way to the front of the queue.

I'd like a hard-sleeper berth.	我想坐硬卧。 Wǒ xiǎng zuò yìngwò.
I'd like a soft-sleeper berth.	我想坐软卧。 Wǒ xiǎng zuò ruǎnwò.
I'd like a bottom berth.	我想睡下铺。 Wǒ xiǎng shuì xiàpù.
I'd like a middle berth.	我想睡中铺。 Wǒ xiǎng shuì zhōngpù.
I'd like an upper berth.	我想睡上铺。 Wǒ xiǎng shuì shàngpù.
I'd like an aisle seat.	我想要靠走廊的座位。 Wǒ xiǎngyào kào zǒuláng de zuòwèi.
I'd like a window seat.	我想要靠窗户的座位。 Wǒ xiǎngyào kào chuānghu de zuòwèi.
I'd like a (non)smoking seat.	我想要(不)吸烟的座位。 Wǒ xiǎngyào (bù) xīyān de zuòwèi.

PRACTICAL TRANSPORT

🔊 LISTEN FOR

到哪里?	Dào nǎli?	Where to?
旅行社	lǚxíng shè	travel agent
满	mǎn	full
取消	qǔxiāo	cancelled
时刻表	shíkè biǎo	timetable
售票窗	shòupiào chuāng	ticket window
晚点	wǎndiǎn	delayed
站台	zhàntái	platform
这个/那个	zhège/nàge	this one/that one

| Is there (a) ...? | 有……吗？ |
| | Yǒu ... ma? |

air-conditioning	空调	kōngtiáo
blanket	毛毯	máotǎn
sick bag	呕吐袋	ǒutù dài
toilet	厕所	cèsuǒ

| I'd like to cancel my ticket. | 我想退票。 |
| | Wǒ xiǎng tuì piào. |

| I'd like to change my ticket. | 我想改票。 |
| | Wǒ xiǎng gǎi piào. |

| I'd like to confirm my ticket. | 我想确定票。 |
| | Wǒ xiǎng quèdìng piào. |

| Can I get a stand-by ticket? | 能买站台票吗？ |
| | Néng mǎi zhàntái piào ma? |

| How much is a (soft-seat) fare to ...? | 到……的(软座票)多少钱？ |
| | Dào ... de (ruǎnzuò piào) duōshǎo qián? |

| How long does the trip take? | 几个小时到站？ |
| | Jǐge xiǎoshí dàozhàn? |

| Is it a direct route? | 是直达的吗？ |
| | Shì zhídáde ma? |

| What time should I check in? | 什么时候检票？ |
| | Shénme shíhou jiǎnpiào? |

| Which platform does it depart from? | 这列火车从几号站台出发？ |
| | Zhèliè huǒchē cóng jǐhào zhàntái chūfā? |

Luggage

| Can I have some coins/ tokens? | 我想换一些硬币。 |
| | Wǒ xiǎng huàn yīxiē yìngbì. |

PRACTICAL TRANSPORT

🔊 LISTEN FOR

超重行李	chāozhòng xíngli	excess baggage
手提行李	shǒutí xíngli	carry-on baggage
行李票	xíngli piào	ticket

Where can I find ...?		……在哪里？ ... zài nǎli?
the baggage claim	取行李	Qǔ xíngli
the left-luggage office	行李寄存处	Xíngli jìcún chù
a luggage locker	行李 暂存箱	Xíngli zàncúnxiāng
a trolley	小推车	Xiǎo tuīchē

My luggage has been damaged.	我的行李被摔坏了。 Wǒde xíngli bèi shuāihuài le.
My luggage has been lost.	我的行李被弄丢了。 Wǒde xíngli bèi nòngdiū le.
My luggage has been stolen.	我的行李被偷走了。 Wǒde xíngli bèi tōuzǒu le.

Plane

Where does flight (BJ8) depart?	(BJ8) 飞机在哪里起飞？ (BJ8)* bā fēijī zài nǎli qǐfēi?
Where does flight (BJ8) arrive?	(BJ8) 飞机在哪里抵达？ (BJ8)* bā fēijī zài nǎli dǐdá?

* use English pronunciation for flight number

Where's ...?	……在哪里？ ... zài nǎli?	
the airport shuttle	机场巴士	Jīchǎng bāshì
arrivals	入境口	Rùjìng kǒu
departures	出境口	Chūjìng kǒu
the duty-free shop	免税店	Miǎnshuì diàn
gate (8)	(8号)登机口	(Bā hào) dēngjī kǒu

Bus & Coach

How often do buses come?	多久来一班车？ Duōjiǔ lái yībān chē?	
Which number bus goes to (Harbin)?	到(哈尔滨)坐几号车？ Dào (Hā'ěrbīn) zuò jǐhào chē?	
Does it stop at (Harbin)?	在(哈尔滨)能下车吗？ Zài (Hā'ěrbīn) néng xià chē ma?	
What's the next stop?	下一站是哪里？ Xiàyī zhàn shì nǎli?	
I'd like to get off at (Harbin).	我在(哈尔滨)下车。 Wǒ zài (Hā'ěrbīn) xià chē.	
Please stop pushing!	不要挤！ Bùyào jǐ!	
boarding pass	登机牌 dēngjī pái	
passport	护照 hùzhào	
transfer	转机 zhuǎnjī	
transit	过境 guòjìng	

city a	市内 shìnèi
city bus	市内大巴 shìnèi dàbā
intercity a	长途 chángtú
intercity bus	长途车 chángtú chē
local a	本地 běndì
private-run bus	小巴 xiǎobā
sleeper bus	卧铺长途车 wòpù chángtú chē

Subway & Train

Which platform for the ... train?	……列火车到 几号站台? ... liè huǒchē dào jǐhào zhàntái?
What station is this?	这是哪个站? Zhè shì nǎge zhàn?
What's the next station?	下一站是哪里? Xiàyī zhàn shì nǎli?
Does it stop at (Tianjin)?	在(天津)能下车吗? Zài (Tiānjīn) néng xià chē ma?
Do I need to change?	需要换车吗? Xūyào huànchē ma?
Which line goes to ...?	到……坐哪条线? Dào ... zuò nǎtiáo xiàn?
How many stops to ...?	到……坐几站? Dào ... zuò jǐzhàn?

Is it direct?	是直达车吗？ Shì zhítōng chē ma?
Is it express?	是特快车吗？ Shì tèkuài chē ma?
Which carriage is for dining?	吃饭到几号车厢？ Chīfàn dào jǐhào chēxiāng?
Which carriage has the soft-sleeper seats?	软卧在几号车厢？ Ruǎnwò zài jǐhào chēxiāng?

Boat

How long is the trip to ...?	几个小时到……？ Jǐge xiǎoshí dào ...?
Is there a fast boat?	有快艇吗？ Yǒu kuàitǐng ma?
How long will we stop here?	这里停留多久？ Zhèlǐ tíngliú duōjiǔ?
What time should we be back on board?	几点钟再上船？ Jǐdiǎnzhōng zài shàngchuán?
Is there karaoke on the boat?	船上有卡拉OK吗？ Chuánshàng yǒu kǎlā ōkèi ma?
Are there life jackets on the boat?	船上有救生衣吗？ Chuánshàng yǒu jiùshēng yī ma?
Is there a toilet on the boat?	船上有厕所吗？ Chuánshàng yǒu cèsuǒ ma?
What's the sea like today?	今天海浪大不大？ Jīntiān hǎilàng dàbùdà?
I feel seasick.	我有点恶心。 Wǒ yǒudiǎn ěxin.

cabin	船舱 chuáncāng
captain	船长 chuánzhǎng
deck	甲板 jiǎbǎn
ferry	渡船 dùchuán
lifeboat	救生艇 jiùshēng tǐng
life jacket	救生衣 jiùshēng yī
yacht	帆船 fānchuán

GETTY CITY COMMISSION/LONELY PLANET IMAGES ©

还等人吗?
Háiděng rén ma?
Are you waiting for more people?

Hire Car & Taxi

I'd like a taxi to depart at (9am).	我要订一辆出租车，(早上9点钟)出发。 Wǒ yào dìng yīliàng chūzū chē, (zǎoshàng jiǔ diǎn zhōng) chūfā.
I'd like a taxi now.	我要订一辆出租车，现在。 Wǒ yào dìng yīliàng chūzū chē, xiànzài.
I'd like a taxi tomorrow.	我要订一辆出租车，明天。 Wǒ yào dìng yīliàng chūzū chē, míngtiān.
Where's the taxi rank?	在哪里打出租车？ Zài nǎli dǎ chūzū chē?
Is this taxi free?	这出租车有人吗？ Zhè chūzū chē yǒurén ma?
✂ Is it free?	有人？ Yǒurén?
Please put the meter on.	请打表。 Qǐng dǎbiǎo.
(The Great Wall), if that's OK.	(长城)，好吗？ (Chángchéng), hǎo ma?
How much is it to (the Great Wall)?	到(长城)多少钱？ Dào (Chángchéng) duōshǎo qián?
I'd like to hire a self-drive car.	我想租一辆轿车。 Wǒ xiǎng zū yīliàng jiàochē.
I'd like to hire a car with a driver.	我想包一辆车。 Wǒ xiǎng bāo yīliàng chē.
How much to hire a car with a driver to ...?	包一辆车到……多少钱？ Bāo yīliàng chē dào ... duōshǎo qián?

Is it air-conditioned?	有空调吗？ Yǒu kōngtiáo ma?
Is petrol included?	包括汽油吗？ Bāokuò qìyóu ma?
Are tolls included?	包括路费吗？ Bāokuò lùfèi ma?
Could I have a receipt for the toll?	请给我发票。 Qǐng gěi wǒ fāpiào.
How much is it (to this address)?	(到这个地址) 多少钱？ (Dào zhège dìzhǐ) duōshǎo qián?
Please take me to (this address).	请带我到 (这个地址)。 Qǐng dàiwǒ dào (zhège dìzhǐ).
✂ **To ...**	去…… Qù ...
Something's wrong with your meter.	你的表有问题。 Nǐde biǎo yǒuwèntí.
I'll write down your licence number and call 110.	我会记下你的车号， 打110。 Wǒ huì jìxià nǐde chēhào, dǎ yāo yāo líng.
Where are we going?	我们到哪儿去？ Wǒmen dào nǎr qù?
Please slow down.	请慢点开。 Qǐng màndiǎn kāi.
Please stop here.	请在这儿停。 Qǐng zài zhèr tíng.
Please wait here.	请在这儿等。 Qǐng zài zhèr děng.

Bicycle

Bicycles are an excellent method for getting around Chinese cities or patrolling tourist sites. In a country with more than 300 million bikes, some organisation is required to prevent cycle chaos. In cities you'll be required to park your bike at a bicycle parking lot known as a cúnchēchù 存车处 overseen by an attendant.

I'd like my bicycle repaired.	我想修这辆自行车。 Wǒ xiǎng xiū zhèliàng zìxíng chē.
I'd like to buy a bicycle.	我想买一辆自行车。 Wǒ xiǎng mai yīliàng zìxíng chē.
I'd like to hire a bicycle.	我想租一辆自行车。 Wǒ xiǎng zū yīliàng zìxíngchē.
I'd like a mountain bike.	我要辆山地车。 Wǒ yàoliàng shāndì chē.
I'd like a racing bike.	我要辆赛车。 Wǒ yàoliàng sài chē.
I'd like a second-hand bike.	我要辆二手车。 Wǒ yàoliàng èrshǒu chē.
How much is it per day?	一天多少钱？ Yī tiān duōshǎo qián?
How much is it per hour?	一小时多少钱？ Yī xiǎoshí duōshǎo qián?
Do I have to pay a deposit?	要给押金吗？ Yào gěi yājīn ma?
How much is the deposit?	押金多少？ Yājīn duōshǎo?
I have a puncture.	车胎被戳破了。 Chētāi bèi chuōpò le.

Could you pump up my tyres, please?	能帮我打气吗? Néng bāngwǒ dǎqì ma?
How much to have this repaired?	修这些多少钱? Xiū zhèxiē duōshǎo qián?
Where's the bicycle parking lot?	存车处在哪儿? Cúnchēchù zài nǎr?
My bike's been stolen.	我的自行车被偷走了。 Wǒde zìxíngchē bèi tōu zǒu le

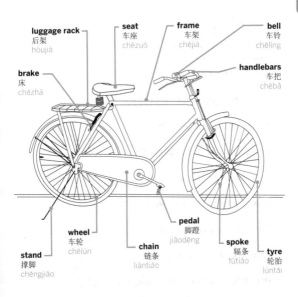

luggage rack
后架
hòujià

seat
车座
chēzuò

frame
车架
chējià

bell
车铃
chēlíng

brake
床
chēzhá

handlebars
车把
chēbǎ

wheel
车轮
chēlún

stand
撑脚
chēngjiǎo

chain
链条
liàntiáo

pedal
脚蹬
jiǎodēng

spoke
辐条
fútiáo

tyre
轮胎
lúntāi

PRACTICAL TRANSPORT

CULTURE TIP **Chinese Dynasties**

The abbreviations BCE and CE stand for 'Before Common Era' and 'Common Era' and are equivalent to the terms BC and AD.

Xia dynasty (2070–1600BCE)
夏朝
Xiàcháo

Shang dynasty (1600–1046BCE)
商朝
Shāngcháo

Zhou dynasty (1046–256BCE)
周朝
Zhōucháo

Spring and Autumn period (770–476BCE)
春秋时期
Chūnqiū shíqī

Warring States period (475–221BCE)
战国时期
Zhànguó shíqī

Qin dynasty (221–207BCE)
秦朝
Qíncháo

Han dynasty (206BCE–220CE)
汉朝
Hàncháo

Tang dynasty (618–907CE)
唐朝
Tángcháo

Song dynasty (960–1279CE)
宋朝
Sòngcháo

Yuan dynasty (1279–1368)
元朝
Yuáncháo

Ming dynasty (1368–1644)
明朝
Míngcháo

Qing dynasty (1644–1911)
清朝
Qīngcháo

Republic of China (1911–1949)
民国时期
Mínguó shíqī

People's Republic (1949–present)
解放后
Jiěfàng hòu

Border Crossing

KEY PHRASES

I'm here for ... days.	我要住……天。	Wǒ yào zhù ... tiān.
I'm staying at ...	我住……	Wǒ zhù ...
I have nothing to declare.	我没有东西申报。	Wǒ méiyǒu dōngxi shēnbào.

Passport Control

I'm ...	我是……来的。 Wǒ shì ... láide.

in transit	过境	guòjìng
on business	出差	chūchāi
on holiday	度假	dùjià
on a student visa	持学生签证	chí xuéshēng qiānzhèng

I'm here for (three) days.	我要住(三)天。 Wǒ yào zhù (sān) tiān.
I'm here for (three) weeks.	我要住(三)个星期。 Wǒ yào zhù (sān)ge xīngqī.
I'm here for (three) months.	我要住(三)个月。 Wǒ yào zhù (sān)ge yuè.
I'm going to (Beijing).	我到(北京)去。 Wǒ dào (Běijīng) qù.
I'm staying at (the Pujiang Hotel).	我住(浦江宾馆)。 Wǒ zhù (Pǔjiāng Bīnguǎn).

PRACTICAL BORDER CROSSING

 LISTEN FOR

一家	yījiā	family
团体	tuántǐ	group
护照	hùzhào	passport
签证	qiānzhèng	visa

The children are on this passport.	孩子在这个护照上。
	Háizi zài zhège hùzhào shàng.
My visa is in order.	我的签证办好了。
	Wǒde qiānzhèng bànhǎole.
Do I have to pay extra for that?	这样要加钱吗？
	Zhèyàng yào jiāqián ma?

Customs

I have nothing to declare.	我没有东西申报。
	Wǒ méiyǒu dōngxi shēnbào.
I have something to declare.	我有东西申报。
	Wǒ yǒu dōngxi shēnbào.
Do I have to declare this?	这个要申报吗？
	Zhège yào shēnbào ma?
I didn't know I had to declare it.	我不知道这个要申报。
	Wǒ bù zhīdào zhège yào shēnbào.

LOOK FOR

一海关	hǎiguān	Customs
免税	miǎnshuì	Duty Free
入境	rùjìng	Immigration
护照检查	hùzhào jiǎnchá	Passport Control
检疫	jiǎnyì	Quarantine

Directions

KEY PHRASES

Where's ...?	……在哪儿?	... zài nǎr?
What's the address?	什么地址?	Shénme dìzhǐ?
How far is it?	有多远?	Yǒu duō yuǎn?

What's the address?	什么地址? Shénme dìzhǐ?
❓ **Where's (a bank)?**	(银行) 在哪儿? (Yínháng) zài nǎr?
💬 **It's ...**	在…… Zài ...
It's straight ahead.	一直往前。 Yīzhí wǎngqián.
It's close.	离这儿不远。 Lí zhèr bù yuǎn.
Turn at the corner.	在拐角拐弯。 Zài guǎijiǎo guǎiwān.
Turn at the intersection.	在十字路口拐弯。 Zài shízì lùkǒu guǎiwān.
Turn at the traffic lights.	在红绿灯拐弯。 Zài hónglǜdēng guǎiwān.
Turn towards the left.	往左拐。 Wǎng zuǒ guǎi.
Turn towards the right.	往右拐。 Wǎng yòu guǎi.

🔊 LISTEN FOR

……的对面	... de duìmiàn	opposite ...
……的前面	... de qiánmian	in front of ...
……的后面	... de hòumian	behind ...
……附近	... fùjìn	near ...
拐角	guǎijiǎo	on the corner
那里	nàli	there
……旁边	... pángbiān	next to ...
这里	zhèli	here

How do I get there?	怎么走？ Zěnme zǒu?
How far is it?	有多远？ Yǒu duō yuǎn?
Can you show me on the map where I am?	请帮我找我在 地图上的位置。 Qǐng bāngwǒ zhǎo wǒ zài dìtú shàng de wèizhi.
Can you show me on the map where it is?	请帮我找它在 地图上的位置。 Qǐng bāngwǒ zhǎo tā zài dìtú shàng de wèizhi.
by bus	坐车去 zuòchē qù
by subway	坐地铁去 zuò dìtiě qù
by taxi	打车去 dǎchē qù
by train	坐火车去 zuò huǒchē qù
on foot	走路去 zǒulù qù

north	北 běi
south	南 nán
east	东 dōng
west	西 xī

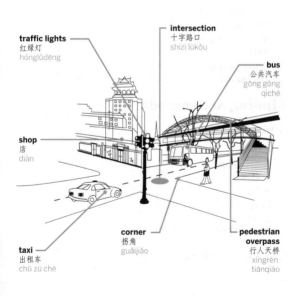

traffic lights
红绿灯
hónglǜdēng

intersection
十字路口
shízì lùkǒu

bus
公共汽车
gōng gòng qìchē

shop
店
diàn

corner
拐角
guǎijiǎo

pedestrian overpass
行人天桥
xíngrén tiānqiáo

taxi
出租车
chū zū chē

Accommodation

KEY PHRASES

Where's a hotel?	哪里有酒店?	Nǎli yǒu jiǔdiàn?
Do you have a double room?	有没有套房?	Yǒuméiyǒu tào fáng?
How much is it per night?	每晚多少钱?	Měi wǎn duōshǎo qián?
When's breakfast served?	几点钟吃早饭?	Jǐdiǎn zhōng chī zǎofàn?
What time is checkout?	几点钟退房?	Jǐdiǎnzhōng tuìfáng?

Finding Accommodation

Where's a ...?	哪里有……?	
	Nǎli yǒu ...?	

guesthouse	宾馆	bīnguǎn
hostel	招待所	zhāodàisuǒ
hotel	酒店	jiǔdiàn
luxury hotel	高级酒店	gāojí jiǔdiàn
university dormitory	学校招待所	xuéxiào zhāodàisuǒ

For addresses, see **directions**, page 63.

Can you recommend somewhere ...?	你能推荐一个…… 的地方住吗?	Nǐ néng tuījiàn yīge ... de dìfang zhù ma?

cheap	便宜	piányi
good	好	hǎo
luxurious	舒服	shūfu
nearby	比较近	bǐjiào jìn
romantic	有情调	yǒu qíngdiào

Booking Ahead & Checking In

Can foreigners stay here?	外国人能住这里吗?	Wàiguó rén néng zhù zhèlǐ ma?
I'll arrange it with the PSB.	我到公安局跟他们协商。	Wǒ dào gōng'ānjú gēn tāmen xiéshāng.
I'd like to book a room, please.	我想订房间。	Wǒ xiǎng dìng fángjiān.
✂ Are there rooms?	有空房吗?	Yǒu kōngfáng ma?
I have a reservation.	我有预订。	Wǒ yǒu yùdìng.
For (three) nights.	住(三)天。	Zhù (sān) tiān.
For (three) weeks.	住(三)个星期。	Zhù (sān)ge xīngqī.
From (2 July) to (6 July).	从(7月2号)到(7月6号)。	Cóng (qīyuè èrhào) dào (qīyuè liùhào).
Do you have a room with a bathroom?	有带浴室的房间吗?	Yǒu dài yùshì de fángjiān ma?

PRACTICAL ACCOMMODATION

住几天?	Zhù jǐtiān?	How many nights?
护照	hùzhào	passport
住满	zhùmǎn	full
前台	qiántái	reception
钥匙	yàoshi	key

Do you have a double room?	有没有套房？ Yǒuméiyǒu tào fáng?
Do you have a single room?	有没有单人房？ Yǒuméiyǒu dānrén fáng?
Do you have a twin room?	有没有双人房？ Yǒuméiyǒu shuāngrén fáng?
Can I see the room?	能看房间吗？ Néng kàn fángjiān ma?
I'll take it.	我订这间。 Wǒ dìng zhèjiān.
I won't take it.	我不要。 Wǒ bùyào.
How much is it per night?	每晚多少钱？ Měi wǎn duōshǎo qián?
How much is it per person?	每人多少钱？ Měi rén duōshǎo qián?
How much is it per week?	每星期多少钱？ Měi xīngqī duōshǎo qián?
Is breakfast included?	早餐包括在内吗？ Zǎocān bāokuò zàinèi ma?
Do I need to pay upfront?	预先付钱吗？ Yùxiān fù qián ma?
Do you give student discounts?	学生可以打折吗？ Xuéshēng kěyǐ dǎzhé ma?

For methods of payment, see **money & banking**, page 94.

Finding a Room

 Do you have a ... room?
有没有……房？
Yǒuméiyǒu ... fáng?

 double
套
tào

single
单人
dānrén

 How much is it per ...?
每……多少钱？
Měi ... duōshǎo qián?

 night
晚
wǎn

person
人
rén

 Is breakfast included?
早餐包括在内吗？
Zǎocān bāokuò zàinèi ma?

 Can I see the room?
能看房间吗？
Néng kàn fángjiān ma?

 I'll take it.
我订这间。
Wǒ dìng zhèjiān.

 I won't take it.
我不要。
Wǒ bùyào.

🔍 LOOK FOR

浴室	Yù shì	Bathroom
入口	Rù kǒu	Entry
出口	Chū kǒu	Exit
女	Nǚ	Female
男	Nán	Male
前台	Qiántái	Reception

Requests & Queries

When is breakfast served?	几点钟吃早饭？ Jǐdiǎn zhōng chī zǎofàn?
Where is breakfast served?	在哪里吃早饭？ Zài nǎli chī zǎofàn?
Please wake me at (7am).	(早上七点钟) 请叫醒我。 (Zǎoshàng qīdiǎnzhōng) qǐng jiàoxǐng wǒ.
Is there hot water all day?	全天有热水吗？ Quántiān yǒu rèshuǐ ma?
Is there heating?	有暖气吗？ Yǒu nuǎnqì ma?
What times does the heating come on?	暖气几点钟开？ Nuǎnqì jǐdiǎnzhōng kāi?
What times does the hot water come on?	热水几点钟开？ Rèshuǐ jǐdiǎnzhōng kāi?
Can I use the kitchen?	能用一下厨房吗？ Néng yòng yī xià chúfáng ma?
Can I use the laundry?	能用一下洗衣房吗？ Néng yòng yī xià xǐyīfáng ma?
Can I use the telephone?	能用一下电话吗？ Néng yòng yī xià diànhuà ma?

| **Do you have a/an ...?** | 有没有……？ |
| | Yǒuméiyǒu ...? |

elevator	电梯	diàntī
laundry service	洗衣服务	xǐyī fúwù
message board	信息栏	xìnxī lán
safe	保险箱	bǎoxiǎn xiāng
swimming pool	游泳池	yóuyǒng chí

| **Do you arrange tours here?** | 你们能安排旅行团吗？ |
| | Nǐmen néng ānpái lǚxíng tuán ma? |

| **Do you change money here?** | 你们能换钱吗？ |
| | Nǐmen néng huànqián ma? |

| **Could I have ..., please?** | 能不能给我……？ |
| | Néngbùnéng gěi wǒ ...? |

an extra blanket	多一条毛毯	duō yītiáo máotǎn
my key	房间钥匙	fángjiān yàoshi
a mosquito net	一顶蚊帐	yīdǐng wénzhàng
a receipt	发票	fāpiào
some soap	一块肥皂	yīkuài féizào
a towel	一块毛巾	yīkuài máojīn

| **Is there a message for me?** | 有人给我留言吗？ |
| | Yǒu rén gěi wǒ liúyán ma? |

| **Can I leave a message for someone?** | 我能留个条吗？ |
| | Wǒ néng liú ge tiáo ma? |

| **I'm locked out of my room.** | 我进不了房间。 |
| | Wǒ jìnbùliǎo fángjiān. |

Complaints

The room's too ...		房间太……了。 Fángjiān tài ... le.
bright	亮	liàng
cold	冷	lěng
dark	暗	àn
expensive	贵	guì
noisy	吵	chǎo
small	小	xiǎo

The ... doesn't work.		……有毛病。 ... yǒu máobìng.
air-conditioning	空调	Kōngtiáo
fan	电风扇	Diànfēngshàn
light	电灯	Diàndēng
shower	淋浴头	Línyù tóu
tap (faucet)	水龙头	Shuǐlóngtóu
toilet	厕所	Cèsuǒ

I saw a big rat in my room.	我房间里有一个大老鼠。 Wǒ fángjiānlǐ yǒu yīge dà lǎoshǔ.
I saw cockroaches in my room.	我房间里有蟑螂。 Wǒ fángjiānlǐ yǒu zhāngláng.
I saw mice in my room.	我房间里有耗子。 Wǒ fángjiānlǐ yǒu hàozi.
Can I get an extra (blanket)?	我能多拿一条(毛毯)吗? Wǒ néng duōná yītiáo (máotǎn) ma?
This (pillow) isn't clean.	这个(枕头)有点脏。 Zhège (zhěntou) yǒudiǎn zāng.

Answering the Door

Who is it?	是谁？ Shì shéi?
Just a moment.	等一下。 Děng yī xià.
Come in.	请进。 Qǐng jìn.
Come back later, please.	请过一会儿再来。 Qǐng guòyīhuìr zài lái.

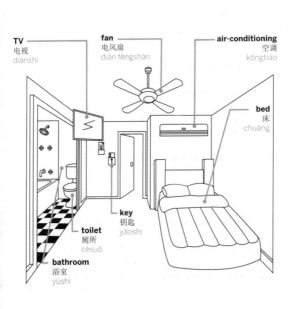

TV
电视
diànshì

fan
电风扇
diàn fēngshàn

air-conditioning
空调
kōngtiáo

bed
床
chuáng

key
钥匙
yàoshi

toilet
厕所
cèsuǒ

bathroom
浴室
yùshì

Checking Out

What time is checkout?	几点钟退房？ Jǐdiǎnzhōng tuìfáng?
Can I have a late checkout?	我能晚点退房吗？ Wǒ néng wǎndiǎn tuìfáng ma?
Can you call a taxi for me (for 11am)?	请帮我订一辆 （早上十一点的）车。 Qǐng bāng wǒ dìng yīliàng (zǎoshàng shíyīdiǎn de) chē.
I'm leaving now.	我现在走。 Wǒ xiànzài zǒu.
Can I leave my bags here?	能放一下行李吗？ Néng fàngyīxià xíngli ma?
There's a mistake in the bill.	帐单上有问题。 Zhàngdān shàng yǒu wèntí.
What's that charge for?	这项是什么？ Zhè xiàng shì shénme?
I had a great stay, thank you.	我在这儿住得很开心，谢谢。 Wǒ zài zhèr zhùde hěn kāixīn, xièxie.
I'll recommend it to my friends.	我会给朋友推荐这个地方。 Wǒ huì gěi péngyou tuījiàn zhège dìfang.
I'll be back in (three) days.	我过（三）天再回来。 Wǒ guò (sān) tiān zài huílái.
I'll be back on (Tuesday).	我下个（星期二）再回来。 Wǒ xiàge (xīngqī èr) zài huílái.
Could I have my deposit, please?	我想拿回我的押金。 Wǒ xiǎng náhuí wǒde yājīn.
Could I have my passport, please?	我想拿回我的护照。 Wǒ xiǎng náhuí wǒde hùzhào.

| Could I have my valuables, please? | 我想拿回我的贵重物品。
Wǒ xiǎng náhuí wǒde guìzhòng wùpǐn. |

Camping

Where can we spend the night?	晚上我们住哪里？ Wǎnshang wǒmen zhù nǎli?
Can we camp here?	我们能在这里露营吗？ Wǒmen néng zài zhèlǐ lùyíng ma?
Can we light a fire here?	能在这里生火吗？ Néng zài zhèlǐ shēnghuǒ ma?
Is it safe to sleep in this place?	住这里安全吗？ Zhù zhèlǐ ānquán ma?

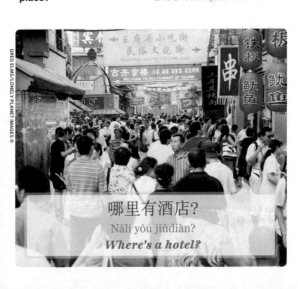

哪里有酒店？
Nǎli yǒu jiǔdiàn?
Where's a hotel?

PRACTICAL ACCOMMODATION

Renting

I'm here about the ... for rent.	我是租……来的。 Wǒ shì zū ... lái de.
Do you have a/an ... for rent?	你有……出租吗? Nǐyǒu ... chūzū ma?

apartment	公寓	gōngyù
house (basic)	房子	fángzi
room	房间	fángjiān
villa (luxurious)	别墅	biéshù

furnished	带家具的 dài jiājù de
partly furnished	带部分家具的 dài bùfen jiājù de
unfurnished	不带家具的 bù dài jiājù de

Staying with Locals

Can I stay at your place?	我能在你家住吗? Wǒ néng zài nǐ jiā zhù ma?
Is there anything I can do to help?	有什么事能帮你吗? Yǒu shénme shì néng bāng nǐ ma?
I have my own mattress.	我带了自己的褥子。 Wǒ dàile zìjǐ de rùzi.
I have my own sleeping bag.	我带了自己的睡袋。 Wǒ dàile zìjǐ de shuìdài.
Can I bring anything for the meal?	我能带一些吃的来吗? Wǒ néng dài yīxiē chī de lái ma?

PRACTICAL ACCOMMODATION

CULTURE TIP **Thanking Hosts**
Food has great significance in Chinese culture.
If you're staying in a Chinese home or have just been invited to share a meal, the surest way to gladden the hearts of your hosts is to heartily express your appreciation of their culinary prowess. Here are two handy phrases:

The food was delicious!	真好吃！ Zhēn hǎochī!
My stomach is very happy.	吃的真饱。 Chīde zhēn bǎo.

In return, you can expect to hear this constant encouragement from your hosts to overindulge yourself:

Eat up!	多吃一点！ Duō chī yīdiǎn!

For more dining-related phrases, see **eating out**, page 176.

Can I do the dishes?	我能帮你洗盘子吗？ Wǒ néng bāng nǐ xǐ pánzi ma?
Thanks for your hospitality.	谢谢你的款待。 Xièxie nǐ de kuǎndài.

Shopping

KEY PHRASES

I'd like to buy ...	我想买……	Wǒ xiǎng mǎi ...
Can I look at it?	我能看看吗？	Wǒ néng kànkan ma?
Can I try it on?	能穿上试试吗？	Néng chuān shàng shìshi ma?
How much is it?	多少钱？	Duōshǎo qián?
That's too expensive.	太贵了。	Tàiguì le.

Looking for ...

Where's a/an ...?	……在哪儿？	... zài nǎr?

antique shop	古董市场	Gǔdǒng shìchǎng
market	市场	Shìchǎng
shopping centre	商场	Shāngchǎng
supermarket	超市	Chāoshì

Where can I buy (a padlock)?	哪里能买到(锁)？
	Nǎli néng mǎidào (suǒ)?

For phrases on directions, see **directions**, page 63.

Making a Purchase

I'm just looking.	我先看看。
	Wǒ xiān kànkan.

I'd like to buy (an adaptor plug).	我想买(一个插座)。 Wǒ xiǎng mǎi (yīge chāzuò).
How much is it?	多少钱? Duōshǎo qián?
Can I look at it?	我能看看吗? Wǒ néng kànkan ma?
Please write down the price.	请把价钱写下来。 Qǐng bǎ jiàqián xiěxià lái.
Do you have any others?	有没有别的? Yǒuméiyǒu biéde?
Do you accept credit cards?	你们收信用卡吗? Nǐmen shōu xìnyòng kǎ ma?
Do you accept debit cards?	你们收借记卡吗? Nǐmen shōu jièjìkǎ ma?
Do you accept travellers cheques?	你们收旅行支票吗? Nǐmen shōu lǚxíng zhīpiào ma?
Can I have a bag, please?	请给我一个袋子。 Qǐng gěi wǒ yīge dàizi.
Can I have a receipt, please?	请给我发票。 Qǐng gěi wǒ fāpiào.
✂ Receipt, please.	发票,谢谢。 Fāpiào, xièxie.
Could I have it wrapped?	能包装一下吗? Néng bāozhuāng yīxià ma?
Does it have a guarantee?	有保修期吗? Yǒu bǎoxiūqī ma?
Can I have it sent overseas?	你能寄到国外吗? Nǐ néng jìdàoguówài ma?
Will I be allowed to take this out of the country?	我能带出境吗? Wǒ néng dài chūjìng ma?
Can you order one for me?	能帮我定购一个吗? Néng bāngwǒ dìnggòuyīge ma?

Can I pick it up later?	过一会儿来拿，好吗？ Guò yīhuìr lái ná, hǎo ma?
It's faulty.	有毛病。 Yǒu máobìng.
This item is a fake.	这是假货。 Zhèshì jiǎhuò.
I don't want to pay the full price.	请帮我打个折扣。 Qǐng bāngwǒdǎ ge zhékòu.
I'd like my change, please.	可以找零钱吗？ Kěyǐ zhǎo língqián ma?
I'd like a refund, please.	可以退钱吗？ Kěyǐ tuì qián ma?
I'd like to return this, please.	可以退换这个吗？ Kěyǐ tuìhuàn zhège ma?

Bargaining

You're kidding!	开什么玩笑！ Kāi shénme wánxiào!
That's too expensive.	太贵了。 Tàiguì le.
Can you lower the price?	能便宜一点吗？ Néng piányi yīdiǎn ma?
Do you have something cheaper?	有便宜一点的吗？ Yǒu piányi yīdiàn de ma?
I'll give you (five kuai).	给你（五块）钱。 Gěinǐ (wǔkuài) qián.
That's my final offer.	就给这么多。 Jiù gěi zhème duō.

Books & Reading

Is there an English-language bookshop?	附近有英文书店吗？ Fùjìn yǒu Yīngwén shūdiàn ma?

Making a Purchase

I'd like to buy ...
我想买……
Wǒ xiǎng mǎi ...

How much is it?
多少钱？
Duōshǎo qián?

— OR —

Can you write down the price?
请把价钱写下来。
Qǐng bǎ jiàqián xiěxià lái.

Do you accept credit cards?
你们收信用卡吗？
Nǐmen shōu xìnyòng kǎ ma?

Could I have a ..., please?
请给我……
Qǐng gěi wǒ ...

 receipt
发票
fāpiào

 bag
一个袋子
yīge dàizi

🔊 LISTEN FOR

实惠	shíhuì	a bargain
大甩卖	dàshuǎimài	grand sale
打折扣	dǎ zhékòu	on special
真宰人	zhēn zǎirén	a rip-off
砍价	kǎnjià	to bargain

Is there an English-language section?	附近有英文书吗？ Fùjìn yǒu Yīngwén shū ma?
Do you have a book by (Jin Yong)?	有没有(金庸)的书？ Yǒuméiyǒu (Jīn Yōng) de shū?
Do you have an entertainment guide?	有没有娱乐指南？ Yǒuméiyǒu yúlè zhǐnán?
I'd like a ...	我想买…… Wǒ xiǎng mǎi ...

copy of the *China Daily*	一份中国日报	yīfèn Zhōngguó Rìbào
dictionary	一本词典	yīběn cídiǎn
newspaper (in English)	一张(英文)报纸	yīzhāng (Yīngwén) bàozhǐ
notepad	一本笔记本	yīběn bǐjìběn

Can you recommend a book to me?	你能给我推荐一本好书吗？ Nǐ néng gěi wǒ tuījiàn yīběn hǎo shū ma?
Do you have Lonely Planet guidebooks?	有没有孤独星球出版社的旅行指南书？ Yǒuméiyǒu Gūdú Xīngqiú chūbǎnshède lǚxíng zhǐnán shū?

CULTURE TIP

Chinese Writers

China has a rich literary tradition. Unfortunately, unless would-be readers master the language, most of it is inaccessible to foreigners. Much of the Chinese literary heritage (particularly poetry) is untranslatable, although scholars persevere. However, some 20th century Chinese classics are available in translation. Look out for the works of literati such as Shen Congwen, Wang Shuo, Lao She, Ba Jin, Feng Jicai and Gao Xingjian.

Clothes

My size is ...	我穿……号。 Wǒ chuān ... hào.

(40)	(40)	(sìshí)
extra large	特大	tèdà
large	大	dà
medium	中	zhōng
small	小	xiǎo

Can I try it on?	能穿上试试吗？ Néng chuān shàng shìshi ma?
Is there a mirror?	有镜子吗？ Yǒu jìngzi ma?
It doesn't fit.	穿得不合身。 Chuānde bù héshēn.
Where can I find a tailor?	哪里能找个裁缝？ Nǎli néngzhǎogecáifeng?

For clothing items, see the **dictionary**.

Music

I'd like a CD.	我想买一个CD。 Wǒ xiǎng mǎi yīge CD.
I'd like a DVD.	我想买一个DVD。 Wǒ xiǎng mǎi yīge DVD.
What region is this DVD for?	这碟片是哪个区域的? Zhè diépiàn shì nǎgè qūyù de?
I'm looking for something by (Zhou Huajian).	我在找 (周华健) 的歌。 Wǒ zài zhǎo (Zhōu Huájiàn) de gē.
What's his/her best recording?	他/她最好的CD是哪个? Tā zuì hǎo de CD shì nǎge?
Can I listen to this?	我能听一下吗? Wǒ néng tīng yīxià ma?

Photography

Can you develop this film?	能洗这个胶卷吗? Néng xǐ zhège jiāojuǎn ma?
Can you load my film?	能安装这个胶卷吗? Néng ānzhuāng zhège jiāojuǎn ma?
Can you print digital photos?	你能打印数码照片吗? Nǐ néng dǎyìn shùmǎ zhàopiān ma?
Can you recharge the battery?	你能给电池充电吗? Nǐ néng gěi diànchí chōngdiàn ma?

RAY LASKOWITZ/LONELY PLANET IMAGES ©

多少钱?
Duōshǎo qián?
How much is it?

Can you transfer my photos to CD?	你能拷贝我的 照片到CD吗? Nǐ néng kǎobèi wǒde zhàopiān dào CD ma?
Do you have batteries for this camera?	你有这个相机的电池吗? Nǐ yǒu zhègè xiàngjī de diànchí ma?
Do you have memory cards for this camera?	你有这个相机的内存卡吗? Nǐ yǒu zhègè xiàngjī de nèicún kǎ ma?

I want to buy ... film for this camera.	我想买这个机子的……胶卷。 Wǒ xiǎng mǎi zhège jīzi de ... jiāojuǎn.

B&W	黑白	hēibái
colour	彩色	cǎisè
slide	幻灯	huàndēng
... speed	……感光度	... gǎn guāngdù

When will it be ready?	什么时候来取？ Shénme shíhòu lái qǔ?
I need a passport photo taken.	我想拍一张护照照片。 Wǒ xiǎng pāi yīzhānghùzhào zhàopiān.
I'm not happy with these photos.	这卷洗得不好。 Zhè juǎn xǐde bùhǎo.

◀)) **LISTEN FOR**

还要别的吗？	Hái yào biéde ma? Anything else?
我能帮你吗？	Wǒ néng bāng nǐ ma? Can I help you?
没有。	Méiyǒu. No, we don't have any.

Repairs

| Can I have my ... repaired here? | 你能修我的……吗?
Nǐ néngxiū wǒde ... ma? |
| When will my ... be ready? | 什么时候来拿……?
Shénme shíhòu láiná ...? |

backpack	背包	bèibāo
camera	照相机	zhàoxiàngjī
glasses	眼镜	yǎnjìng
shoes	鞋子	xiézi
sunglasses	墨镜	mòjìng

Souvenirs

bronze	青铜器 qīngtóngqì
calligraphy	书法 shūfǎ
ink painting	水墨画 shuǐmòhuà
jade	玉器 yùqì
oil painting	油画 yóuhuà
scroll	国画 guóhuà
woodblock print	木刻 mùkè

Communications

KEY PHRASES

Where's the local internet cafe?	附近有网吧吗?	Fùjìn yǒu wǎngbā ma?
I'd like to check my email.	我想查一下电子信箱。	Wǒ xiǎng chá yīxiàdiànzǐ xìnxiāng.
I want to send a parcel.	我想寄一个包裹。	Wǒ xiǎng jì yī gè bāoguǒ.
I want to call ...	我想打电话到……	Wǒ xiǎng dǎ diànhuà dào ...
I'd like a SIM card.	我想买一张SIM卡。	Wǒ xiǎng mǎi yī zhāng SIM kǎ.

The Internet

Where's the local internet cafe?	附近有网吧吗? Fùjìn yǒu wǎngbā ma?
Do you have internet access?	你这儿能上网吗? Nǐ zhè'er néng shàngwǎng ma?
Is there wireless internet access here?	这里有无线网络讯号吗? Zhèlǐ yǒu wúxiàn wǎngluò xùnhào ma?
Can I get an account with a local internet provider?	我能开一个 IP账户吗? Wǒ néng kāiyīge IP zhànghù ma?

I'd like to ...	我想……	
	Wǒ xiǎng ...	

check my email	查一下电子信箱	chá yīxiàdiànzǐ xìnxiāng
download my photos	下载我的照片	xiàzǎi wǒde zhàopià
get internet access	上网	shàngwǎng
use a printer	打印	dǎyìn
use a scanner	扫描	sǎomiáo
use Skype	用Skype	yòng Skype

Do you have PCs?	有个人电脑吗?
	Yǒu gèrén diànnǎo ma?

Do you have Macs?	有苹果电脑吗?
	Yǒu píngguǒ diànnǎo ma?

Can I connect my laptop here?	我能在这里连接我的笔记本电脑吗?
	Wǒ néng zài zhèlǐ liánjiē wǒde bǐjìběn diànnǎo ma?

Do you have headphones (with a microphone)?	你有耳机（耳麦）吗?
	Nǐ yǒu ěrjī (ěrmài) ma?

How much per hour?	每小时多少钱?
	Měi xiǎoshí duōshǎoqián?

How much per (five) minutes?	每(五)分钟多少钱?
	Měi (wǔ)fēnzhōng duōshǎoqián?

How much per page?	每页多少钱?
	Měi yè duōshǎoqián?

How do I log on?	我怎么登录?
	Wǒ zěnme dēnglù?

Please change it to English-language preference.	请帮我换成英文格式。 Qǐng bāngwǒhuànchéng Yīngwén géshì.
This connection's really slow.	网速太慢了。 Wǎngsù tài màn le.
It's crashed.	死机了。 Sǐjī le.
I've finished.	上完了。 Shàng wán le.

Mobile/Cell Phone

I'd like a ...	我想买一…… Wǒ xiǎng mǎi yī ...	
charger for my phone	个充电器	ge chōngdiàn qì
mobile/cell phone	个手机	ge shǒujī
(100 yuan) prepaid card	张(一百块的) 预付卡	zhāng (yībǎi kuài de) yùfùkǎ
SIM card	张SIM卡	zhāng SIM kǎ

What are the rates?	电话费怎么算？ Diànhuàfèi zěnme suàn?
(30 fen) per minute.	每分钟(三毛钱)。 Měifēnzhōng (sānmáoqián).

Phone

Q What's your phone number?	您的电话号码是多少？ Nín de diànhuà hàomǎ shì duōshǎo?
A The number is ...	号码是…… Hàomǎ shì ...

Where's the nearest public phone?	最近的公用电话在哪里? Zuìjìn de gōngyòng diànhuà zài nǎli?
Can you help me find the number for ...?	请帮我找一下…… 的号码。 Qǐng bāngwǒ zhǎoyīxià ... de hàomǎ.
I want to ...	我想…… Wǒ xiǎng ...

buy a phonecard	买一张 电话卡	mǎi yīzhāng diànhuà kǎ
call (Singapore)	打电话到 (新加坡)	dǎ diànhuà dào (Xīnjiāpō)
make a (local) call	打(市内) 电话	dǎ (shìnèi) diànhuà
reverse the charges	打对方付款 的电话	dǎ duìfāng fùkuǎn de diànhuà
speak for (three) minutes	讲(三) 分钟	jiǎng (sān) fēnzhōng

How much does it cost per minute?	打一分钟多少钱? Dǎ yīfēnzhōng duōshǎo qián?
What's the code for (New Zealand)?	(新西兰)的区号是多少? (Xīnxīlán) de qūhào shì duōshǎo?
It's engaged.	占线了。 Zhànxiàn le.
I've been cut off.	断掉了。 Duàndiào le.
The connection's bad.	线路不好。 Xiànlù bùhǎo.
Hello.	喂。 Wèi.

🔊 LISTEN FOR

打错了。	Dǎcuò le.	Wrong number.
你是谁?	Nǐ shì shéi?	Who's calling?
你找谁?	Nǐ zhǎo shéi?	Who do you want to speak to?
(他/她)不在。	(Tā) bùzài.	(He/She) is not here.
等一下。	Děngyīxià.	One moment.

Can I speak to ...?	我找…… Wǒ zhǎo ...
It's ...	这是…… Zhè shì ...
Is ... there?	……在吗? ... zài ma?
Please tell him/her I called.	请告诉他/她我打过电话。 Qǐng gàosù tā wǒ dǎguò diànhuà.
Can I leave a message?	我能留言吗? Wǒ néng liúyán ma?
My number is ...	我的号码是…… Wǒde hàomǎ shì ...
I don't have a contact number.	我在这儿没有联系电话。 Wǒ zài zhèr méiyǒuliánxì diànhuà.
I'll call back later.	我晚点再打过来。 Wǒ wǎndiǎn zài dǎguòlái.

Post Office

I want to send a letter.	我想寄一封信。 Wǒ xiǎng jì yī fēng xìn.
I want to send a parcel.	我想寄一个包裹。 Wǒ xiǎng jì yī gè bāoguǒ.

I want to send a postcard.	我想寄一张明信片。 Wǒ xiǎng jì yī zhāng míngxìnpiàn.
I want to buy an envelope.	我想买一个信封。 Wǒ xiǎng mǎi yī ge xìnfēng.
I want to buy a stamp.	我想买一张邮票。 Wǒ xiǎng mǎi yī zhāng yóupiào.
Please send it by airmail/surface mail to (Australia).	请寄航空信/ 平信到(澳大利亚)。 Qǐng jì hángkōng xìn/ píngxìn dào (Àodàlìyà).
It contains (souvenirs).	里面有(纪念品)。 Lǐmian yǒu (jìniànpǐn).
Where's the poste restante section?	留局待取写在哪里？ Liújú dàiqǔ xiě zài nǎli?
Is there any mail for me?	有没有我的信？ Yǒuméiyǒu wǒde xìn?
customs declaration	海关报税 hǎiguān bàoshuì
domestic	国内 guónèi
international	国际 guójì
postal service	信件 xìnjiàn

◀)) **LISTEN FOR**

航空信	hángkōng xìn	air
特快	tèkuài	express
挂号	guàhào	registered
(陆运)平信	(lùyùn) píngxìn	surface (land)
(海运)平信	(hǎiyùn) píngxìn	surface (sea)

Money & Banking

KEY PHRASES

How much is it?	多少钱?	Duōshǎo qián?
What's the exchange rate?	兑换率是多少?	Duìhuànlǜ shì duōshǎo?
Where's an ATM?	自动取款机在哪儿?	Zìdòng qǔkuǎnjī zài nǎr?
I'd like to change money.	我要换钱。	Wǒ yào huànqián.
What's the charge for that?	手续费是多少?	Shǒuxùfèi shì duōshǎo?

Paying the Bill

Q How much is it?	多少钱?	Duōshǎo qián?
A It's (1200) RMB.	是(1200)元。	Shì (yīqiān liǎngbǎi) yuán.
A It's free.	是免费的。	Shì miǎnfèi de.
Please write down the price.	请把价钱写下来。	Qǐng bǎ jiàqián xiě xiàlái.
Do you accept credit cards?	你们收信用卡吗?	Nǐmen shōu xìnyòng kǎ ma?
Do you accept debit cards?	你们收借记卡吗?	Nǐmen shōu jièjìkǎ ma?
Do you accept travellers cheques?	你们收旅行支票吗?	Nǐmen shōu lǚxíng zhīpiào ma?

LISTEN FOR

护照	hùzhào	passport
证件	zhèngjiàn	identification
签字。	Qiānzì.	Sign here.
你的帐户 没有钱。	Nǐde zhànghù méiyǒu qián.	You have no funds left.
我们不能办。	Wǒmen bùnéng bàn.	We can't do that.
有问题。	Yǒu wèntí.	There's a problem.

PRACTICAL MONEY & BANKING

There's a mistake in the bill.	帐单上有问题。 Zhàngdān shàng yǒu wèntí.
I'd like my change, please.	可以找零吗？ Kěyǐ zhǎo líng ma?
I'd like a refund, please.	可以退款吗？ Kěyǐ tuì kuǎn ma?

Banking

What time does the bank open?	银行什么时候开门？ Yínháng shénme shíhòu kāimen?
Where can I ...?	我在哪里能……？ Wǒ zài nǎli néng ...?
I'd like to ...	我要…… Wǒ yào ...

cash a cheque	兑现一张 支票	duìxiàn yīzhāng zhīpiào
change a travellers cheque	换旅行 支票	huàn lǚxíng zhīpiào
change money	换钱	huànqián
get a cash advance	现金透支	xiànjīn tòuzhī
withdraw money	取现金	qǔ xiànjīn

CULTURE TIP

Chinese Currency

RMB (Renminbi rénmínbì) – 'People's Money' – is the official term for the Chinese currency.

元	yuán	the official name for the basic unit of RMB
块	kuài	commonly used colloquial term for a yuan
角	jiǎo	the official term; 10 jiao make up one yuan
毛	máo	commonly used colloquial term for a jiao
分	fēn	the official term; 10 fen make up one jiao

Where's an ATM?	自动取款机在哪儿? Zìdòng qǔkuǎnjī zài nǎr?
Where's a place to change foreign money?	换外币的地方在哪儿? Huàn wàibì de dìfang zài nǎr?
What's the exchange rate?	兑换率是多少? Duìhuànlǜ shì duōshǎo?
What's the charge for that?	手续费是多少? Shǒuxùfèi shì duōshǎo?
The ATM took my card.	取款机吃了我的卡。 Qǔkuǎnjī chīle wǒde kǎ.
I've forgotten my PIN.	我忘了我的密码。 Wǒ wàngle wǒde mìmǎ.
Can I use my credit card to withdraw money?	能用信用卡取现金吗? Néng yòng xìnyòngkǎ qǔ xiànjīn ma?
Has my money arrived yet?	我的汇款到了没有? Wǒde huìkuǎn dàole méiyǒu?
How long will it take to arrive?	还要等多久? Háiyàoděng duōjiǔ?

Business

KEY PHRASES

I'm attending a conference.	我来参加一个研讨会。	Wǒ lái cānjiā yīge yántǎohuì.
I have an appointment with ...	我跟……有约。	Wǒ gēn ... yǒuyuē.
Shall we go for a meal?	咱们是不是出去吃顿饭？	Zánmen shìbùshì chūqù chīdùnfàn?

Where's the business centre?	商务中心在哪儿？ Shāngwù zhōngxīn zài nǎr?
Where's the conference?	研讨会在哪儿？ Yántǎohuì zài nǎr?
Where's the meeting?	会议在哪儿？ Huìyì zài nǎr?

I'm attending a ...　　我来参加一个……
Wǒ lái cānjiā yīge ...

conference	研讨会	yántǎohuì
course	培训班	péixùnbān
meeting	会议	huìyì
trade fair	洽谈会	qiàtánhuì

| I'm here for (two) days. | 我要呆（两）天。
Wǒ yào dāi (liǎng)tiān. |
| I'm here for (two) weeks. | 我要呆（两）个星期。
Wǒ yào dāi (liǎng)ge xīngqī. |

CULTURE TIP

Time in China

The Chinese tend to view punctuality as a virtue and you should find that people arrive on time for meetings and social events. They may even arrive a little ahead of time, just to be on the safe side. In business dealings, punctual attendance at appointments can be interpreted as a sign of earnestness.

When planning events, note that the Chinese are very superstitious about numbers. When setting a date, you might be wise to check with your Chinese counterparts that the numbers contained in the proposed date are favourable. The number four (sì 四), in particular, is considered unlucky as it sounds a lot like the word for 'death' (sǐ 死).

I'm staying at ..., room ...	我住在……, ……号房间。 Wǒ zhù zài ..., ... hào fángjiān.
I'm with (China Travel Co).	我跟(中旅公司) 一块来的。 Wǒ gēn (Zhōnglǔ gōngsī) yīkuàilái de.
I'm with my colleague(s).	我跟(几个) 同事一块来的。 Wǒ gēn (jǐge) tóngshì yīkuàilái de.
I'm with (two) others.	我跟(两个) 人一块来的。 Wǒ gēn (liǎngge) rén yīkuàilái de.
I'm alone.	我一个人来的。 Wǒ yīgerén lái de.
I have an appointment with ...	我跟……有约。 Wǒ gēn ... yǒuyuē.

I need ...	我需要……	Wǒ xūyào ...

a computer	一个电脑	yīge diànnǎo
an internet connection	上网	shàng wǎng
an interpreter	一位翻译	yīwèi fānyì
to send a fax	发一个 传真	fā yīge chuánzhēn

That went very well.	刚才开得很好。 Gāngcái kāide hěnhǎo.
Thank you for your time.	谢谢你们的关照。 Xièxie nǐmende guānzhào.
Shall we go for a drink?	咱们是不是出去喝杯酒？ Zánmen shìbùshì chūqù hēbēijiǔ?
Shall we go for a meal?	咱们是不是出去吃顿饭？ Zánmen shìbùshì chūqù chīdùnfàn?
It's on me.	我请客。 Wǒ qǐng kè.

PRACTICAL BUSINESS

CULTURE TIP

Doing Business in China

The notion of guānxì 关系 (connections) is central to doing business in China. In a country where people often have to compete for goods and services in short supply, a network of advantageous reciprocal connections in places of power is all-important. Obtaining goods and services through such channels is colloquially known as 'going through the back door' (zǒuhòumén 走后门). Typical displays of guānxì are lavish banquets fuelled with Chinese spirit (báijiǔ 白酒). If you want to cut any deals while in China, you may be wise to adopt the local custom in this regard.

Sightseeing

KEY PHRASES

I'd like a guide.	我想买一本指南书。	Wǒ xiǎng mǎi yī běn zhǐnán shū.
Can I take photos?	可以照相吗？	Kěyǐ zhàoxiàng ma?
When does the museum open?	博物馆几点开门？	Bówùguǎn jǐdiǎn kāimén?
I'm interested in ...	我对……感兴趣。	Wǒ duì ... gǎnxìngqù.
When's the next (tour)?	下一个(向导游)是什么时候？	Xiàyīge (xiàngdǎoyóu) shì shénme shíhòu?

Requests & Queries

I'd like a/an ...	我想买一……	
	Wǒ xiǎng mǎi yī ...	
audio set	个语音向导	ge yǔyīn xiàngdǎo
catalogue	本画册	běn huàcè
guide	本指南书	běn zhǐnán shū
guidebook in English	本英文指南书	běn Yīngwén zhǐnán shū
(local) map	张(本地)地图	zhāng (běndì) dìtú

Do you have information on local culture?	有没有关于地方文化的资料？
	Yǒuméiyǒu guānyú dìfāng wénhuà de zīliào?

几点回来?

Jǐdiǎn huílái?

What time should we be back?

Do you have information on local history?	有没有关于地方史的资料? Yǒuméiyǒu guānyú dìfāng shǐ de zīliào?
Do you have information on local religion?	有没有关于地方宗教的资料? Yǒuméiyǒu guānyú dìfāng zōngjiào de zīliào?
I'd like to see ...	我想看…… Wǒ xiǎng kàn ...
What's that?	那是什么? Nà shì shénme?
Who made it?	是谁做的? Shì shéi zuòde?
How old is it?	有多久的历史? Yǒu duōjiǔ de lìshǐ?

Can I take photos?	可以照相吗？ Kěyǐ zhàoxiàng ma?
Could you take a photo of me?	你能帮我照相吗？ Nǐ néng bāng wǒ zhàoxiàng ma?
Can I take a photo (of you)?	我能拍(你)吗？ Wǒ néng pāi(nǐ) ma?
I'll send you the photograph.	我会把照片寄给你。 Wǒ huì bǎ zhàopiàn jìgěi nǐ.
Please write down your name and address.	请写下你的名字和地址。 Qǐng xiěxià nǐde míngzì hé dìzhǐ.
I've been to ...	我去过…… Wǒ qùguò ...
I'm planning to go to (the) ...	我打算去…… Wǒ dǎsuàn qù ...

Army of Terracotta Warriors in Xi'an	西安 兵马俑	Xī'ān Bīngmǎyǒng
Forbidden City	故宫	Gùgōng
Great Wall	长城	Chángchéng
Guilin	桂林	Guìlín
Pingyao	平遥	Píngyáo
Tai Shan	泰山	Tàishān
West Lake of Hangzhou	杭州西湖	Hángzhōu Xīhú

Getting In

What time does it open?	几点开门？ Jǐdiǎn kāimén?
What time does it close?	几点关门？ Jǐdiǎn guānmén?

What's the admission charge?	门票多少钱？	Ménpiào duōshǎo qián?
Is there a discount for ...?	给……打折扣吗？	Gěi ... dǎzhékòu ma?

children	儿童	értóng
families	家庭	jiātíng
groups	团体	tuántǐ
older people	老年人	lǎoniánrén
students	学生	xuéshēng

Galleries & Museums

When does the gallery open?	艺术馆几点开门？	Yìshùguǎn jǐdiǎn kāimén?
When does the museum open?	博物馆几点开门？	Bówùguǎn jǐdiǎn kāimén?
Q **What kind of art are you interested in?**	你喜欢什么样的艺术？	Nǐ xǐhuān shénmeyàng de yìshù?
A **I'm interested in ...**	我对……感兴趣。	Wǒ duì ... gǎnxìngqù.
Q **What's in the collection?**	这里收藏了什么？	Zhè lǐ shōucáng le shénme?
A **It's a/an ... exhibition.**	是一个……展览。	Shì yīge ... zhǎnlǎn.
Q **What do you think of ...?**	你觉得……怎么样？	Nǐ juéde ... zěnmeyàng?
A **I like the works of ...**	我喜欢……的作品。	Wǒ xǐhuān ... de zuòpǐn.
A **It reminds me of ...**	让我想到……	Ràng wǒ xiǎngdào ...

... art		……艺术 ... yìshù
comic	漫画	mànhuà
graphic	版画	bǎnhuà
modern	现代派	xiàndài pài
realist	现实主义	xiànshí zhǔyì

Tours

Can you recommend a (boat trip)?	你能推荐一个 (游船)吗? Nǐ néng tuījiàn yīge (yóuchuán) ma?
Can you recommend a (day trip)?	你能推荐一个 (一日游)吗? Nǐ néng tuījiàn yīge (yīrìyóu) ma?
When's the next (tour)?	下一个(向导游) 是什么时候? Xiàyīge (xiàngdǎoyóu) shì shénme shíhòu?
Is ... included?	包括……吗? Bāokuò ... ma?

accommodation	住宿	zhùsù
the admission price	门票钱	ménpiàoqián
food	饮食	yǐnshí
transport	交通	jiāotōng

The guide will pay.	导游会付钱。 Dǎoyóu huì fùqián.
The guide has paid.	导游已经付了钱。 Dǎoyóu yǐjīng fùle qián.

CULTURE TIP

Lǎowài

One of the mild annoyances you're likely to face on the road, if you venture outside the cosmopolitan centres, is the incessant exclamation 老外 lǎowài, or even 'Hello lǎowài, hello!' The first character means 'old' and is a mark of respect in Chinese. The second character literally means 'outside'.

The expression is not exactly polite, but it shouldn't cause offence. You could think of it as something like 'Hey Old Stranger!' It's certainly a lot better than outmoded forms of address such as 'Foreign Devil' or 'American Spy'. If you answer with 'Hello!' be prepared for your audience to break into hysterical laughter.

How long is the tour?	向导游要多长时间？ Xiàngdǎoyóu yào duōcháng shíjiān?
What time should we be back?	几点回来？ Jǐdiǎn huílái?
I'm with them.	我跟他们在一块。 Wǒ gēn tāmen zài yīkuài.
I've lost my group.	我找不到我的团队。 Wǒ zhǎobùdào wǒde tuánduì.

PRACTICAL

SENIOR & DISABLED TRAVELLERS

Senior & Disabled Travellers

KEY PHRASES

I need assistance.	我需要帮助。	Wǒ xūyào bāngzhù.
Is there wheelchair access?	轮椅能进门吗？	Lúnyǐ néng jìn mén ma?
Could you help me cross the street safely?	能帮我过马路吗？	Néng bāngwǒ guò mǎlù ma?

In China older people are revered. To be called an 'old man' (dàye 大爷 – literally 'great father') or an 'old woman' (dàmā 大妈 – literally 'great mother') is a compliment, a tribute to your maturity and wisdom. Disabled people, on the other hand, will not find getting around China easy as there are precious few facilities for the disabled.

I'm deaf.	我耳朵聋了。 Wǒ ěrduǒ lóng le.
I have a hearing aid.	我带有助听器。 Wǒ dàiyǒu zhùtīngqì.
I have a disability.	我有残疾。 Wǒ yǒu cánjí.
I need assistance.	我需要帮助。 Wǒ xūyào bāngzhù.
Is there wheelchair access?	轮椅能进门吗？ Lúnyǐ néng jìn mén ma?
How wide is the entrance?	门口有多宽？ Ménkǒu yǒu duōkuān?
How many steps are there?	有多少台阶？ Yǒu duōshǎo táijiē?

Is there a lift?	有电梯吗？ Yǒu diàntī ma?
Are there rails in the bathroom?	浴室里有扶手吗？ Yùshì lǐ yǒu fúshǒu ma?
Is there somewhere I can sit down?	哪里可以坐下休息？ Nǎli kěyǐ zuòxià xiūxi?
Could you help me cross the street safely?	能帮我过马路吗？ Néng bāngwǒ guò mǎlù ma?
older person	老年人 lǎoniánrén
person with a disability	残疾人 cánjí rén
ramp	坡道 pōdào
walking frame	拐杖架子 guǎizhàng jiàzi
walking stick	拐杖 guǎizhàng
wheelchair	轮椅 lúnyǐ

Travel with Children

KEY PHRASES

Are children allowed?	能带小孩去吗？	Néng dài xiǎohái qù ma?
Is there a child discount?	这儿有没有给儿童打折扣？	Zhèr yǒuméiyǒu gěi értóng dǎ zhékòu?
Are there any good places to take children around here?	附近有孩子玩的地方吗？	Fùjìn yǒu háizi wánde dìfang ma?

Chinese people find foreign children fascinating. You may find that travelling with children greatly facilitates striking up conversations with locals and getting to know them.

Is there a ...?　　　　　　　　这儿有没有······？
　　　　　　　　　　　　　　　　Zhèr yǒuméiyǒu ...?

child discount	给儿童打折扣	gěi értóng dǎ zhékòu
child-minding service	保姆服务	bǎomǔ fúwù
child's portion	儿童份量（的饭菜）	értóng fènliàng (de fàncài)
crèche	幼儿园	yòu'éryuán
family ticket	家庭票	jiātíng piào

I need a/an ...	我在找一……	Wǒ zài zhǎo yī ...
baby seat	个婴儿座	ge yīng'ér zuò
(English-speaking) babysitter	位(会说英文的)保姆	wèi (huì shuō Yīngwén de) báomǔ
cot	张婴儿床	zhāng yīng'ér chuáng
highchair	张高凳子	zhāng gāodèngzi
plastic bag	个塑料袋	ge sùliào dài
plastic sheet	块塑料布	kuài sùliào bù
potty	个婴儿马桶	ge yīng'ér mǎtǒng
pram	辆小推车	liàng xiǎotuīchē
sick bag	个呕吐袋	ge ǒutù dài
stroller	辆婴儿推车	liàng yīng'ér tuīchē

Do you sell ...?	你们卖……吗?	Nǐmen mài ... ma?
baby wipes	婴儿纸巾	yīng'ér zhǐjīn
disposable nappies	一次性尿裤	yīcìxìng niàokù
painkillers for infants	孩子止痛药	háizi zhǐtòng yào
tissues	纸巾	zhǐjīn

Where's the nearest ...?	最近的……在哪里?	Zuìjìn de ... zài nǎli?
park	公园	gōngyuán
playground	孩子活动地方	háizi huódòng dìfang
swimming pool	游泳池	yóuyǒng chí
tap	水龙头	shuǐlóngtóu
theme park	游乐园	yóulèyuán
toyshop	玩具店	wánjù diàn

Do you hire prams/ strollers?	这儿能租用婴儿推车吗？ *Zhèr néng zūyòng yīng'ér tuīchē ma?*
Is there space for a pram/ stroller?	有地方放推车吗？ *Yǒu dìfang fàng tuīchē ma?*
Are children allowed?	能带小孩去吗？ *Néng dài xiǎohái qù ma?*
Are there any good places to take children around here?	附近有孩子玩的地方吗？ *Fùjìn yǒu háizi wánde dìfang ma?*
Is this suitable for ...-year-old children?	对……岁孩子合适吗？ *Duì ... suì háizi héshì ma?*
Do you mind if I breastfeed here?	这儿喂奶你介意吗？ *Zhèr wèinǎi nǐ jièyì ma?*
Could I have some paper and pencils, please?	能借用纸和笔吗？ *Néng jièyòng zhǐ hé bǐ ma?*
Do you know a dentist who's good with children?	哪个儿科牙医比较好？ *Nǎge érkē yáyī bǐjiào hǎo?*
Do you know a doctor who's good with children?	哪个儿科医生比较好？ *Nǎge érkē yīshēng bǐjiào hǎo?*

If your child is sick, see **health**, page 166.

Social

Meeting People

KEY PHRASES

My name is ...	我叫……	Wǒ jiào ...
I'm from ...	我从……来。	Wǒ cóng ... lái.
I'm ...	我是个……	Wǒ shì gè ...
I'm ... years old.	我……岁。	Wǒ ... suì.
And you?	你呢？	Nǐ ne?

Basics

Note that in Mandarin, the word 'please' (qǐng 请) always precedes a request. You're likely to become familiar with the two phrases at the top of the opposite page as Chinese people use them a lot.

Yes.	是。 Shì.
No.	不是。 Bùshì.
Please ...	请…… Qǐng ...
Thank you (very much).	（非常）谢谢你。 (Fēicháng) xièxie nǐ.
You're welcome.	不客气。 Bù kèqi.
Excuse me. **(to get attention)**	劳驾。 Láojià.
Excuse me. **(to get past)**	借光。 Jièguāng.
Sorry.	对不起。 Duìbùqǐ.

As you please.	随便。
	Suíbiàn.
No problem.	没关系。
	Méiguānxi.

Greetings & Goodbyes

In common parlance, nǐ 你 ('you' singular) can have the polite form nín 您. This polite form is particularly common in Beijing. You'll encounter it as part of some common greetings.

Greetings all.	大家好。
	Dàjiā hǎo.
Hello. (general)	你好。
	Nǐhǎo.
Hello. (Beijing)	您好。
	Nínhǎo.

我很喜欢这里。
Wǒ hěn xǐhuān zhèlǐ.
I love it here!

Hi. (lit: Have you eaten?)	吃饭了吗？	Chīfàn le ma?
Good afternoon.	下午好。	Xiàwǔ hǎo.
Good evening.	晚上好。	Wǎnshàng hǎo.
Good morning. (after breakfast)	早上好。	Zǎoshàng hǎo.
🅀 **How are you? (general)**	你好吗？	Nǐhǎo ma?
🄰 **How are you? (Beijing)**	您好吗？	Nínhǎo ma?
🄰 **Fine. And you?**	好。你呢？	Hǎo. Nǐ ne?
What's your name?	你叫什么名字？	Nǐ jiào shénme míngzi?
My name is ...	我叫……	Wǒ jiào ...
I'd like to introduce you to ...	给你介绍……	Gěi nǐ jièshào ...
✂ **This is ...**	这是……	Zhèshì ...
I'm pleased to meet you.	幸会。	Xìnghuì.
This is my ...	这是我的……	Zhè shì wǒde ...

child	孩子	háizi
colleague	同事	tóngshì
friend	朋友	péngyou
partner (intimate)	对象	duìxiàng

For other family members, see **family**, page 120.

Goodbye.	再见。 Zàijiàn.
See below	
Bye.	拜拜。 Bàibai.
See you later.	回头见。 Huítóu jiàn.
Good night.	晚安。 Wǎn'ān.

Titles & Addressing People

China is host to a wealth of titles and terms of address, reflecting the richness of China's feudal past. Travellers to China can get by using the three titles given below. The last term xiǎojiě 小姐 is becoming the generic term for women of unspecified marital status. Be aware that it can carry a derogatory overtone of 'prostitute', but only if used in sexually suggestive contexts.

Mr/Sir (lit: first-born)	先生 xiānsheng
Mrs/Madam	女士 nǚshì
Ms/Miss (lit: little sister)	小姐 xiǎojiě

Making Conversation

Here are some common greetings and conversation starters that you may encounter or that may help you to break the ice.

Have you eaten?	吃饭了吗？ Chīfàn le ma?
Stepping out?	出去吗？ Chūqù ma?
You've arrived!	你来啦！ Nǐ lái la!

CULTURE TIP **Family & Friends**

In China, the friendliest way to address people is by using kinship terms. You can call a woman of an older generation āyí 阿姨 (auntie). It's polite to give people the benefit of the doubt on the upwards side when guessing their age.

In Beijing, gēmenr 哥们儿 (buddy) and jiěmenr 姐们儿 (sis) are popular for men and women respectively, reflecting Beijing's laid-back youth culture. Elsewhere, the terms dàgē 大哥 (big brother) and jiějie 姐姐 (big sister) are commonly used. On the less friendly side, to call one of your peers sūnzi 孙子 (grandchild) – a rank two full generations below yours – is a popular insult.

Off to the market?	买菜去？ Mǎicài qù?
Do you live here?	你住这里吗？ Nǐ zhù zhèlǐ ma?
Where are you going?	上哪儿去？ Shàngnǎr qù?
What are you doing?	你在干吗？ Nǐ zài gànma?
🗨 **Do you like it here?**	喜欢这里吗？ Xǐhuān zhèlǐ ma?
🗨 **I love it here.**	我很喜欢这里。 Wǒ hěn xǐhuān zhèlǐ.
🗨 **Are you here on holidays?**	你来这里旅游吗？ Nǐ lái zhèlǐ lǚyóu ma?
🗨 **I'm here for a holiday.**	我来这里旅游。 Wǒ lái zhèlǐ lǚyóu.
🗨 **I'm here on business.**	我来这里出差。 Wǒ lái zhèlǐ chūchāi.

A I'm here to study.	我来这里留学。 Wǒ lái zhèlǐ liúxué.	
Q How long are you here for?	你在这里住多久? Nǐ zài zhèlǐ zhù duōjiǔ?	
A I'm here for (four) weeks.	我住(四)个星期。 Wǒ zhù (sì)ge xīngqī.	
Can I take a photo (of you)?	我可以拍(你)吗? Wǒ kěyǐ pāi (nǐ) ma?	
That's (beautiful), isn't it?	太(好看)了! Tài (hǎokàn) le!	
Just joking.	开玩笑。 Kāiwánxiào.	
What's this called?	这个叫什么? Zhège jiào shénme?	

Nationalities

Q Where are you from?	你从哪儿来? Nǐ cóngnǎr lái?	
A I'm from Australia.	我从澳大利亚来。 Wǒ cóng Àodàlìyà lái.	
A I'm from Canada.	我从加拿大来。 Wǒ cóng Jiānádà lái.	
A I'm from Singapore.	我从新加坡来。 Wǒ cóng Xīnjiāpō lái.	

For more nationalities, see the **dictionary**.

Age

Try not to be too ruffled if everyone asks how many years you've managed to pack on over your life's journey. They don't mean to cause offence, but are simply curious to know how old you are – age is an indication of status and wealth in traditional China.

🔊 LISTEN FOR

People are often curious to know how foreigners get over their initial culture shock. You may well have locals ask you this question.

你在这儿习惯吗?   Nǐ zài zhèr xíguàn ma?
Are you accustomed to life here?

Q How old are you?	你多大了? Nǐ duōdà le?
A I'm ... years old.	我……岁。 Wǒ ... suì.
Q How old is your daughter?	你的女儿多大了? Nǐde nǚ'ér duōdà le?
Q How old is your son?	你的儿子多大了? Nǐde érzi duōdà le?
A He/She is ... years old.	他/她……岁。 Tā ... suì.
Too old!	太老了! Tài lǎo le!
I'm younger than I look.	我还小了。 Wǒ hái xiǎo le.

For your age, see **numbers & amounts**, page 34.

Occupations & Studies

Expect inquisitive locals to ask 'How much do you earn?' (Nǐ zhèng duōshǎo qián? 你挣多少钱?), as this is one of the top 10 questions asked of foreigners. This curiosity is probably explained by the rise of the free market and free-market jobs in China – a new and exciting phenomenon.

Q What's your occupation?   你做什么工作?
 Nǐ zuò shénme gōngzuò?

🅰 I'm a/an ... 　　　　　　我是个……
Wǒ shì gè ...

accountant	会计	kuàijì
chef	厨师	chúshī
engineer	工程师	gōngchéngshī
journalist	记者	jìzhě
teacher	老师	lǎoshī

🅰 I do business. 　　　　　我做生意。
Wǒ zuò shēngyì.

🅰 I do casual work. 　　　　我打工。
Wǒ dǎgōng.

🅰 I work in administration. 　我做秘书工作。
Wǒ zuò mìshū gōngzuò.

🅰 I work in health. 　　　　我做卫生工作。
Wǒ zuò wèishēng gōngzuò.

🅰 I work in sales and marketing. 　我做销售工作。
Wǒ zuò xiāoshòu gōngzuò.

🅰 I'm retired. 　　　　　　我退休了。
Wǒ tuìxiū le.

LANGUAGE TIP

Conversation Starters

When trying to start up a conversation in China, never be afraid to ask, or state, the obvious. If a friend is coming out of a restaurant with red-fried pork smeared all over their face, best check to see whether they've eaten by asking Chīfàn le ma? 吃饭了吗? ('Have you eaten?'). If you can't think of an obvious question to ask, try stating the obvious. It's as easy as talking about the weather. If a friend has just arrived at your house, let them know they've arrived with a gleeful Nǐ lái la! 你来啦! ('You've arrived!').

🇦 I'm self-employed.	我下海了。 Wǒ xiàhǎi le.
🇦 I'm unemployed.	我下岗了。 Wǒ xiàgǎng le.
🇶 What are you studying?	你学什么？ Nǐ xué shénme?
🇦 I'm studying humanities.	我学文科。 Wǒ xué wénkē.
🇦 I'm studying (Mandarin) Chinese.	我学中文。 Wǒ xué Zhōngwén.
🇦 I'm studying science.	我学理科。 Wǒ xué lǐkē.

For more occupations and studies, see the **dictionary**.

Family

Mandarin kinship terms can get very complicated as there are different titles according to age, hierarchy and whether the relationship is maternal or paternal. Included here are the terms for immediate family members and a selection of extended-family terms.

🇶 Are you married?	你结婚了吗？ Nǐ jiéhūn le ma?
🇦 I live with someone.	我有伴儿。 Wǒ yǒu bànr.
🇦 I'm ...	我…… Wǒ ...

divorced	离婚了	líhūn le
in a relationship	有伴	yǒubàn
married	结婚了	jiéhūn le
separated	分手了	fēnshǒu le
single	单身	dānshēn

Q Do you have a family of your own?	你成家了吗?
	Nǐ chéngjiā le ma?
A Do you have a/an ...?	你有……吗?
	Nǐ yǒu ... ma?
A I (don't) have a/an ...	我(没)有……
	Wǒ (méi) yǒu ...

brother	兄弟	xiōngdì
daughter	女儿	nǚ'ér
father	父亲	fùqīn
granddaughter	孙女	sūnnǚ
grandson	孙子	sūnzi
husband	丈夫	zhàngfu
mother	母亲	mǔqīn
partner (intimate)	对象	duìxiàng
sister	姐妹	jiěmèi
son	儿子	érzi
wife	太太	tàitai

SOCIAL MEETING PEOPLE

Farewells

I'm leaving tomorrow.	明天我要走了。
	Míngtiān wǒ yào zǒu le.
If you come to (Scotland), you can stay with me.	有机会来(苏格兰), 可以住我那儿。
	Yǒu jīhuì lái (Sūgélán) kěyǐ zhù wǒ nàr.
Keep in touch!	保持联系!
	Bǎochí liánxì!
It's been great meeting you.	认识你实在很高兴。
	Rènshi nǐ shízài hěn gāoxìng.

Q What's your (email address)?	你的(网址)是什么？ Nǐde (wǎngzhǐ)shì shénme?
A Here's my (address).	给你我的(地址)。 Gěi nǐ wǒde (dìzhǐ).
A Here's my (phone number).	给你我的 (电话号码)。 Gěi nǐ wǒde (diànhuà hàomǎ).

Well-Wishing

Bon voyage!	一路平安！ Yīlù píngān!
Congratulations!	恭喜，恭喜！ Gōngxǐ, gōngxǐ!
Good luck!	祝你好运！ Zhù nǐ hǎoyùn!
Happy birthday!	生日快乐！ Shēngrì kuàilè!
Happy (Chinese) New Year!	新年好！ Xīnnián hǎo!
Congratulations! May you make lots of money!	恭喜发财！ Gōngxǐ fācái!

This last expression is a popular Chinese New Year greeting, especially in southern China.

Interests

KEY PHRASES

What do you do in your spare time?	你有什么爱好吗?	Nǐ yǒu shénme àihào ma?
Do you like ...?	你喜欢……吗?	Nǐ xǐhuān ... ma?
I (don't) like ...	我(不)喜欢……	Wǒ (bù) xǐhuān ...

Common Interests

Q What do you do in your spare time?	你有什么爱好吗? Nǐ yǒu shénme àihào ma?
Q Do you like ...?	你喜欢……吗? Nǐ xǐhuān ... ma?

calligraphy	书法	shūfǎ
climbing mountains	爬山	páshān
computer games	电子游戏	diànzǐ yóuxì
films	看电影	kàn diànyǐng
music	听音乐	tīngyīnyuè
photography	摄影	shèyǐng
sport	体育	tǐyù
surfing the internet	上网	shàngwǎng
window shopping	逛商店	guàngshāngdiàn

A I (don't) like ... | 我(不)喜欢……
Wǒ (bù) xǐhuān ...

cooking	做饭	zuòfàn
dancing	跳舞	tiàowǔ
drawing	画画	huàhuà
drinking	喝酒	hējiǔ
eating	吃饭	chīfàn
gardening	养花	yǎnghuā
reading	看书	kànshū
talking	聊天	liáotiān
travelling	旅游	lǚyóu
walking	散步	sànbù
watching TV	看电视	kàn diànshì

For sporting activities, see **sports**, page 148.

Music

Do you like to ...? | 你爱……吗？
Nǐ ài ... ma?

dance	跳舞	tiàowǔ
go to concerts	参加音乐会	cānjiā yīnyuèhuì
listen to music	听音乐	tīngyīnyuè
play an instrument	弹乐器	tán yuèqì
sing	唱歌	chànggē

Which bands do you like?	你喜欢什么乐队？ Nǐ xǐhuān shénme yuèduì?
What music do you like?	你喜欢什么音乐？ Nǐ xǐhuān shénme yīnyuè?
Which singers do you like?	你喜欢什么歌手？ Nǐ xǐhuān shénme gēshǒu?

alternative music	非主流音乐 fēizhǔliú yīnyuè
blues	蓝调音乐 lándiào yīnyuè
Chinese traditional music	中国传统音乐 Zhōngguó chuántǒng yīnyuè
classical music	古典音乐 gǔdiǎn yīnyuè
easy listening	轻音乐 qīng yīnyuè
electronic music	电子音乐 diànzǐ yīnyuè
folk music	民谣 mínyáo
heavy metal	重金属音乐 zhòngjīnshǔ yīnyuè
hip hop	说唱音乐 shuōchàng yīnyuè
jazz	爵士乐 juéshì yuè
Peking opera	京剧 jīngjù
pop	流行音乐 liúxíng yīnyuè
rock	摇滚 yáogǔn
world music	国际民谣音乐 guójì mínyáo yīnyuè

Planning to go to a concert? See **buying tickets**, page 46, and **going out**, page 134.

Cinema & Theatre

I feel like going to a (ballet).	我想去看(芭蕾)。 Wǒ xiǎngqù kàn (bālěi).
I feel like going to a (film).	我想去看(电影)。 Wǒ xiǎngqù kàn (diànyǐng).
What's showing tonight?	今晚有什么节目? Jīnwǎn yǒu shénme jiémù?
Is it in English?	是英文版吗? Shì Yīngwén bǎn ma?
Does it have (English) subtitles?	有(英文)字幕吗? Yǒu (Yīngwén) zìmù ma?
Is this seat taken?	这座有人吗? Zhè zuò yǒu rén ma?
Have you seen ...?	你看过……吗? Nǐ kànguò ... ma?
Q Who's in it?	是谁演的? Shì shéi yǎnde?
A It stars ...	主角是…… Zhǔjué shì ...
Q Did you like the (play)?	你喜欢(戏剧)吗? Nǐ xǐhuān (xìjù) ma?
A I thought it was excellent.	我觉得很好看。 Wǒ juéde hěn hǎokàn.
A I thought it was long.	我觉得有点长。 Wǒ juéde yǒu diǎn cháng.
A I thought it was OK.	我觉得还行。 Wǒ juéde háixíng.

Games & Entertainment

In China you won't go far without seeing groups of people (often retired men) playing board games or cards in public places like teahouses or parks. The most popular game is mah-jong májiàng 麻将. The shuffling of mah-jong tiles is often accompanied by the hum of conversation, which sometimes becomes animated as money is won or lost on the game.

Some claim that the game of chess was invented in China. While this is hard to prove, it is true that both Chinese chess xiàngqí 象棋 and international chess guójì xiàngqí 国际象棋 are very popular. The Chinese love of gambling extends to numerous forms of card games pūkè pái 扑克牌, with bridge being very popular.

SOCIAL INTERESTS

| I (don't) like ... | 我 (不) 喜欢…… |
| | Wǒ (bù) xǐhuān ... |

action movies	动作片	dòngzuò piàn
animated films	动画片	dònghuà piàn
Chinese cinema	中国 电影	Zhōngguó diànyǐng
comedies	喜剧片	xǐjù piàn
documentaries	纪录片	jìlù piàn
drama	戏剧	xìjù
Hong Kong cinema	香港 电影	Xiānggǎng diànyǐng
horror movies	恐怖片	kǒngbù piàn
kung fu movies	武打片	wǔdǎ piàn
sci-fi movies	科幻片	kēhuàn piàn
short films	短篇 电影	duǎnpiān diànyǐng
thrillers	惊险片	jīngxiǎn piàn
war movies	战争片	zhànzhēng piàn

Feelings & Opinions

KEY PHRASES

Are you ...?	你……吗？	Nǐ ... ma?
I'm (not) ...	我(不)……	Wǒ (bù) ...
What do you think of it?	你觉得怎么样？	Nǐ juéde zěnme yàng?
I thought it was OK.	我觉得还行。	Wǒ juéde háixíng.
Did you hear about ...?	你听说过……吗？	Nǐ tīngshuōguò ... ma?

Feelings

Physical sensations (hot, hungry, etc) are expressed in the form 'I am ...', while sentiments (depressed, disappointed, etc) are expressed in the form 'I feel ...' . These phrases could come in handy in China as friendliness is often expressed through an exaggerated concern for the welfare of others.

Q Are you ...?	你……吗？ Nǐ ... ma?
A I'm (not) ...	我(不)…… Wǒ (bù) ...

cold	冷	lěng
hot	热	rè
hungry	饿	è
thirsty	渴	kě
tired	累	lèi

Q Do you feel ...?		你感到……吗？ Nǐ gǎndào ... ma?
A I (don't) feel ...		我（不）感到…… Wǒ (bù) gǎndào ...

annoyed	生气	shēngqì
depressed	郁闷	yùmèn
disappointed	失望	shīwàng
embarrassed	不好意思	bùhǎo yìsi
happy	高兴	gāoxìng
sad	难过	nánguò
surprised	惊讶	jīngyà
worried	着急	zháojí

If you're feeling unwell, see **health**, page 166.

Opinions

Q Did you like it?	你觉得好吗？ Nǐ juéde hǎo ma?
A I thought it was ...	我觉得…… Wǒ juéde ...
Q What do you think of it?	你觉得怎么样？ Nǐ juéde zěnme yàng?
A It's ...	它…… Tā ...

awful	很差劲	hěn chàjìn
beautiful	好美	hǎoměi
boring	很无聊	hěn wúliáo
great	很棒	hěn bàng
interesting	很有意思	hěn yǒu yìsi
strange	奇怪	qíguài

a little	有一点 yǒu yìdiǎn
I'm a little sad.	我有一点难过。 Wǒ yǒu yìdiǎn nánguò.
very	很 hěn
I'm very surprised.	我很惊讶。 Wǒ hěn jīngyà.
extremely	非常 fēicháng
I'm extremely happy.	我非常高兴。 Wǒ fēicháng gāoxìng.

Politics & Social Issues

When talking about social, political and environmental issues, keep in mind that certain issues are too politically sensitive to discuss with strangers. In addition, your status as a foreigner who can afford to travel may affect how your questions are understood. Unqualified criticism of things Chinese is not likely to win you any friends.

Q	Who do you vote for?	你投票给哪个党？ Nǐ tóupiào gěi nǎge dǎng?
A	I support the ... party.	我支持……党。 Wǒ zhīchí ... dǎng.
A	I'm a member of the ... party.	我是……人士。 Wǒ shì ... rénshì.
	communist party	共产党 gòngchǎndǎng
	conservative	保守派 bǎoshǒu pài
	green activists	环保 huánbǎo
	leftist	左翼 zuǒyì

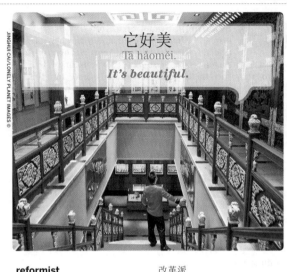

它好美
Tā hǎoměi.
It's beautiful.

SOCIAL

FEELINGS & OPINIONS

reformist	改革派 gǎigé pài
rightist	右翼 yòuyì
social democratic party	社会民主党 shèhuì mínzhǔdǎng
socialist	社会党 shèhuì dǎng
Did you hear about ...?	你听说过……吗? Nǐ tīngshuōguò ... ma?
Do you agree?	你同意吗? Nǐ tóngyì ma?
I (don't) agree with ...	我(不)同意…… Wǒ (bù) tóngyì ...

CULTURE TIP **Smoothing Social Situations**
If someone looks worried that they may have offended you, try letting them know that everything is OK with a long, slow méishì 没事 ('No problem.'). If you're worried that you may have caused offence, turn this into a question Méishì ba? 没事吧? ('There's no problem, is there?'). If you're worried that they might have meant to cause offence, then ask Yǒushì ma? 有事吗? ('Got a problem?') to find out for sure. Armed with these phrases you should be able to remedy any awkward situations that you might find yourself in.

How do people feel about ...?	人们觉得……怎么样? Rénmen juéde … zěnmeyàng?
crime	犯罪活动 fànzuì huódòng
the economy	经济 jīngjì
education	教育 jiàoyù
the environment	环境 huánjìng

The Environment

You may find that concern about many issues, including environmental ones, tends to be very far removed from the minds of most Chinese, who generally contend with more pressing issues of local importance.

Is this a protected forest?	这个是被保护森林吗? Zhège shì bèibǎohù de sēnlín ma?
Is this a protected park?	这个是被保护公园吗? Zhège shì bèibǎohù de gōngyuán ma?

Is this a protected species?	这个是被保护物种吗？ Zhège shì bèibǎohù de wùzhǒng ma?
Is there a ... problem here?	本地有……问题吗？ Běn dì yǒu ... wèntí ma?
What should be done about ...?	……应该怎么处理？ ... yīnggāi zěnme chǔlǐ?
ozone layer	臭氧层 chòuyǎngcéng
pollution	污染 wūrǎn
recycling programme	回收措施 huíshōu cuòshī
the Three Gorges Project	三峡工程 sānxiá gōngchéng

SOCIAL GOING OUT

Going Out

What's on tonight?	今天晚上有什么活动？	Jīntiān wǎnshàng yǒu shénme huódòng?
Where can I find clubs?	夜总会怎么找？	Yèzǒnghuì zěnme zhǎo?
Would you like to go for a coffee?	你想去喝咖啡吗？	Nǐ xiǎng qù hē kāfēi ma?
When will we meet?	几点钟碰头？	Jǐdiǎnzhōng pèngtóu?
Where will we meet?	在哪里碰头？	Zài nǎli pèngtóu?

Where to Go

What's there to do in the evenings?	晚上有什么好玩的吗？ Wǎnshàng yǒu shénme hǎowán de ma?
What's on ...?	……有什么活动？ ... yǒu shénme huódòng?

locally	这儿附近	Zhèr fùjìn
this weekend	这个周末	Zhège zhōumò
today	今天	Jīntiān
tonight	今天晚上	Jīntiān wǎnshàng

Where can I find ...?	……怎么找？	
	... zěnme zhǎo?	
clubs	夜总会	Yèzǒnghuì
gay venues	同志吧	Tóngzhìbā
places to eat	吃饭的地方	Chīfàn de dìfang
pubs	酒吧	Jiǔbā

Is there a local entertainment guide?	有没有本地的娱乐指南？
	Yǒuméiyǒu běndì de yúlè zhǐnán?

Is there a local film guide?	有没有本地的电影指南？
	Yǒuméiyǒu běndì de diànyǐng zhǐnán?

Is there a local music guide?	有没有本地的音乐指南？
	Yǒuméiyǒu běndì de yīnyuè zhǐnán?

I feel like going to a ...	我想到……去。	
	Wǒ xiǎng dào ... qù.	
bar/pub	酒吧	jiǔbā
cafe	咖啡屋	kāfēiwū
nightclub	夜总会	yèzǒnghuì
party	聚会	jùhuì
restaurant	饭馆	fànguǎn

I feel like going to ...	我想去……	
	Wǒ xiǎng qù ...	

listen to a concert	听音乐会	tīng yīnyuè huì
see a film	看电影	kàn diànyǐng
see a show	看演出	kàn yǎnchū
sing karaoke	唱卡拉OK	chàng kǎlā ōkèi
see Peking opera	看京剧	kàn jīngjù
see some acrobats	看杂技	kàn zájì
watch a ballet	看芭蕾	kàn bālěi

For more on bars and drinks, see **romance**, page 140, and **eating out**, page 176.

Invitations

What are you doing now?	你现在做什么？
	Nǐ xiànzài zuò shénme?
What are you doing this weekend?	你这个周末做什么？
	Nǐ zhège zhōumò zuò shénme?
What are you doing tonight?	你今天晚上做什么？
	Nǐ jīntiān wǎnshàng zuò shénme?
Do you know a good restaurant?	你知道哪里有好饭店？
	Nǐ zhīdào nǎli yǒu hǎo fàndiàn?
Do you want to come to the concert with me?	你想跟我去音乐会吗？
	Nǐ xiǎng gēn wǒ qù yīnyuè huì ma?
We're having a party/banquet.	我们要开聚会/宴会。
	Wǒmen yàokāi jùhuì/yànhuì.
You should come.	你应该来。
	Nǐ yīnggāi lái.

The drinks are on me.	我请客。 Wǒ qǐngkè.
Q Would you like to go (for a) ...?	你想去……吗? Nǐ xiǎng qù ... ma?
A I feel like going (for a) ...	我想去…… Wǒ xiǎng qù ...

banquet	大吃大喝	dàchī dàhē
coffee	喝咖啡	hē kāfēi
dancing	跳舞	tiàowǔ
drink	喝酒	hējiǔ
meal	吃饭	chīfàn
out somewhere	外面玩儿	wàimian wánr
walk	散步	sànbù

SOCIAL　GOING OUT

Responding to Invitations

Sure!	好! Hǎo!
Yes, I'd love to.	好,我愿意。 Hǎo, wǒ yuànyì.
That's very kind of you.	你太客气了。 Nǐ tài kèqi le.
Where shall we go?	我们到哪儿去? Wǒmen dàonǎr qù?
No, I'm afraid I can't.	不行,我不能来。 Bùxíng, wǒ bùnéng lái.
Sorry, I can't sing/dance.	不好意思,我不会 唱歌/跳舞。 Bùhǎo yìsi, wǒ bùhuì chànggē/tiàowǔ.
What about tomorrow?	明天行吗? Míngtiān xíng ma?

Arranging to Meet

Q **When will we meet?**	几点钟碰头? Jǐdiǎnzhōng pèngtóu?
A **Let's meet at (eight) o'clock.**	我们在(八)点钟见面。 Wǒmen zài (bā)diǎn zhōng jiànmiàn.
Q **Where will we meet?**	在哪里碰头? Zài nǎli pèngtóu?
A **Let's meet at (the entrance).**	我们在(门口)见面。 Wǒmen zài (ménkǒu) jiànmiàn.
I'll pick you up.	我来接你。 Wǒ lái jiē nǐ.
Q **Are you ready?**	准备好了吗? Zhǔnbèi hǎo le ma?
A **I'm ready.**	准备好了。 Zhǔnbèi hǎo le.
A **I'll be coming later.**	我要晚一点来。 Wǒ yào wǎnyīdiǎn lái.
Where will you be?	我在哪里找你? Wǒ zài nǎli zhǎo nǐ?
If I'm not there by (nine) o'clock, don't wait for me.	如果到了(九)点钟我还没来,就不要等我。 Rúguǒ dàole (jiǔ)diǎn zhōng wǒ hái méilái, jiù bùyào děngwǒ.
I'll see you then.	不见不散。 Bùjiàn bùsàn.
See you later.	回头见。 Huítóu jiàn.
See you tomorrow.	明天见。 Míngtiān jiàn.

CULTURE TIP

Street Life
In China's crowded cities, a lot of life – particularly in summer – is lived out on the streets and in the precious open spaces and parks. An evening's entertainment might consist of activities such as kite flying (fàng fēngzheng 放风筝) or playing pool (dǎtáiqiú 打台球). In the warmer months, young people indulge in open-air dancing to rock music (bēngdí 蹦迪) while older people gather in the parks for ballroom dancing sessions (tiào jiāoyì wǔ 跳交谊舞).

I'm looking forward to it.	我期待它的到来。 Wǒ qīdài tāde dàolái.
Sorry I'm late.	不好意思，来晚了。 Bùhǎo yìsi, láiwǎn le.
Never mind.	没事。 Méishì.

Drugs

I don't take drugs.	我不吸毒。 Wǒ bù xīdú.
I take ... occasionally.	我偶尔吃⋯⋯ Wǒ ǒu'ěr chī ...
Do you want to have a smoke?	想抽一点吗？ Xiǎng chōuyìdiǎn ma?
Do you have a light?	有火吗？ Yǒu huǒ ma?

Romance

KEY PHRASES

Would you like to do something (tomorrow)?	(明天)想出去玩吗?	(Míngtiān) xiǎng chūqù wán ma?
I love you.	我爱你。	Wǒ ài nǐ.
Leave me alone!	别烦我!	Bié fán wǒ!

Asking Someone Out

Where would you like to go (tonight)?	(今天晚上)想去哪里玩? (Jīntiān wǎnshàng) xiǎng qù nǎli wán?
Q Would you like to do something (tomorrow)?	(明天)想出去玩吗? (Míngtiān) xiǎng chūqù wán ma?
A Yes, I'd love to.	好啊,很想去。 Hǎo a, hěn xiǎngqù.
A I'm busy.	对不起,我有事。 Duìbùqǐ, wǒ yǒushì.

Pick-up Lines

Would you like a drink?	你想喝点什么? Nǐ xiǎng hē diǎn shénme?
You look like some cousin of mine.	你长得像我的表妹。 Nǐ zhǎngde xiàng wǒde biǎomèi.
You're a fantastic dancer.	你跳得真好。 Nǐ tiàode zhēnhǎo.

Can I be with you forever?	我能陪你一起到老吗？
	Wǒ néng péinǐ yīqǐ dàolǎo ma?
Can I dance with you?	我能跟你跳个舞吗？
	Wǒ néng gēnnǐ tiàogewǔ ma?
Can I sit here?	我能坐这儿吗？
	Wǒ néng zuò zhèr ma?

Rejections

I'm here with my boyfriend/girlfriend.	我同男朋友/女朋友一起来的。
	Wǒ tóng nánpéngyou/nǚpéngyou yīqǐ lái de.
Excuse me, I have to go now.	对不起，我要走了。
	Duìbùqǐ, wǒ yào zǒule.
I'd rather not.	我不想。
	Wǒ bù xiǎng.
No, thank you.	不行，谢谢。
	Bùxíng, xièxie.
Go and play somewhere else!	到一边玩去！
	Dào yībiān wán qù!
Leave me alone!	别烦我！
	Bié fán wǒ!

Getting Closer

I like you very much.	我很喜欢你。
	Wǒ hěn xǐhuān nǐ.
You're great.	你真棒。
	Nǐ zhēn bàng.
Let's kiss!	咱们亲一下！
	Zánmen qīnyīxià!

CULTURE TIP

Body Language

Beware of inadvertently sending the wrong signals with your body language while in China. Squeezing hard on people's hands when shaking hands is an attribute only of foreigners. Chinese handshakes are soft – more of a gentle clasp really. Foreigners' habit of looking at locals while they speak to them is also off-putting, as the norm in China is not to look people in the eye when talking to them. When someone is addressing you, however, it's all right to look at them.

Don't be put off by people gesturing at their noses as if they have an itch. The nose, as opposed to the heart, is the symbolic centre of the self in China. Don't kiss anyone by way of greeting unless you want to frighten or titillate: it's not socially acceptable.

Do you want to come inside for a while?	想进来坐坐吗？ Xiǎng jìnlái zuòzuo ma?
Do you want a massage?	你想按摩吗？ Nǐ xiǎng ànmó ma?

Sex

Do you have a (condom)?	你带 (避孕套) 了吗？ Nǐ dài (bìyùntào) le ma?
Let's use a (condom).	咱们用 (避孕套) 吧。 Zánmen yòng (bìyùntào) ba.
I won't do it without protection.	没有防备，我不玩。 Méiyǒu fángbèi, wǒ bù wán.
Kiss me!	亲我！ Qīn wǒ!
I want you.	我要你。 Wǒ yào nǐ.

I want to make love to you.	我想跟你做爱。 Wǒ xiǎng gēnnǐ zuò'ài.
It's my first time.	这是我的第一次。 Zhè shì wǒde dìyīcì.
How about going to bed?	咱们上床，好吗？ Zánmen shàngchuáng, hǎo ma?
Touch me here.	摸我这儿。 Mō wǒ zhèr.
❓ Do you like this?	喜欢这样吗？ Xǐhuān zhèyàng ma?
🅰 I (don't) like that.	我 (不) 喜欢这样。 Wǒ (bù) xǐhuān zhèyàng.
I think we should stop now.	我想我们现在该结束了。 Wǒ xiǎng wǒmen xiànzài gāi jiéshù le.
Oh yeah!	真是！ Zhēn shì!
That's great!	真棒！ Zhēnbàng!
Easy tiger!	慢点来！ Màndiǎn lái!
That was amazing.	刚才真不可思议。 Gāngcái zhēn bùkě sīyì.
That was weird.	刚才真有点奇怪。 Gāngcái zhēn yǒudiǎn qíguài.
That was wild.	刚才真疯狂。 Gāngcái zhēn fēngkuáng.
Can I call you?	我可以给你打电话吗？ Wǒ kěyǐ gěi nǐ dǎ diànhuà ma?
Can I see you?	我可以见你吗？ Wǒ kěyǐ jiànnǐ ma?
Can I stay over?	我可以在这儿过夜吗？ Wǒ kěyǐ zài zhèr guòyè ma?

LANGUAGE TIP

Terms for Gays & Lesbians
Following the Communist Revolution, the officially sanctioned term of address for both men and women was 'comrade' (tóngzhì 同志). In today's China this word isn't commonly used as a term of address and has undergone a shift in meaning – yesterday's 'comrade' is now a slang word for 'gay'. It's a kind of play on words, as the literal meaning of 'comrade' in Chinese is 'of the same mindset'. While in revolutionary circles this mindset entailed a vision of a new society, today's mindset is a particular vision of sexuality. The self-appellation of tóngzhì as used by China's gay community can be seen as a subversive means of challenging the more official tag of 'homosexual' (tóngxìng liàn 同性恋, literally 'same-sex love').

Love

I love you.	我爱你。 Wǒ ài nǐ.
I think we're good together.	我觉得我们俩挺般配。 Wǒ juéde wǒmen liǎ tǐng bānpèi.
Will you go out with me?	你能跟我谈朋友吗？ Nǐ néng gēn wǒ tán péngyou ma?
Will you live with me?	你能跟我住一起吗？ Nǐ néng gēn wǒ zhù yīqǐ ma?
Will you marry me?	你能跟我结婚吗？ Nǐ néng gēn wǒ jiéhūn ma?

Beliefs & Culture

KEY PHRASES

What's your religion?	你信什么教？	Nǐ xìn shénme jiào?
I'm ...	我信……	Wǒ xìn ...
I'm sorry, it's against my beliefs.	不好意思，这是违背我的信仰的。	Bùhǎo yìsi, zhèshì wéibèi wǒde xìnyǎng de.

Religion

Q Are you religious?
你信教吗？
Nǐ xìnjiào ma?

Q What's your religion?
你信什么教？
Nǐ xìn shénme jiào?

A I'm ...
我信……
Wǒ xìn ...

agnostic	不可知论	bùkězhī lùn
an atheist	无神论	wúshénlùn
Buddhist	佛教	Fójiào
Catholic	天主教	Tiānzhǔjiào
Christian	基督教	Jīdūjiào
Hindu	印度教	Yìndùjiào
Jewish	犹太教	Yóutàijiào
Muslim	伊斯兰教	Yīsīlánjiào

I (don't) believe in ...		我 (不) 信…… Wǒ (bù) xìn ...
astrology	星象	xīngxiàng
Confucianism	儒教	Rújiào
Daoism	道教	Dàojiào
fate	命运	mìngyùn
fengshui	风水	fēngshuǐ
God	上帝	shàngdì

Can I attend a service here?	我能在这里做礼拜吗？ Wǒ néng zài zhèlǐ zuò lǐbài ma?
Where can I pray?	我在哪里可以祈祷？ Wǒ zài nǎli kěyǐ qídǎo?
Where can I meditate?	我在哪里可以静坐？ Wǒ zài nǎli kěyǐ jìngzuò?

Cultural Differences

Is this a local custom?	这是地方风俗吗？ Zhè shì dìfāng fēngsú ma?
I don't want to offend you.	我不想得罪你们。 Wǒ bù xiǎng dézuì nǐmen.
I'm not used to this.	我没有这个习惯。 Wǒ méiyǒu zhège xíguàn.
I'd rather not join in.	我最好不参加。 Wǒ zuìhǎo bù cānjiā.
I'll try it.	我可以试试。 Wǒ kěyǐ shìshi.
I didn't mean to do anything wrong.	我不想做错什么。 Wǒ bùxiǎng zuòcuò shénme.

CULTURE TIP

Communicating with the Chinese

Whether you're wheeling and dealing in China, or just trying to get a few yuan knocked off the price of a portrait of Mao, there are a few points to keep in mind to help your negotiations go smoothly.

The concept of 'saving face' (miànzi 面子) is important in Chinese culture. Essentially it's about avoiding being made to look stupid or to back down in front of others – a concept which isn't limited to the Chinese, of course. Negotiated settlements that provide benefits to both parties are preferable to confrontation. A desire to save face may lead people to disguise uncomfortable truths.

Chinese men and women are generally reserved with hand and facial movements. The animated gesticulating of foreigners can seem undignified and even comical to them. Also, a smile doesn't necessarily mean happiness. Chinese people may also smile when they're embarrassed or worried.

For more on body language, see **romance**, page 142.

I'm sorry, it's against my beliefs.	不好意思，这是违背我的信仰的。 Bùhǎo yìsi, zhèshì wéibèi wǒde xìnyǎng de.
I'm sorry, it's against my religion.	不好意思，这是违背我的宗教的。 Bùhǎo yìsi, zhèshì wéibèi wǒde zōngjiào de.
This is different.	这有点与众不同。 Zhè yǒudiǎn yǔzhòng bùtóng.
This is fun.	这有点好玩。 Zhè yǒudiǎn hǎowán.
This is interesting.	这有点意思。 Zhè yǒudiǎn yìsi.

Sports

KEY PHRASES

What sport do you play?	你喜欢玩什么体育项目?	Nǐ xǐhuān wán shénme tǐyù xiàngmù?
What's your favourite team?	你最喜欢的球队是谁?	Nǐ zuì xǐhuān de qiúduì shì shéi?
What's the score?	几比几?	Jǐbǐjǐ?

Sporting Interests

In Mandarin any sport can be 'played' using the verb wán 玩, but generally this has light-hearted connotations, as in 'to have a kick of the ball', expressing such a playful interest in sport.

Q What sport do you play?
你喜欢玩什么体育项目?
Nǐ xǐhuān wán shénme tǐyù xiàngmù?

A I play/do ...
我喜欢玩……
Wǒ xǐhuān wán ...

To say that you really play a sport, you need to use an appropriate verb such as 'hit' (dǎ 打) or 'kick' (tī 踢). If you follow a sport, use the verb 'follow' (kàn 看).

I play (football/soccer).
我喜欢踢(足球)。
Wǒ xǐhuān tī (zúqiú).

I follow (rugby).
我喜欢看
(英式橄榄球)。
Wǒ xǐhuān kàn
(yīngshì gǎnlǎnqiú).

I play ...	我喜欢打······	
	Wǒ xǐhuān dǎ ...	
I follow ...	我喜欢看······	
	Wǒ xǐhuān kàn ...	

badminton	羽毛球	yǔmáoqiú
basketball	篮球	lánqiú
handball	手球	shǒuqiú
hockey	曲棍球	qūgùnqiú
table tennis	乒乓球	pīngpāng qiú
tennis	网球	wǎngqiú
(beach) volleyball	(沙滩)排球	(shātān) páiqiú
water polo	水球	shuǐqiú

The verb 'do' (gǎo 搞) can be used when you're not sure whether you should hit, kick or train harder (as in cycling or athletics).

I do ...	我喜欢搞······	
	Wǒ xǐhuān gǎo ...	
I follow ...	我喜欢看······	
	Wǒ xǐhuān kàn ...	

archery	射箭	shèjiàn
fencing	剑术	jiànshù
long-distance running	长跑	chángpǎo
rowing	划船	huáchuán
sailing	帆船	fānchuán
scuba diving	潜水	qiánshuǐ
shooting	射击	shèjī
swimming	游泳	yóuyǒng
track & field	田径	tiánjìng
weightlifting	举重	jǔzhòng

Some sports (such as gymnastics and martial arts) are identified not by hits or kicks but by the rigorous 'repetitive training' required of the practitioner, expressed by the verb liàn 练.

I play/do …	我喜欢练……	
	Wó xǐhuān liàn …	
I follow …	我喜欢看……	
	Wó xǐhuān kàn …	

gymnastics	体操	tǐcāo
judo	柔道	róudào
karate	空手道	kōngshǒudào
martial arts	武术	wǔshù
(Chinese kung fu)	(中国功夫)	(Zhōngguó gōngfu)
tae kwon do	跆拳道	táiquándào
t'ai chi	太极拳	tàijíquán

I like to cycle.	我喜欢骑自行车。
	Wǒ xǐhuān qí zìxíngchē.
I like to run.	我喜欢跑步。
	Wǒ xǐhuān pǎobù.
I like to walk.	我喜欢散步。
	Wǒ xǐhuān sànbù.
Who's your favourite sportsperson?	你最喜欢的球星是谁？
	Nǐ zuì xǐhuān de qiúxīng shì shéi?
Who's your favourite team?	你最喜欢的球队是谁？
	Nǐ zuì xǐhuān de qiúduì shì shéi?
Q Do you like to play (table tennis)?	你喜欢打 (乒乓球) 吗？
	Nǐ xǐhuān dǎ (pīngpāngqiú) ma?
A Yes, very much.	很喜欢。
	Hěn xǐhuān.

A Not really.	不太喜欢。 Bùtài xǐhuān.
A I like watching it.	我喜欢看。 Wǒ xǐhuān kàn.
Q What's the score?	几比几？ Jǐbǐjǐ?
A draw/even	打平 dǎ píng
A love/zero	零 líng
A match point	赛点 sàidiǎn

Going to a Game

Would you like to go to a game with me?	你想跟我去看球赛吗？ Nǐ xiǎng gēn wǒ qù kàn qiúsài ma?
Who are you supporting?	你支持哪个队？ Nǐ zhīchí nǎge duì?
Who's playing?	谁在打？ Shéi zài dǎ?
Who's winning?	谁占上风？ Shéi zhànshàngfēng?

🔊 LISTEN FOR

进门！	Jìnmén!	What a goal!
好球！	Hǎoqiú!	What a hit!
踢得好！	Tīde hǎo!	What a kick!
传得好！	Chuánde hǎo!	What a pass!
真精彩！	Zhēn jīngcǎi!	What a performance!

Come on!	加油！ Jiāyóu!
That was a bad game!	比赛打得真差劲！ Bǐsài dǎde zhēn chàjìn!
That was a great game!	比赛打得真精彩！ Bǐsài dǎde zhēn jīngcǎi!

Playing Sport

Q Do you want to play?	你想玩吗？ Nǐ xiǎng wán ma?
A I have an injury.	我受伤了。 Wǒ shòushāng le.
Q Can I join in?	我可以跟你们一起玩吗？ Wǒ kěyǐ gēn nǐmen yīqǐ wán ma?
A Great.	好。 Hǎo.
Your/My point.	你/我得分。 Nǐ/Wǒ dé fēn.
Kick/Pass it to me!	踢/传给我！ Tī/Chuán gěi wǒ!
You're a good player.	你打得很好。 Nǐ dǎde hěnhǎo.
Thanks, I enjoyed the game.	多谢你，我打得很开心。 Duōxiè nǐ, wǒ dǎ de hěn kāixīn.
Do I have to be a member to attend?	只对会员开放吗？ Zhǐ duì huìyuán kāifàng ma?
Is there a women-only session?	有女子班吗？ Yǒu nǚzǐ bān ma?
Where are the changing rooms?	更衣室在哪儿？ Gēngyīshì zài nǎr?

| **Where's the nearest ...?** | 最近的……在哪里？ |
| | Zuìjìnde ... zài nǎli? |

golf course	高尔夫球场	gāo'ěrfū qiúchǎng
gym	健美中心	jiànměi zhōngxīn
swimming pool	游泳池	yóuyǒng chí
tennis court	网球场	wǎngqiú chǎng

| **What's the charge per ...?** | 每……要花多少钱？ |
| | Měi ... yàohuā duōshǎo qián? |

day	天	tiān
game	场	chǎng
hour	小时	xiǎoshí
visit	次	cì

真精彩！
Zhēn jīngcǎi!
What a performance!

Can I hire a ...?		我可以租一……吗？ Wǒ kěyǐ zū yī ... ma?
ball	个球	ge qiú
bicycle	辆自行车	liàng zìxíngchē
court	个场地	ge chǎngdì
racquet	副拍子	fù pāizi

Table Tennis

I'd like to play table tennis.	我想打乒乓球。 Wǒ xiǎng dǎ pīngpāng qiú.
Do you know where I can find a table-tennis table?	哪里有乒乓球桌？ Nǎli yǒu pīngpāng qiú zhuō?
Can I book a table?	我可以预订一个乒乓球桌吗？ Wǒ kěyǐ yùdìng yīge pīngpāng qiú zhuō ma?
bat	拍子 pāizi
net	网 wǎng
serve	发球 fāqiú
table	球桌 qiúzhuō
table-tennis ball	乒乓球 pīngpāng qiú

CULTURE TIP | **Chinese Martial Arts**

In Mandarin, the many styles of martial arts are collectively known as wǔshù (Zhōngguó gōngfu) 武术(中国功夫). Each style embodies its own particular spirit and philosophy (drawing on Confucianism, Taoism, Buddhism and Zen). Here are a few styles that travellers to China may see:

Bagua Zhang (Eight-Trigram Boxing) | 八卦掌 | Bāguà zhǎng

The characteristics of this martial art style, in which practitioners wheel around in circles kicking and landing palm strikes, are the skills of subterfuge, evasion, speed and unpredictability.

Shaolin Boxing | 少林拳 | Shàolín quán

Originating at the Shaolin monastery and still practised there today, this major martial art form draws on Zen Buddhist beliefs and bases its forms on five animals: dragon, snake, tiger, leopard and crane.

Taijiquan | 太极拳 | Tàijíquán

Known in the West as t'ai chi, this graceful centuries-old Chinese system promotes flexibility, circulation, strength, balance, meditation and relaxation. Based on Taoist beliefs, it's traditionally practiced as a form of self-defence without the use of force.

Xingyi Quan (Body-Mind Boxing) | 形意拳 | Xíngyì quán

Often mentioned in the same breath as *taijiquan,* this martial art is more dynamic and powerful. The movements of this – perhaps the oldest form of martial art still practised in China – are performed in a relaxed state but quickly and directly.

SOCIAL SPORTS

Outdoors

KEY PHRASES

Where can I buy supplies?	在哪里能买到预备品？	Zài nǎli néng mǎidào yùbèipǐn?
Do we need a guide?	需要向导吗？	Xūyào xiàngdǎo ma?
Is it safe?	安全吗？	Ānquán ma?
I'm lost.	我迷路了。	Wǒ mílù le.
What's the weather like?	天气怎么样？	Tiānqì zěnmeyàng?

Hiking

Where can I buy supplies?	在哪里能买到预备品？ Zài nǎli néng mǎidào yùbèipǐn?
Where can I find someone who knows this area?	在哪里能找路熟的人？ Zài nǎli néng zhǎo lùshú de rén?
Where can I get a map?	在哪里能买地图？ Zài nǎli néng mǎi dìtú?
Do we need to take bedding?	需要带上被褥吗？ Xūyào dàishàng bèirù ma?
Do we need to take food?	需要带上食品吗？ Xūyào dàishàng shípǐn ma?
Do we need to take water?	需要带上饮用水吗？ Xūyào dàishàng yǐnyòngshuǐ ma?
How high is the climb?	山有多高？ Shān yǒu duō gāo?

How long is the trail?	步行有多远？ Bùxíng yǒu duō yuǎn?
Do we need a guide?	需要向导吗？ Xūyào xiàngdǎo ma?
Are there guided treks?	有徒步旅行团吗？ Yǒu túbù lǚxíng tuán ma?
Is it safe?	安全吗？ Ānquán ma?
Is the track easy to follow?	路好找吗？ Lù hǎozhǎo ma?
Is the track open?	路开通了吗？ Lù kāitōng le ma?
Is the track scenic?	路边风景好吗？ Lù biān fēngjǐng hǎo ma?
Which is the easiest route?	哪条路最容易？ Nǎtiáo lù zuì róngyì?
Which is the most interesting route?	哪条路最有意思？ Nǎtiáo lù zuì yǒu yìsi?
Which is the shortest route?	哪条路最短？ Nǎtiáo lù zuì duǎn?
Is there somewhere to spend the night?	有地方住吗？ Yǒu dìfang zhù ma?
When does it get dark?	天什么时候变黑？ Tiān shénme shíhòu biànhēi?
Where's the nearest village?	最近的村子在哪里？ Zuìjìn de cūnzi zài nǎli?
Where have you come from?	你从哪边过来的？ Nǐ cóng nǎbiān guòlái de?
How long did it take?	走了有多久？ Zǒule yǒu duōjiǔ?
Does this path go to ...?	这条路到……吗？ Zhètiáo lù dào ... ma?

Can I go through here?	我能从这里穿过吗? Wǒ néng cóng zhèlǐ chuānguò ma?
Is the water OK to drink?	这水能喝吗? Zhè shuǐ nénghē ma?
I'm lost.	我迷路了。 Wǒ mílù le.

At the Beach

Where's the best beach?	最好的海滩在哪里? Zuìhǎo de shātān zài nǎlǐ?
Where's the nearest beach?	最近的海滩在哪里? Zuìjìn de shātān zài nǎlǐ?
Where's the public beach?	公共的海滩在哪里? Gōnggòng de shātān zài nǎlǐ?
Is it safe to swim here?	这里游泳安全吗? Zhèlǐ yóuyǒng ānquán ma?
What time is high/low tide?	涨/退潮是几点钟? Zhǎng/Tuì cháo shì jǐdiǎnzhōng?
Do we have to pay?	要买票吗? Yào mǎipiào ma?

Weather

| ❖ What's the weather like? | 天气怎么样? Tiānqì zěnmeyàng? |
| ❖ What will the weather be like tomorrow? | 明天天气会怎么样? Míngtiān tiānqì huì zěnmeyàng? |

A It's ...

天气……
Tiānqì ...

cloudy	多云	duō yún
cold	冷	lěng
fine	晴	qíng
freezing	很冷	hěnlěng
hot	热	rè
raining	下雨	xiàyǔ
snowing	下雪	xiàxuě
sunny	晴朗	qínglǎng
warm	暖和	nuǎnhuo
windy	刮风	guāfēng

Where can I buy a rain jacket?	在哪里能买到雨衣？ Zài nǎli néng mǎidào yǔyī?
Where can I buy an umbrella?	在哪里能买到雨伞？ Zài nǎli néng mǎidào yǔsǎn?
dry season	旱季 hànjì
monsoon season	季风季节 jìfēng jìjié
wet season	雨季 yǔjì

Flora & Fauna

What ... is that?	那个……是什么？ Nàge ... shì shénme?

animal	动物	dòngwù
flower	花	huā
plant	植物	zhíwù
tree	树	shù

SOCIAL OUTDOORS

◀)) LISTEN FOR

大熊猫	dà xióng māo	giant panda
荷花	héhuā	lotus
牡丹花	mǔdān huā	peony
丹顶鹤	dāndǐng hè	red-necked crane
小熊猫	xiǎo xióng māo	red panda
东北虎	dōngběi hǔ	Siberian tiger

Is it ...?

是……的吗?
Shì ... de ma?

common	常见	chángjiàn
dangerous	危险	wēixiǎn
endangered	濒危	bīnwēi
protected	受保护	shòu bǎohù

| **What's it used for?** | 它用来做什么?
Tā yònglái zuò shénme? |
| **Can you eat the fruit?** | 果子能吃吗?
Guǒzi néngchī ma? |

Safe Travel

Emergencies

KEY PHRASES

Help!	救命！	Jiùmìng!
It's an emergency.	有急事。	Yǒu jíshì.
Where are the toilets?	厕所在哪儿？	Cèsuǒ zài nǎr?

Help!	救命！ Jiùmìng!
Stop!	站住！ Zhànzhù!
Go away!	走开！ Zǒukāi!
Thief!	小偷！ Xiǎotōu!
Fire!	着火啦！ Zháohuǒ la!
Watch out!	小心！ Xiǎoxīn!
It's an emergency.	有急事。 Yǒu jíshì.
Call a doctor!	请叫医生来！ Qǐng jiào yīshēng lái!
Call an ambulance!	请叫一辆急救车！ Qǐng jiào yīliàng jíjiù chē!
I'm ill.	我生病了。 Wǒ shēngbìng le.

LOOK FOR

急诊科	Jízhěn Kē	Emergency Department
医院	Yīyuàn	Hospital
警察	Jǐngchá	Police
派出所	Pàichūsuǒ	Police Station

My friend/child is ill.
我的朋友/孩子
生病了。
Wǒde péngyou/háizi
shēngbing le.

He/She is having a/an ...
他/她……
Tā ...

allergic reaction	过敏症发作	guòmǐnzhèng fāzuò
asthma attack	哮喘发病	xiàochuǎn fābìng
baby	在生孩子	zài shēng háizi
epileptic fit	癫痫病发作	diānxiánbìng fāzuò
heart attack	心脏病发作	xīnzàngbìng fāzuò

I'm lost.
我迷路了。
Wǒ mílù le.

Could you please help?
你能帮我吗?
Nǐ néng bāngwǒ ma?

Can I use your phone?
我能借用你的电话吗?
Wǒ néng jièyòng nǐde
diànhuà ma?

Where are the toilets?
厕所在哪儿?
Cèsuǒ zài nǎr?

Police

KEY PHRASES

Where's the police station?	派出所在哪里?	Pàichūsuǒ zài nǎli?
I want to contact my embassy/ consulate.	我要联系我的大使馆/领事馆。	Wǒ yào liánxì wǒde dàshǐguǎn/lǐngshìguǎn.
I've lost my bags.	我的行李丢了。	Wǒde xíngli diū le.

In China, it's the Public Security Bureau or PSB (gōng'ānjú 公安局) that's responsible for introducing and enforcing regulations concerning foreigners. Turn to them for mediation in disputes with hotels, restaurants or taxi drivers.

Where's the police station?	派出所在哪里? Pàichūsuǒ zài nǎli?
Please telephone 110.	请打110。 Qǐng dǎ yāo yāo líng.
I want to report an offence.	我要报案。 Wǒ yào bào'àn.
It was him/her.	是他/她做的。 Shì tā zuòde.
I've been (assaulted).	我被(侵犯)了。 Wǒ bèi (qīnfàn)le.
I've been (robbed).	我被(抢劫)了。 Wǒ bèi (qiǎngjié)le.
He/She has been (raped).	他/她被(强奸)了。 Tā bèi (qiángjiān)le.

I've lost my ...		我的……丢了。 Wǒde ... diū le.
bags	行李	xíngli
jewellery	首饰	shǒushì
money	钱	qián
papers	文件	wénjiàn
passport	护照	hùzhào

What am I accused of?	我被指控犯了什么罪? Wǒ bèi zhǐkòng fànle shénme zuì?
I didn't do it.	不是我做的。 Bùshì wǒ zuòde.
I want to contact my embassy/consulate.	我要联系我的大使馆/领事馆。 Wǒ yào liánxì wǒde dàshǐguǎn/lǐngshìguǎn.
Can I have a lawyer who speaks English?	我想找一个会说英文的律师。 Wǒ xiǎng zhǎo yíge huìshuō Yīngwén de lǜshī.
This drug is for personal use.	这个药品是私用的。 Zhège yàopǐn shì sīyòngde.
I have a prescription for this drug.	这个药我有处方。 Zhège yào wǒ yǒu chǔfāng.

🔊 LISTEN FOR

你被指控犯了 破坏秩序。	Nǐ bèi zhǐkòng fànle pòhuài zhìxù. You're charged with disturbing the peace.
他/她被指控犯了 随带禁物。	Tā bèi zhǐkòng fànle suídài jìnwù. He/She is charged with possession of illegal substances.
他/她被指控犯了盗窃。	Tā bèi zhǐkòng fànle dàoqiè. He/She is charged with theft.

Health

KEY PHRASES

Where's the nearest hospital?	最近的医院在哪儿?	Zuìjìnde yīyuàn zài nǎr?
I'm sick.	我病了。	Wǒ bìng le.
I need a doctor (who speaks English).	我要看(会说英文的)医生。	Wǒ yào kàn (huìshuō Yīngwénde) yīshēng.
I'm on medication for ...	我有……的处方药。	Wǒ yǒu ... de chǔfāngyào.
I'm allergic to ...	我对……过敏。	Wǒ duì ... guòmǐn.

Doctor

Where's the nearest ...?	最近的……在哪儿? Zuìjìnde ... zài nǎr?	
(night) pharmacist	(昼夜)药房	(zhòuyè) yàofáng
dentist	牙医	yáyī
doctor	医生	yīshēng
emergency department	急诊科	jízhěn kē
hospital	医院	yīyuàn
optometrist	眼科	yǎnkē

I need a doctor (who speaks English).	我要看(会说英文的)医生。 Wǒ yào kàn (huìshuō Yīngwénde) yīshēng.

🔊 LISTEN FOR

哪儿疼呢？	Nǎr téng ne? Where does it hurt?
发烧吗？	Fāshāo ma? Do you have a temperature?
这个情况持续了多久？	Zhège qíngkuàng chíxùle duōjiǔ? How long have you been like this?
以前有过这样的 情况吗？	Yǐqián yǒuguò zhèyàngde qíngkuàng ma? Have you had this before?
你喝酒吗？	Nǐ hējiǔ ma? Do you drink?
你抽烟吗？	Nǐ chōuyān ma? Do you smoke?
你吸毒吗？	Nǐ xīdú ma? Do you take drugs?
你有过敏症吗？	Nǐ yǒu guòmǐnzhèng ma? Are you allergic to anything?
你有处方药吗？	Nǐ yǒu chǔfāngyào ma? Are you on medication?

Could I see a female doctor?	最好要看一位女医生。 Zuìhǎo yàokàn yīwèi nǚyīshēng.
Could the doctor come here?	医生能到这儿来吗？ Yīshēng néng dào zhèr lái ma?
Is there an after-hours emergency number?	有晚上急诊电话号码吗？ Yǒu wǎnshàng jízhěn diànhuà hàomǎ ma?
I've run out of my medication.	我用完了我的处方药。 Wǒ yòngwánle wǒde chǔfāngyào.
This is my usual medicine.	我平时服这个药。 Wǒ píngshí fú zhège yào.

What's the correct dosage?	剂量是多少？	Jìliàng shì duōshǎo?
I don't want a blood transfusion.	我不要输血。	Wǒ bùyào shūxuè.
Please use a new syringe.	请用一个新针头。	Qǐng yòngyīge xīn zhēntóu.
I've been vaccinated against ...	我打过……的免疫针。	Wǒ dǎguò ... de miǎnyì zhēn.

hepatitis A/B/C	甲/乙/丙肝炎	jiǎ/yǐ/bǐng gānyán
rabies	狂犬病	kuángquǎnbìng
tetanus	破伤风	pòshāngfēng
typhoid	伤寒	shānghán

I need new contact lenses.	我要买新的隐形眼镜。	Wǒ yàomǎi xīnde yǐnxíng yǎnjìng.
I need new glasses.	我要买新的眼镜。	Wǒ yàomǎi xīnde yǎnjìng.
Can I have a receipt for my insurance?	能给我保险发票吗？	Néng gěi wǒ bǎoxiǎn fāpiào ma?

Symptoms & Conditions

I'm sick.	我病了。	Wǒ bìng le.
My friend is sick.	我的朋友病了。	Wǒde péngyou bìng le.
My child is sick.	我的孩子病了。	Wǒde háizi bìng le.
It hurts here.	这里痛。	Zhèlǐ tòng.
I'm dehydrated.	我脱水了。	Wǒ tuōshuǐ le.

◀)) LISTEN FOR

| 你需要住院。 | Nǐ xūyào zhùyuàn.
You need to be admitted to hospital. |
| 你回国要做检查。 | Nǐ huíguó hòu yàozuò jiǎnchá.
You should have it checked when you go home. |

SAFE TRAVEL

HEALTH

I feel ... 我感到……
Wǒ gǎndào ...

dizzy	头晕	tóuyūn
hot and cold	忽冷忽热	hūlěng hūrè
nauseous	恶心	ěxīn
shivery	全身发抖	quánshēn fādǒu

I've been (injured).	我(受伤)了。 Wǒ (shòushāng)le.
He/She has been (vomiting).	他/她(常呕吐)了。 Tā (cháng ǒutù)le.
I'm on medication for ...	我有……的处方药。 Wǒ yǒu ... de chǔfāngyào.
I have ...	我有…… Wǒ yǒu ...
I've recently had ...	我最近有…… Wǒ zuìjìn yǒu ...

Women's Health

| (I think) I'm pregnant. | 我(好像)怀孕了。
Wǒ (hǎoxiàng) huáiyùn le. |
| I'm on the pill. | 我用避孕药。
Wǒ yòng bìyùn yào. |

◀)) **LISTEN FOR**

你有性生活吗？	Nǐ yǒu xìngshēnghuó ma? Are you sexually active?
你有过非安全 性交吗？	Nǐ yǒuguò fēi ānquán xìngjiāo ma? Have you had unprotected sex?
你用避孕措施吗？	Nǐ yòng bìyùn cuòshī ma? Are you using contraception?
你的月经还来吗？	Nǐde yuèjīng háilái ma? Are you menstruating?
上次月经是什么 时候？	Shàngcì yuèjīng shì shénme shíhòu? When did you last have your period?
你怀孕了吗？	Nǐ huáiyùn le ma? Are you pregnant?
你怀孕了。	Nǐ huáiyùn le. You're pregnant.

I haven't had my period for (six) weeks.	我(六)个星期没来月经了。 Wǒ (liù)ge xīngqī méi lái yuèjīng le.
I need contraception.	我要买避孕品。 Wǒ yàomǎi bìyùn pǐn.
I need the morning-after pill.	我要买事后避孕药。 Wǒ yàomǎi shìhòu bìyùn yào.
I need a pregnancy test.	我要做一个怀孕测试。 Wǒ yàozuò yīge huáiyùn cèshì.
I've noticed a lump here.	我发现这儿长了一个疙瘩。 Wǒ fāxiàn zhèr zhǎngle yīge gēda.

Allergies

I have a skin allergy.	我皮肤过敏。 Wǒ pífū guòmǐn.

I'm allergic to ... 我对……过敏。
Wǒ duì ... guòmǐn.

anti-inflammatories	抗炎药	kàngyányào
codeine	可待因	kědàiyīn
penicillin	青霉素	qīngméisù
sulphur-based drugs	硫基药物	liújī yàowù

Alternative Treatments

Herbal medicine (zhōngyào 中药) and acupuncture (zhēnjiǔ 针灸) are the most common medical systems in China.

I don't use (Western medicine). 我不吃(西药)。
Wǒ bùchī (Xīyào).

Can I see someone who practises ...? 哪里能看……大夫?
Nǎli néngkàn ... dàifu?

acupuncture	针灸	zhēnjiǔ
Chinese herbal medicine	中药	zhōngyào
Chinese medicine	中医	zhōngyī
meridian massage	经络按摩	jīngluò ànmó

🔍 LOOK FOR

不许吸烟	Bùxǔ xīyān	No Smoking
不许吐痰	Bùxǔ tǔtán	No Spitting

Parts of the Body

My ... hurts.	我的……疼。 Wǒde ... téng.
I can't move my ...	我的……不能动。 Wǒde ... bùnéng dòng.
I have a cramp in my ...	我的……抽筋了。 Wǒde ... chōujīn le.
My ... is swollen.	我的……发肿了。 Wǒde ... fāzhǒng le.

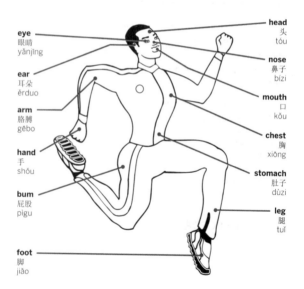

eye
眼睛
yǎnjīng

ear
耳朵
ěrduo

arm
胳膊
gēbo

hand
手
shǒu

bum
屁股
pìgu

foot
脚
jiǎo

head
头
tóu

nose
鼻子
bízi

mouth
口
kǒu

chest
胸
xiōng

stomach
肚子
dùzi

leg
腿
tuǐ

🔊 LISTEN FOR

必须用完。	Bìxū yòngwán. You must complete the course.
以前吃过吗?	Yǐqián chīguò ma? Have you taken this before?
一天两次(与饭一起吃)。	Yītiān liǎngcì (yǔ fàn yīqǐ chī). Twice a day (with food).

Chemist/Pharmacist

I need something for ...	我要……的药。 Wǒ yào ... de yào.
Do I need a prescription for ...?	……需要处方吗? ... xūyào chǔfāng ma?
I have a prescription.	我有处方。 Wǒ yǒu chǔfāng.
My prescription is ...	我的处方是…… Wǒ de chǔfāng shì ...
How many times a day?	每天吃几次? Měitiān chī jǐcì?
Will it make me drowsy?	吃后犯困吗? Chīhòu fànkùn ma?

Dentist

I have a toothache.	我有牙疼。 Wǒ yǒu yáténg.
I have a broken tooth.	我有崩牙。 Wǒ yǒu bēngyá.
I have a cavity.	我有牙洞。 Wǒ yǒu yádòng.

🔊 LISTEN FOR

张开口。	Zhāngkāi kǒu.	Open wide.
咬一下。	Yǎoyīxià.	Bite down on this.
漱口！	Shùkǒu!	Rinse!

I've lost a filling.	我的牙齿填充物掉了。 Wǒ de yáchǐ tiánchōngwù diàole.
My dentures are broken.	我的假牙坏了。 Wǒde jiǎyá huàile.
My gums hurt.	我齿龈好痛。 Wǒ chǐyín hǎotòng.
I need an anaesthetic.	我需要麻醉药。 Wǒ xūyào mázuì yào.
I need a filling.	我需要补牙。 Wǒ xūyào bǔyá.

Food

Eating Out

KEY PHRASES

Can you recommend a restaurant?	你可以推荐一个饭馆吗？	Nǐ kěyǐ tuījiàn yīge fànguǎn ma?
I'd like a table for (five).	我要一张（五个人的）桌子。	Wǒ yào yīzhāng (wǔge rén de) zhuōzi.
I'd like a menu (in English).	我要（英文）菜单。	Wǒ yào (Yīngwén) càidān.
I'll have (a beer).	我来一个（啤酒）。	Wǒ lái yīge (píjiǔ).
Bill, please!	买单！	Mǎidān!

Basics

Chinese meals come earlier than you may be used to, so get ready to wind your stomach clock back a couple of hours. Lunch is the main meal of the day and often includes a selection of stir-fried dishes and rice. Dinner is much the same as lunch but often with beer taking the place of rice. All meals are served hot – hot food is believed to be better for the digestion.

breakfast	早饭 zǎofàn
lunch	午饭 wǔfàn
dinner	晚饭 wǎnfàn
snack	小吃 xiǎochī

to eat	吃	
	chī	
to drink	喝	
	hē	
I'm starving!	我饿坏了！	
	Wǒ è huài le!	

Finding a Place to Eat

Can you recommend a ...?	你可以推荐一个……吗？	
	Nǐ kěyǐ tuījiàn yīge ... ma?	

bar	酒吧	jiǔbā
cafe	咖啡屋	kāfēiwū
noodle house	面馆	miànguǎn
restaurant	饭馆	fànguǎn
snack shop	小吃店	xiǎochī diàn
(won ton) stall	(馄饨) 摊	(húntun) tān
street vendor	街头小吃	jiētóu xiǎochī
teahouse	茶馆	cháguǎn

Where would you go for (a) ...?	……该到哪里去？	
	... gāi dàonǎli qù?	

banquet	办宴席	Bàn yànxí
celebration	举行庆祝会	Jǔxíng qìngzhù huì
cheap meal	吃得便宜一点的	Chīde piányi yīdiǎn de
local specialities	地方小吃	Dìfang xiǎochī
yum cha	饮茶	Yǐnchá

🔊 LISTEN FOR

关门了。	Guānmén le.	We're closed.
客满了。	Kè mǎn le.	We're full.
请等一下。	Qǐng děng yīxià.	One moment.
坐哪里？	Zuò nǎli?	Where would you like to sit?

I'd like to reserve a table for (two) people.	我想预订一张（两个）人的桌子。 Wǒ xiǎng yùdìng yīzhāng (liǎngge) rén de zhuōzi.
I'd like to reserve a table for (eight) o'clock.	我想预订一张（八）点钟的桌子。 Wǒ xiǎng yùdìng yīzhāng (bā) diǎn zhōng de zhuōzi.
Are you still serving food?	你们还营业吗？ Nǐmen hái yíngyè ma?
How long is the wait?	吃饭要等多久？ Chīfàn yàoděng duōjiǔ?

At the Restaurant

The Chinese have a word, rènào 热闹 (literally 'hot and noisy', ie 'bustling'), which typifies the atmosphere of their restaurants. When the Chinese eat out, they like to have raucous, lip-smacking fun. The style of whispering couples sipping expensive wine by candlelight is not their thing.

What would you recommend for the main meal?	有什么主菜可以推荐的？ Yǒu shénme zhǔcài kěyǐ tuījiàn de?
What would you recommend for dessert?	有什么甜点可以推荐的？ Yǒu shénme tiándiǎn kěyǐ tuījiàn de?
What would you recommend for drinks?	有什么饮料可以推荐的？ Yǒu shénme yǐnliào kěyǐ tuījiàn de?

What's in that dish?	这道菜用什么东西做的？ Zhèdào cài yòng shénme dōngxi zuòde?
I'll have that.	来一个吧。 Lái yīge ba.
I'd like a/the …	我要…… Wǒ yào …

drink list	酒水单	jiǔshuǐ dān
half portion	半份	bànfèn
menu in English	英文菜单	Yīngwén càidān
nonsmoking table	不吸烟的桌子	bùxīyān de zhuōzi
smoking table	吸烟的桌子	xīyān de zhuōzi
table for (five)	一张(五个 人的)桌子	yīzhāng (wǔge rén de) zhuōzi

✂ For two, please.	两个人， 谢谢。	Liǎngge rén, xièxie.

Can I see the menu, please?	能不能给我看一下菜单？ Néng bù néng gěiwǒ kàngyīxià càidān?

✂ Menu, please.	菜单，谢谢。	Càidān, xièxie.

Is it self-serve?	这里是自助的吗？ Zhèlǐ shì zìzhù de ma?
Are these complimentary?	这是赠送的吗？ Zhè shì zèngsòng de ma?
I'd like the beef noodle soup.	我想吃牛肉面。 Wǒ xiǎng chī niúròu miàn.
I'd like a local speciality.	我想吃一个地方特色菜。 Wǒ xiǎng chī yīge dìfāng tèsè cài.
I'd like a meal fit for a king.	我想吃山珍海味。 Wǒ xiǎng chī shānzhēn hǎiwèi.

FOOD EATING OUT

🔊 LISTEN FOR

想点什么？	Xiǎng diǎn shénme?	What can I get for you?
你喜欢……吗？	Nǐ xǐhuān ... ma?	Do you like ...?
我建议……	Wǒ jiànyì ...	I suggest the ...
上菜了！	Shàng cài le!	Here you go!

Requests

Please bring a ...		请拿一……来。 Qǐng ná yī ... lái.
cloth	块抹布	kuài mābù
glass	个杯子	ge bēizi
knife and fork	副刀叉	fù dāochā
serviette	块餐巾	kuài cānjīn
wineglass	个葡萄酒杯	ge pútáo jiǔbēi

I'd like it with ...		多放一点…… Duōfàng yīdiǎn ...
I'd like it without ...		不要放…… Bùyàofàng ...
chilli	辣椒	làjiāo
garlic	大蒜	dàsuàn
nuts	果仁	guǒrén
oil	油	yóu
MSG	味精	wèijīng

For phrases relating to allergies and food choices, see **vegetarian & special meals**, page 196.

Eating Out

 Can I see the menu, please?
能不能给我看一下菜单?
Néng bù néng gěiwǒ kàngyīxià càidān?

 What would you recommend for ...?
有什么……可以推荐的?
Yǒu shénme ... kěyǐ tuījiàn de?

 the main meal
主菜
zhǔcài

 dessert
甜点
tiándiǎn

 drinks
饮料
yǐnliào

 Can you bring me some ..., please?
请拿些……来。
Qǐng ná xiē ... lái.

 Please bring the bill.
请给我账单。
Qǐng gěiwǒ zhàngdān.

I (don't) want it ...		我(不)要……的。 Wǒ (bù)yào ... de.
barbecued	烧烤	shāokǎo
boiled	煮	zhǔ
braised	煎	jiān
deep-fried	油炸	yóuzhá
grilled	铁板烤	tiěbǎn kǎo
medium	半生半熟	bànshēng bànshú
rare	半生	bànshēng
reheated	重热	chóngrè
roasted	烤	kǎo
steamed	蒸	zhēng
stir-fried	炒	chǎo
well done	熟	shú

Do you have ...?		有没有……? Yǒuméiyǒu ...?
chilli sauce	辣椒酱	làjiāo jiàng
dipping sauce	蘸酱	zhànjiàng
garlic	大蒜	dàsuàn
soy sauce	酱油	jiàngyóu
vinegar	醋	cù

For additional items, see the **menu decoder**, page 199.

Compliments & Complaints

I love this dish.	这道菜真香。 Zhè dào cài zhēnxiāng.
I love the local cuisine.	这个地方的菜真好吃。 Zhège dìfāng de cài zhēn hǎochī.

That was delicious!	真好吃！ Zhēn hǎochī!
I'm full.	吃饱了。 Chībǎo le.
This dish is (too) cold.	这个菜(太)凉了。 Zhège cài (tài) liáng le.
This dish is (too) spicy.	这个菜(太)辣了。 Zhège cài (tài) là le.
This dish is superb.	这个菜好极了。 Zhège cài hǎojí le.

FOOD EATING OUT

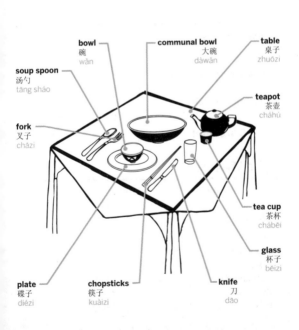

soup spoon
汤勺
tāng sháo

bowl
碗
wǎn

communal bowl
大碗
dàwǎn

table
桌子
zhuōzi

fork
叉子
chāzi

teapot
茶壶
cháhú

tea cup
茶杯
chábēi

glass
杯子
bēizi

plate
碟子
diézi

chopsticks
筷子
kuàizi

knife
刀
dāo

> **CULTURE TIP** **Bill-Paying Etiquette**
> A favourite Chinese sport is fighting over the bill in restaurants. It's considered polite in China to offer to pay the bill once or even twice, even if you're clearly the guest. A protest along the following lines may be made loudly, to show sincerity, even when it's a bluff:
>
> 你请客，我买单。 Nǐ qǐngkè, wǒ mǎidān.
> You were tonight's host, but I'll pay the bill.

Paying the Bill

Is service included in the bill?	帐单中包括服务费吗？ Zhàngdān zhōng bāokuò fúwù fèi ma?
There's a mistake in the bill.	帐单上有问题。 Zhàngdān shàng yǒu wèntí.
Please bring the bill.	请给我账单。 Qǐng gěiwǒ zhàngdān.
✂ **Bill, please!**	买单！　　　Mǎidān!

Light Meals

What's that called?	那个叫什么？ Nàge jiào shénme?	
I'd like ..., please.	请给我…… Qǐng gěi wǒ ...	
one slice	一块	yīkuài
a piece	一份	yīfèn
a sandwich	一个三明治	yīge sānmíngzhì
that one	那一个	nàyīge
two	两个	liǎngge

🔍 LOOK FOR

t–凉菜	Liángcài	Appetisers (cold)
主菜	Zhǔ cài	Main Courses (usually meat dishes)
海鲜	Hǎixiān	Seafood Dishes
汤类	Tānglèi	Soups
蔬菜	Shūcài	Vegetable Dishes (may contain meat)
主食	Zhǔshí	Staples
甜品	Tiánpǐn	Desserts
啤酒	Píjiǔ	Beer
果汁	Guǒzhī	Fruit Juice
汽水	Qìshuǐ	Soft Drinks
香槟	Xiāngbīn	Sparkling Wines
白酒	Báijiǔ	Spirits
白兰地	Báilándì	Cognac
加饭酒	Jiāfànjiǔ	Digestifs

For more words you might see on a menu, see the **menu decoder**, page 199.

FOOD EATING OUT

Nonalcoholic Drinks

... water	······水 ... shuǐ	
boiled	开	kāi
cold	凉开	liáng kāi
sparkling mineral	矿泉汽	kuàngquán qì
still mineral	矿泉	kuàngquán

CULTURE TIP

Sharing Meals

Meals in Chinese restaurants typically come in communal plates (dàpán 大盘) rather than individual servings, and diners eat directly from them. This style of eating contributes to the fun, social atmosphere of dining in China. It also contributes to the high rates of hepatitis B infection in China, so make sure you're immunised before you go.

fresh drinking yogurt	酸奶	suānnǎi
(orange) juice	(橙)汁	(chéng) zhī
lychee juice	荔枝汁	lìzhī zhī
soft drink	汽水	qìshuǐ
sour plum drink	酸梅汤	suānméitāng
cup of coffee with (milk)	一杯咖啡加(牛奶)	yībēi kāfēi jiā (niúnǎi)
cup of tea without (sugar)	一杯茶不加(糖)	yībēi chá bù jiā (táng)
... coffee	……咖啡	... kāfēi

black	黑	hēi
decaffeinated	低咖啡因	dī kāfēiyīn
espresso	浓缩	nóngsuō
iced	冰	bīng
strong	特浓	tènóng
weak	淡	dàn
white	白	bái

Alcoholic Drinks

Keep an eye out for people tapping their fingers on the tablecloth as their glass is filled – a custom that conquered China from the south in the early 1990s. It indicates appreciation of the service rendered.

beer	啤酒 píjiǔ
brandy	白兰地 báilándì
Champagne	香槟 xiāngbīn
Chinese spirit	白酒 báijiǔ
cocktail	鸡尾酒 jīwěi jiǔ
maotai (Chinese vodka)	茅台酒 máotái jiǔ
rice wine	黄酒 huángjiǔ

CULTURE TIP

Tea

Generally speaking, the Chinese are tea rather than coffee drinkers. Though the major cities have a nascent coffee culture, coffee can be hard to find outside the major cities. The good news is that China has many delicious teas, just as you might expect.

红茶	hóngchá	black tea
菊花茶	júhuāchá	chrysanthemum tea
绿茶	lǜchá	green tea
花茶	huāchá	jasmine tea
乌龙茶	wūlóngchá	oolong tea

FOOD | EATING OUT

Street Food

China's bustling towns and cities teem with street vendors (jiētóu xiǎochī 街头小吃) selling delicious snacks (xiǎochī 小吃) to eat on the go. Choose from this array of popular treats:

凉粉	liángfěn	cold clear bean-flour noodles
玉米棒	yùmǐ bàng	corn on the cob
饺子	jiǎozi	dumpling (boiled)
锅贴	guōtiē	dumpling (fried)
包子	bāozi	dumpling (steamed)
煎饼	jiānbǐng	egg and spring-onion pancake
烧饼	shāobǐng	flat bread topped with sesame seeds
肉饼	ròubǐng	pork pie (large)
馅饼	xiànbǐng	pork pie (small)
烧卖	shāomài	steamed dumpling with pork, prawn, water-chestnut and bamboo-shoot filling
粽子	zòngzi	sticky rice wrapped in bamboo leaves
馄饨	húntun	wonton soup

a shot of ...　　　　　　　　一樽……
　　　　　　　　　　　　　　　yīzūn ...

gin	金酒	jīnjiǔ
rum	朗姆酒	lǎngmǔjiǔ
tequila	龙舌兰酒	lóngshélán jiǔ
vodka	伏特加	fútèjiā
whisky	威士忌	wēishìjì

a bottle/glass of ... wine	一瓶/一杯……葡萄酒 yīpíng/yībēi ... pútáo jiǔ

dessert	甜	tián
red	红	hóng
sparkling	香槟	xiāngbīn
white	白	bái

a glass of beer	一杯啤酒 yī bēi píjiǔ
a large bottle of beer	一大瓶啤酒 yī dàpíng píjiǔ
a small bottle of beer	一小瓶啤酒 yī xiǎopíng píjiǔ

In the Bar

Excuse me!	劳驾！ Láojià!
Q What would you like to drink?	你想喝什么？ Nǐ xiǎng hē shénme?
A I'll have ...	我来一个…… Wǒ lái yīge ...
Same again, please.	请再来一个。 Qǐng zài lái yīge.
No ice, thanks.	不要加冰块。 Bùyào jiā bīngkuài.

🔊 **LISTEN FOR**

你喝了什么？	Nǐ hē le shénme? What are you having?
你喝多了。	Nǐ hē duō le. I think you've had enough.

CULTURE TIP **Chinese Cuisine**

Chinese cuisine can be divided into four main schools. The character of these regional cuisines is encapsulated by the saying 'The East is sour, the West is spicy, the South is sweet and the North is salty.' (dōng suān, xī là, nán tián, běi xián 东酸, 西辣, 南甜, 北咸).

A number of provincial cooking styles are recognised, too, including the ones given below.

皖菜	Wǎncài	Anhui cuisine
浙菜	Zhècài	Eastern (Shanghai) cuisine
闽菜	Mǐncài	Hokkien cuisine
湘菜	Xiāngcài	Hunan cuisine
苏菜	Sūcài	Jiangsu cuisine
鲁菜	Lǔcài	Northern (Shandong) cuisine
川菜	Chuāncài	Western (Sichuan) cuisine
粤菜	Yuècài	Southern (Cantonese) cuisine

What are you drinking?	喝什么？ Hē shénme?
I'll buy you one.	我请客。 Wǒ qǐng kè.
How much is that?	总共多少钱？ Zǒnggòng duōshǎo qián?
Do you serve meals here?	你们提供饭菜吗？ Nǐmen tígòng fàncài ma?

Drinking Up

Cheers!	干杯！ Gānbēi!
This is hitting the spot.	太顺口了。 Tài shùnkǒu le.

I feel fantastic!	感觉真爽！ Gǎnjué zhēnshuǎng!
I think I've had one too many.	我是不是喝多了。 Wǒ shìbùshì hēduō le.
I'm feeling drunk.	我有点醉。 Wǒ yǒudiǎn zuì.
I'm pissed.	我醉了。 Wǒ zuì le.
I feel ill.	我要呕。 Wǒ yào ǒu.
Where's the toilet?	哪里有厕所？ Nǎli yǒu cèsuǒ?
I'm tired, I'd better go home.	我困了，该回家了。 Wǒ kùn le, gāi huíjiā le.
Can you call a taxi for me?	你能帮我叫个车吗？ Nǐ néng bāngwǒ jiào ge chē ma?

FOOD

EATING OUT

Self-Catering

KEY PHRASES

What's the local speciality?	有什么地方特产？	Yǒu shénme dìfāng tèchǎn?
Where can I find the ... section?	哪里有卖……？	Nǎli yǒu mài ...?
I'd like ...	我要……	Wǒyào ...

Buying Food

What's the local speciality?	有什么地方特产？ Yǒu shénme dìfāng tèchǎn?
What's that?	那是什么？ Nà shì shénme?
Can I taste it?	能尝一下吗？ Néng chángyīxià ma?
Can I have a bag, please?	我买一包吧。 Wǒ mǎi yībāo ba.
How much?	多少钱？ Duōshǎo qián?
How much is (half a kilo of apples)?	（一斤苹果）多少钱？ (Yījīn píngguǒ) duōshǎo qián?
Do you have anything cheaper?	你有便宜一点的吗？ Nǐ yǒu piányi yīdiǎn de ma?
Do you have other kinds?	你有别的吗？ Nǐ yǒu biéde ma?

🔊 LISTEN FOR

你想要什么?	Nǐ xiǎng yào shénme? What would you like?
想点什么呢?	Xiǎng diǎn shénme ne? What can I get for you?
不需要。	Bù xūyào. No, we don't have any.
还要别的吗?	Háiyào biéde ma? Would you like anything else?
总共(五块)钱。	Zǒnggòng (wǔ kuài) qián. That's (five kuai).

FOOD **SELF-CATERING**

I'd like ...	我要…… Wǒyào ...	
half a dozen	半打	bàndá
a dozen	一打	yīdá
a bottle	一瓶	yīpíng
a jar	一罐	yīguàn
a litre	一公升	yīgōngshēng
a packet	一盒	yīhé
a piece	一块	yīkuài
(three) pieces	(三)块	(sān) kuài
a slice	一份	yīfèn
(six) slices	(六)份	(liù) fèn
a tin	一罐	yīguàn
some ...	一些……	yīxiē ...
that one	那个	nàge
this one	这个	zhège

Less.	少一点。	Shǎo yīdiǎn.
A bit more.	多一点。	Duō yīdiǎn.
Enough!	够了，够了！	Gòule, gòule!
Where can I find the ... section?	哪里有卖……？	Nǎli yǒu mài ...?

dairy	奶制品	nǎizhìpǐn
frozen goods	冰冻食品	bīngdòng shípǐn
fruit and vegetable	水果和蔬菜	shuǐguǒ hé shūcài
meat	肉	ròu
poultry	鸡	jī
seafood	海鲜	hǎixiān

Cooking

Could I please borrow a/an ...?	我能借一……吗？	Wǒ néng jiè yī ... ma?
I need a/an ...	我想要一……	Wǒ xiǎngyào yī ...

bottle opener	个开瓶器	ge kāipíng qì
can opener	个开罐器	ge kāiguàn qì
corkscrew	个螺旋开瓶器	ge luóxuán kāipíng qì
frying pan	口炸锅	kǒu zháguō
meat cleaver	把菜刀	bǎ càidāo
rice cooker	个电饭锅	ge diànfànguō
saucepan	口小锅	kǒu xiǎoguō
steamer	个蒸笼	ge zhēnglóng
toaster	个烤面包机	ge kǎomiànbāo jī
wok	口锅	kǒu guō

FOOD SELF-CATERING

GREG ELMS/LONELY PLANET IMAGES ©

能尝一下吗?
Néng chángyīxià ma?
Can I taste it?

cooked	熟 shú
cured	咸 xián
dried	干 gān
fresh	鲜 xiān
frozen	冰冻 bīngdòng
raw	生 shēng
smoked	熏 xūn

Vegetarian & Special Meals

KEY PHRASES

Do you have vegetarian food?	有没有素食食品？	Yǒuméiyǒu sùshí shípǐn?
Could you prepare a meal without ...?	能不能做一个不放……的菜？	Néngbùnéng zuòyīge bùfàng ... de cài?
I'm allergic to ...	我对……过敏。	Wǒ duì ... guòmǐn.

Special Diets & Allergies

I'm allergic to ...	我对……过敏。	
	Wǒ duì ... guòmǐn.	
butter	黄油	huángyóu
chilli	辣椒	làjiāo
dairy produce	奶制品	nǎizhìpǐn
eggs	鸡蛋	jīdàn
gelatine	明胶	míngjiāo
gluten	面筋	miànjīn
honey	蜂蜜	fēngmì
MSG	味精	wèijīng
nuts	果仁	guǒrén
peanuts	花生	huāshēng
seafood	海鲜	hǎixiān
shellfish	贝类海鲜	bèilèi hǎixiān

| I'm on a special diet. | 我在节食。
Wǒ zài jiéshí. |
| I don't eat (pork). | 我不吃(猪肉)。
Wǒ bùchī (zhūròu). |

To explain your dietary restrictions with reference to religious beliefs, see **beliefs & culture**, page 145.

Ordering Food

Do you have halal food?	有没有清真食品? Yǒuméiyǒu qīngzhēn shípín?
Do you have kosher food?	有没有犹太食品? Yǒuméiyǒu yóutài shípín?
Do you have vegetarian food?	有没有素食食品? Yǒuméiyǒu sùshí shípín?
Is there a (vegetarian) restaurant near here?	附近有没有(素食)饭馆? Fùjìn yǒuméiyǒu (sùshí) fànguǎn?
Is it cooked with (meat stock)?	是用(肉)做的吗? Shì yòng (ròu) zuòde ma?
Could you prepare a meal without ...?	能不能做一个不放 ……的菜? Néngbùnéng zuòyīge bùfàng ... de cài?

eggs	鸡蛋	jīdàn
fish	鱼	yú
fish stock	鱼肉	yúròu
MSG	味精	wèijīng
poultry	家禽	jiāqín
red meat	牛羊肉	niúyángròu

Is this ...? 这个是……的吗?
Zhège shì ... de ma?

free of animal produce	没有动物成份	méiyǒu dòngwù chéngfèn
free-range	自由放养	zìyóu fàngyǎng
genetically modified	转基因	zhuǎn jīyīn
gluten-free	无筋面粉	wújīn miànfěn
halal	清真	qīngzhēn
kosher	犹太	yóutài
low fat	低脂肪	dī zhīfáng
low sugar	低糖	dītáng
organic	有机	yǒujī
salt-free	不加盐	bùjiā yán

Menu
~ DECODER ~
饭食词表

These Chinese dishes and ingredients are listed in alphabetical order according to their pronunciation so you can easily understand what's on offer and ask for what takes your fancy when eating out in China. The following abbreviations identify the cuisine to which individual dishes belong:

NC - Northern Cuisine, **SC** - Southern Cuisine,
EC - Eastern Cuisine, **WC** - Western Cuisine

~ B ~

bābǎo fàn 八宝饭 'eight treasure rice' – sweet rice dish traditionally eaten at Chinese New Year containing colourful sugary fruits, nuts & seeds

bābǎo làjiàng 八宝辣酱 (EC) 'eight treasure hot sauce' – made from pressed tofu & chilli

bái hújiāo 白胡椒 white pepper

bái jièmo 白芥末 white mustard

bái mǐfàn 白米饭 rice – the staple & imbued with an almost spiritual significance to the Chinese people

bái pútáo jiǔ 白葡萄酒 white wine

báicài 白菜 Chinese white cabbage

báicù 白醋 white rice vinegar

báijiǔ 白酒 Chinese vodka-like spirit

báilándì 白兰地 brandy

báimǐ 白米 plain rice

báizhuóxiā 白灼虾 (SC) fresh whole prawns that are poached, simmered & served with a peanut-oil & soy-sauce dip

bājiǎo 八角 star anise

bājiǎo fěn 八角粉 powder made from ground star anise

bàn shēng 半生 rare

bànban jī 拌拌鸡 (WC) 'bang-bang chicken' – cold dish featuring cooked shredded chicken, cucumber & cellophane (bean thread) noodles with a sesame-paste, sesame-oil, garlic, ginger & chilli-sauce dressing

bàngzi 蚌子 clam • mussel

bànshēng bànshú 半生半熟 medium

bào 爆 'exploded' – stir-fried in hot oil

bàochǎo miàn 爆炒面 (WC) 'hot-wok noodles' – pan-fried crispy egg noodles often served with meat & vegetables

bàoyú 鲍鱼 abalone

bāozǎi fàn 煲仔饭 'clay-pot rice' – braised rice cooked in a clay pot with Chinese sausage, salted fish, vegetables & mushrooms

bāozi 包子 steamed dumpling

básī píngguǒ 拔丝苹果 apple pieces dipped in batter then deep-fried & coated in toffee

B

C

Běijīng kǎoyā 北京烤鸭 (NC) Peking duck – slices of spice-imbued roast duck often served with pancakes, shallots & plum sauce

biǎndòu 扁豆 green bean

bīngdòng 冰冻 frozen

bǐnggān 饼干 Western-style biscuit

bīngjīlíng 冰激凌 ice cream

bīngkuài 冰块 ice cubes

bōcài 菠菜 spinach

bòhé 薄荷 mint

bōluó 菠萝 pineapple

bùdīng 布丁 (SC) Western-style pudding

~ C ~

càidān 菜单 menu

càihuā 菜花 cauliflower

càishì 菜市 fresh-food market

càitān 菜摊 greengrocer

càixīn 菜心 Chinese flowering cabbage – sometimes known as 'choi sum' or 'choy sum' in English

càiyóu 菜油 vegetable oil

cānguǎn 餐馆 restaurant

cǎoméi 草莓 strawberry

chá 茶 tea

chángfěn 肠粉 (SC) steamed rice-noodle roll stuffed with shrimp, pork or beef & served with soy sauce & sesame oil

chǎo 炒 stir-fried

chǎo shānsù 炒三素 (SC) vegetarian stir-fried dish of mushrooms, lotus root, ginkgo nuts & fresh vegetables

chǎofàn 炒饭 fried rice

chǎofěn 炒粉 fried rice noodles

chǎomiàn 炒面 fried rice noodles

Cháozhōu lúshuǐ é 潮州卤水鹅 (SC) goose stewed in a rich sauce & served with a garlic & vinegar dip

Cháozhōu yīmiàn 潮州伊面 (SC) thin egg noodles pan-fried until crunchy & served with chives, sugar & vinegar

Cháozhōu yútāng 潮州鱼汤 (SC) soup made from sliced fish (usually pomfret), squid, celery, mushrooms & rice cooked in chicken stock & sprinkled with dried fish pieces

Cháozhōucài 潮州菜 Chaozhou cuisine

chāshāo 叉烧 (SC) barbecued sweet roast pork

chāshāobāo 叉烧包 (SC) steamed barbecued pork bun

cháyè dàn 茶叶蛋 (SC) 'tea egg' – marbled hard-boiled egg flavoured with black tea & star anise

chéncù 陈醋 dark vinegar

chéng zhī 橙汁 orange juice

chéngjiàng 橙酱 marmalade

chéngzi 橙子 orange

chénpí 陈皮 (SC) mandarin or tangerine peel used as a flavouring

Chóngqìng huǒguō 重庆火锅 (WC) 'Chongqing hotpot' – cook-it-yourself meal requiring diners to dip various meats & vegetables into a pot of boiling spicy stock

chóngrè 重热 re-heated

chòu dòufu 臭豆腐 (EC) 'stinky tofu' – tofu fermented in cabbage juice with a pungent result

Chuāncài 川菜 Western (Sichuan) cuisine – renowned for its use of the red chilli & fiery peppercorns; pork, poultry, legumes & soybeans are the main staples

chūnjuǎn 春卷 (NC) 'spring roll' – deep-fried pancake stuffed with a mixture that can include vegetables, chicken, pork, prawns, mushrooms, sprouts & noodles

cōngbào yángròu 葱爆羊肉 (NC) hot-wok lamb with shallots

cōngyóubǐng 葱油饼 (NC) 'onion cakes' – pastries filled with spring onion

cù 醋 vinegar

cuì 脆 crisp

cuìpí 脆皮 pork crackling

~ D ~

dà cài 大菜 main course

dà cōng 大葱 oversized spring onions

dàn 蛋 egg

dànbái 蛋白 egg white

dàndàn miàn 担担面 (WC) 'dan-dan noodles' – thin wheat noodles served with pork, scallions & a red-hot chilli-oil, soy-sauce, sesame-paste, garlic, ginger & Sichuan roasted-peppercorn sauce

dàngāo 蛋糕 cake

dànhuáng 蛋黄 egg yolk

dànmiàn 蛋面 (SC) egg noodles – sold dried or fresh

dàntà 蛋挞 (SC) baked puff pastry with an egg custard filling

dàntāng 蛋汤 (SC) 'egg drop soup' – soup based on chicken broth into which raw eggs are whisked & cooked

dàsuàn 大蒜 garlic

dàxiā 大虾 prawn

dàzháxiè 大闸蟹 (SC) 'hairy crab' – so called for the hair-like growths on their legs & underbellies, these crabs are a Shanghainese delicacy

diǎnxīn 点心 (SC) dim sum – an umbrella term for the vast array of steamed & fried dumplings & small delicacies served at a yǐnchá

dìguā 地瓜 sweet potato

dīng 丁 cubed beef, chicken or pork

dīngxiāng 丁香 clove

dōngcài 冬菜 (NC) Tianjin pickled cabbage

dōngguā 冬瓜 winter melon – type of melon with thick white flesh used in soups & other dishes

dòufěn 豆粉 bean noodles

dòufu 豆腐 tofu (soybean curd)

dòufu nǎo 豆腐脑 (NC) salty bean-curd soup

dòufu pí 豆腐皮 dried bean curd

dòufu tāng 豆腐汤 (WC) casserole of bean curd with bamboo shoots, ham, scallions, Chinese cabbage, ginger & shrimps

dòujiāng 豆浆 fresh soy milk

dòujiǎo 豆角 chopped green beans

dòumiáo 豆苗 pea shoots

dòunǎi fěn 豆奶粉 powdered soy milk

dòushā bāo 豆沙包 sweet steamed red-bean-paste bun

dòuyá 豆芽 bean sprout

dòuzi 豆子 bean

dùn 炖 stewed

~ E ~

é 鹅 goose

èlí 鳄梨 avocado

~ F ~

fāngbiàn miàn 方便面 instant noodles

fànguǎn 饭馆 restaurant

fānqié chǎo jīdàn 番茄炒鸡蛋 stir-fried tomato & egg

fānqié jiàng 番茄酱 ketchup • tomato sauce

fèi 肺 lung

féicháng 肥肠 large intestines of pig

fēicháng kělè 非常可乐 'extreme cola' – Chinese version of Coca-Cola

féiròu 肥肉 fatty meat

fēngmì 蜂蜜 honey

fèngzhuǎ (jījiǎo) 凤爪（鸡脚）'phoenix claws' – chicken feet

fěnsī 粉丝 vermicelli

fóshǒu 佛手 (EC) Buddha's hand – fragrant citrus fruit also known as the fingered citron

fǔrǔ 腐乳 fermented tofu cubes, dried, steamed then bottled with wine & possessing a curiously Camembert-like taste & texture

fútèjiā 伏特加 vodka

fǔzhú 腐竹 dried yellow soy-milk sticks

G

~ G ~

gān 干 dried

gān 肝 liver

gānbiǎn 干煸 'dry-fried' – fried with a minimum of liquids which are then boiled away to leave the food coated in sauce

gānbiǎn niúròu 干煸牛肉 (WC) shredded beef, deep-fried then tossed with chillies

gānbiǎn sìjì dòu (WC) 干煸四季豆 deep-fried snake beans stir-fried with garlic, ginger & shrimps & served with soy sauce, wine, vinegar & sesame oil

gǎnlǎn yóu 橄榄油 olive oil

gānzhè 甘蔗 sugar cane

gāodiǎn wū 糕点屋 cake shop

gēzi 鸽子 pigeon

gōngbào jīdīng 宫爆鸡丁 (NC) marinated chicken cubes stir-fried with chillies & peanuts & seasoned with a sweet bean sauce

gōngfu chá 功夫茶 (SC) congou tea – very strong short black tea

gǒuqǐzi 枸杞子 box thorn – similar in texture & nutritional value to spinach

gǒuròu 狗肉 dog

guā 瓜 melon • vegetable marrow

guāzi 瓜子 melon seeds

guìpí 桂皮 cinnamon bark

guǒgān 果干 dried fruit

guǒjiàng 果酱 jam

guǒrén 果仁 nuts

guōtiē 锅贴 fried dumpling

guǒzhī 果汁 juice

gǔsuí 骨髓 bone marrow

~ H ~

hǎidài 海带 kelp

hǎishēn 海参 sea cucumber

hǎixiān 海鲜 seafood

hǎizhé 海蜇 jellyfish – sold in sheets & packed in salt & served shredded

hànbǎobao 汉堡包 hamburger

háoyóu 蚝油 (SC) oyster sauce

háoyóu jièlán 蚝油芥兰 (SC) dish of jièlán (also known as gai lum, Chinese broccoli or Chinese kale) with oyster sauce

háozi 蚝子 oyster

héfàn 盒饭 generic term for a take-away box

héfěn 河粉 thin round or flat slippery rice noodles

hélán dòu 荷兰豆 snow pea

hétáo 核桃 walnut

hóng pútáo jiǔ 红葡萄酒 red wine

hóngchá 红茶 black tea

hóngcù 红醋 red rice vinegar

hóngdòu 红豆 red mung bean

hóngshāo 红烧 (WC) 'red-fried' – braised in a sweet star-anise sauce

hóngshāo páigǔ 红烧排骨 (WC) red-fried pork spare ribs

hóngshāo ròu 红烧肉 (WC) red-fried pork

huāchá 花茶 jasmine tea

Huáiyáng cài 淮扬菜 East Coast cuisine – relatively vegetarian-friendly cuisine that makes use of a wide variety of condiments & fresh ingredients; also home of the red stew (meat simmered in dark soy sauce, sugar & spices)

huángdòu 黄豆 soy bean

huángguā 黄瓜 cucumber

huángjiàng 黄酱 (NC) black-bean dipping sauce

huángjiǔ 黄酒 'yellow wine' – rice wine similar in taste to sherry & best served warm

huángshàn 黄鳝 paddy eel

huángyóu 黄油 butter

huāshēng 花生 peanut

huāshēng jiàng 花生酱 peanut butter

huāshēng yóu 花生油 peanut oil

huíguō ròu 回锅肉 (NC) sweet & sour pork

hújiāo fěn 胡椒粉 pepper (condiment)

húluóbo 胡萝卜 carrot

húntun 馄饨 wonton soup – dumplings stuffed with pork & shrimp served in chicken broth

húntun tān 馄饨摊 wonton stall

huǒjī 火鸡 turkey

huǒtuǐ 火腿 ham

~ J ~

jiān 煎 braised

jiānbǐng 煎饼 egg & spring onion pancake

jiānbǐng 煎饼 (SC) fortune cookies

jiāng 姜 ginger

jiàngyóu 酱油 soy sauce

jiàngzhī páigǔ 酱汁排骨 (EC) barbecued pork ribs – a speciality of the city of Wuxi

jiāobái 茭白 (EC) wild-rice root

jiàohuā jī 叫花鸡 (EC) 'beggar's chicken' – whole, deboned chicken stuffed with pork, vegetables, mushrooms, ginger & other seasonings wrapped in lotus leaves & wet clay or pastry & baked for several hours

jiàomǔ 酵母 yeast

jiǎozi 饺子 boiled dumpling

jiǎyú 甲鱼 tortoise

jīchì 鸡翅 chicken wing

jīdàn 鸡蛋 chicken egg

jièlán 芥兰 gai lum (also known in English as Chinese broccoli or Chinese kale)

jiētóu xiǎochī 街头小吃 street food vendor

jīnqiāng yú 金枪鱼 tuna

jīnsīmiàn 金丝面 (NC) fried Beijing egg noodles – similar to Japanese udon noodles

jīnzhēngū 金针菇 golden needle mushroom (also known as enoki mushroom)

jīròu 鸡肉 chicken

jītāng 鸡汤 chicken stock

jītuǐ 鸡腿 drumstick

jiǔbā 酒吧 bar

jiǔcài 韭菜 Chinese chives

jiǔlèi 酒类 alcoholic drinks

jīwěi jiǔ 鸡尾酒 cocktail

júhuā 菊花 chrysanthemum – flowering plant with a taste similar to lettuce used as an accompaniment to dishes

júhuāchá 菊花茶 chrysanthemum tea

júzi 橘子 mandarin

~ K ~

kāfēi 咖啡 coffee

kāfēiwū 咖啡屋 cafe

kāishuǐ 开水 boiling water

kāixīnguǒ 开心果 pistachio

kǎo 烤 roasted

kǎo miànbāo 烤面包 toast

kǎo yángròu chuàn 烤羊肉串 (WC) chargrilled lamb kebab – a Uighur speciality

kuàngquánshuǐ 矿泉水 mineral water

kǔguā 苦瓜 bitter melon – resembles a knobbly cucumber & has a strong bitter taste

~ L ~

là 辣 hot chilli

làjiāo 辣椒 chilli pepper

làjiāo jiàng 辣椒酱 chilli sauce

Lánzhōu miàn 兰州面 (WC) Lanzhou beef noodles

làzi jīdīng 辣子鸡丁 (WC) tender braised chilli chicken

lí 梨 pear

liáng kāishuǐ 凉开水 chilled boiled water

liángcài 凉菜 appetiser

liángfěn 凉粉 cold bean-flour noodles

lián'ǒu 莲藕 lotus root – the tuber stem of the water lily which can be stuffed with rice & steamed, stir-fried or used in soups & stews

liúlián 榴莲 (SC) durian – spiky fruit prized by the Chinese as the 'king of fruits', with a repellant smelly-sock aroma & a dense creamy flesh

lǐyú 鲤鱼 carp

lìzhī zhī 荔枝汁 lychee-flavoured soft drink

lìzi 栗子 chestnut

lóngxiā 龙虾 rock lobster

Lǔcài 鲁菜 Northern (Shandong) cuisine – typical ingredients are wheat pancakes, spring onions & fermented bean paste

lǜchá 绿茶 green tea

lǜdòu 绿豆 green mung bean

luóbo 萝卜 radish

luóbo gāo 萝卜糕 (SC) fried radish cake containing grated turnip, Chinese sausage, dried shrimp, mushrooms, spring onion & seasonings

luóhàn zhāi 罗汉斋 (SC) vegetarian stew (with many variations) which usually includes wood-ear fungus & lily bud stems

lǘròu 驴肉 donkey

~ M ~

máhuā 麻花 (NC) Tianjin Muslim-style bread twist

málà tàng 麻辣烫 (WC) 'numbingly hot soup' – the standard cooking broth that goes with Chóngqìng huǒguō with liberal doses of mouth-scorching Sichuan pepper & chilli oil

mángguǒ 芒果 mango

mántou 馒头 steamed bun

mányú 鳗鱼 river eel

máodòu 毛豆 fresh soy beans

máotái jiǔ 茅台酒 Chinese-style vodka made from millet

mápó dòufu 麻婆豆腐 (NC) 'ma-po bean curd' – fresh bean curd marinated in spices then deep-fried in chilli oil & garnished with shredded pork & fiery peppercorns

mǎyǐ shàngshù 蚂蚁上树 (NC) 'ants climbing a tree' – cellophane noodles with braised minced pork seasoned with soy sauce & served sprinkled with chopped spring onions

méicài kòuròu 梅菜扣肉 double-cooked steamed pork with pickled salted cabbage

méizi 梅子 plum

miànbāo 面包 bread

miànfěn 面粉 flour

miànguǎn 面馆 noodle house

miànjīn qiú 面筋球 meaty-textured gluten ball made from dough that is washed so only gluten remains – used in vegetarian dishes

miàntiáo 面条 noodles

mǐfěn 米粉 rice noodles

míhóutáo 猕猴桃 kiwi fruit

Mǐncài 闽菜 Hokkien cuisine

mógū 蘑菇 mushroom

mòlì huāchá 茉莉花茶 jasmine tea

mùguā 木瓜 papaya • pawpaw

mùxūròu 木须肉 (NC) stir-fried pork with wood-ear fungus

~ N ~

nǎilào 奶酪 cheese

nǎizhìpǐn 奶制品 dairy

nánguā 南瓜 pumpkin

niángāo 年糕 Chinese New Year sweets • rice cake

níngméng 柠檬 lemon

níngméng jī 柠檬鸡 (SC) lemon chicken

niúròu 牛肉 beef

niúròu tāng 牛肉汤 beef stock

nuòmǐ 糯米 glutinous rice (also known as sticky rice or sweet rice)

~ O ~

Ōushì zǎocān 欧式早餐 continental breakfast

~ P ~

páigǔ 排骨 spare ribs

péigēn 培根 bacon

piàn 片 slice

pídàn shòuròu zhōu 皮蛋瘦肉粥 (SC) preserved duck egg & pork congee

píjiǔ 啤酒 beer

píngguǒ 苹果 apple

pǔ'ěr chá 普洱茶 pu-erh tea – aged black jasmine tea purported to have medicinal qualities & possessing a distinctive aroma & taste

pútáo 葡萄 grapes

pútáo jiǔ 葡萄酒 wine

pútáogān 葡萄干 raisins

~ Q ~

qiǎokèlì 巧克力 chocolate

qiézi 茄子 aubergine • eggplant

qíncài 芹菜 celery

qīngcài 青菜 green leafy vegetables

qīngjiāo 青椒 capsicum • bell pepper

qīngtāng 清汤 light broth

qīngzhēn 清真 halal

qīngzhēng dàxháxiè 清蒸大闸蟹 (EC) stir-fried crab with ginger & shallots

qìshuǐ 汽水 soft drink • soda

quánjiāfú 全家福 (EC) 'family happiness seafood spectacular' – seafood braised with mushrooms & pig tendon

quánmài miànbāo 全麦面包 whole-meal bread

~ R ~

rénshēn 人参 ginseng – prized as a tonic & aphrodisiac

rèqiǎokèlì 热巧克力 hot chocolate

ròu 肉 meat (pork unless specified)

ròubǐng 肉饼 large pork pie

ròudiàn 肉店 butcher's shop

ròujiāmó 肉夹馍 (NC) finely chopped braised pork & coriander stuffed into a pocket of flat bread

ròupái 肉排 steak (beef)

ròuxiàn 肉馅 mince

~ S ~

sānmíngzhì 三明治 sandwich

sānwén yú 三文鱼 salmon

shādiē 沙嗲 satay – originally a Southeast Asian dish but now a popular dim sum item

shāguō dòufu 砂锅豆腐 (EC) bean curd in a clay pot with dried bamboo & vermicelli

shālā 沙拉 salad

shānméi 山梅 raspberry

shāo 烧 spit-roasted meat with a sweet sauce

shāobǐng 烧饼 flat bread topped with sesame seeds

shāokǎo 烧烤 barbecued

shāomài 烧卖 won ton wrappers filled with pork, prawns, water chest-nuts & bamboo shoots then steamed

shātáng 砂糖 sugar

shēng 生 raw

shēngcài 生菜 lettuce

shéròu 蛇肉 snake

shìzi 柿子 persimmon

shòuròu 瘦肉 lean meat

shú 熟 cooked • well done

shuàn yángròu 涮羊肉 (NC) 'Mongolian lamb hotpot' – sliced meat is dipped into a flame-heated hotpot of hot broth brought to the table & cabbage & noodles are later added to make a soup

shūcài 蔬菜 vegetable dishes – not usually vegetarian but featuring a specific vegetable

shuǐguǒ 水果 fruit

shuǐjīng yáoròu 水晶肴肉 (EC) pig's trotter jelly

shuǐzhǔ zhūzá 水煮猪杂 (WC) stewed pig intestines in a fiery blend of chilli powder, chilli paste & fresh mountain chillies

T

Sìchuān jī 四川鸡 (WC) Sichuan chicken
sìjì páigǔ 四季排骨 (SC) braised spare ribs
sōngrén 松仁 pine nut
suān 酸 sour
suānlà 酸辣 'sour & hot' – usually a soupy style of cooking with plenty of Chinese vinegar & chilli oil
suānlà tāng 酸辣汤 'hot & sour soup' – warming Sichuanese winter soup that traditionally included solidified chicken blood & is made with pepper, chillies & vinegar
suānméi 酸梅 dried sour plum
suānméi tāng 酸梅汤 sour plum drink
suànmiáo 蒜苗 garlic chives
suānnǎi 酸奶 fresh drinking yogurt
suànní 蒜泥 'garlic-fried' – cooked with a liberal dose of crushed garlic & oil
Sūcài 苏菜 Jiangsu cuisine
sǔn 笋 bamboo shoot

~ T ~

táng hétao 糖核桃 candied walnut
tángchǎo lìzi 糖炒栗子 hot roasted chestnut – the ideal winter hand warmer
tángcù 糖醋 'sweet & sour' – piquant sauce composed of sugar & vinegar used to flavour meat or for dipping
tángcù lǐyú 糖醋鲤鱼 (EC) sweet & sour fish
tángcù páigǔ 糖醋排骨 (EC) sweet & sour pork ribs
tángguǒ 糖果 lollies • candy
tánghúlu 糖葫芦 (NC) toffeed crab-apple stick
tānglèi 汤类 soup
táozi 桃子 peach
tián 甜 sweet
tiánbǐng 甜饼 cookie • sweet biscuit
tiáncài 甜菜 beetroot
tiánjī 田鸡 'field chicken', ie frog

tiánpǐn 甜品 dessert
tiáowèipǐn 调味品 flavour enhancer
tiěbǎn kǎo 铁板烤 grilled on a hotplate
tǔdòu 土豆 potato
tùròu 兔肉 rabbit

~ W ~

Wǎncài 皖菜 Anhui cuisine
wāndòu 豌豆 pea
wǎnfàn 晚饭 dinner
wèidao 味道 flavour • taste
wèijīng 味精 MSG
wēishìjì 威士忌 whisky
wōwótóu 窝窝头 (NC) steamed yellow corn bun – rather dry & unappetising
wǔfàn 午饭 lunch
wúhuā guǒ 无花果 fig
wūlóngchá 乌龙茶 oolong tea – delicious dark tea that is partially fermented before drying

~ X ~

xī húlu 西葫芦 courgette • zucchini
xī yòuzi 西柚子 grapefruit
xiājiǎo 虾饺 (SC) bonnet-shaped prawn dumpling with translucent dough
xiāmǐ 虾米 dried shrimp
xiān 鲜 fresh
xián 咸 cured • salty • savoury
xiàn bǐng 馅饼 small pork pie
Xī'ān húlu jī 西安葫芦鸡 (WC) Xi'an casseroled griddled chicken
xiánbǐnggān 咸饼干 cracker
xiáncài 咸菜 pickled vegetables
xiāngbīn 香槟 champagne
Xiāngcài 湘菜 Hunan cuisine
xiāngcǎo 香草 vanilla
xiāngcháng 香肠 pork sausage
xiāngjiāo 香蕉 banana
xiāngliào 香料 culinary herbs • spices
xiányā 咸鸭 pickled duck
xiányú 咸鱼 sardine

xiǎo báicài 小白菜 bok choy (cabbage-like vegetable)
xiǎo cōng 小葱 shallot • spring onion
xiǎochī 小吃 snack
xiǎochī diàn 小吃店 snack shop
xiǎomàibù 小卖部 convenience store
xiǎomǐ 小米 millet – the Chinese staple until it was supplanted by rice during the Han dynasty
xiārén guōba 虾仁锅巴 (EC) crisped rice with shrimp
xiāzi 虾子 prawn • shrimp
xīduō 西多 (SC) Cantonese French toast – peanut butter sandwiched between two slices of white bread before cooking
xīguā 西瓜 watermelon
xīhóngshì 西红柿 tomato
xīlánhuā 西兰花 broccoli
xìngrén 杏仁 almond
xìngtáo 杏桃 apricot
xuè dòufu 血豆腐 bean curd soaked in pig's blood, often made into a soup
xūn 熏 smoked

~ Y ~

yā 鸭 duck
yābǐng 鸭饼 (SC) salted, boned & pressed duck immersed in peanut oil then steamed
yán 盐 salt
yáng cōng 洋葱 onion
yángròu 羊肉 lamb
yángròu zhuāfàn 羊肉抓饭 (WC) pilaf – cumin-flavoured rice cooked with carrot & lamb; a Uighur speciality
Yángzhōu chǎofàn 扬州炒饭 (EC) Yangzhou fried rice – there are many variations of this dish but it may include shrimp & pieces of chicken or pork
Yángzhōu shīzi tóu 扬州狮子头 (EC) 'lion's head meatballs' – oversized pork meatballs cooked with bok choy in a clay pot

yánjī 盐鸡 (SC) 'salt-baked chicken' – chicken stuffed with ginger, garlic & green onions & baked with rock salt
yànmài piàn 燕麦片 oats
yāoguǒ 腰果 cashew nut
yāozi 腰子 kidney
yèxiāo 夜宵 practice of eating snacks in the late evening – popular items include eggs, bean curd & vegetables boiled in stock & presented on a stick
yēzi 椰子 coconut
yìdàlì miàn 意大利面 'Italian noodles' – pasta
yīmiàn 伊面 (SC) deep-fried egg noodles
yǐnchá 饮茶 yum cha – a meal of snack-like portions taken from mid-morning to late afternoon
yīngtáo 樱桃 cherry
yǐnliào 饮料 cold drink
yóucài 油菜 mustard greens – term covers a diverse range of greens which are often used in salads when young or pickled
yóuchǎo miàn 油炒面 (NC) oily fried noodles
yóutiáo 油条 fried dough stick – a popular breakfast item
yóuyú 鱿鱼 calamari • squid
yóuzhá 油炸 deep-fried
yòuzi 柚子 grapefruit • pomelo
yú 鱼 fish
yuánliào 原料 ingredient
Yuècài 粤菜 Southern (Cantonese) cuisine – this style has the most varied range of ingredients & the most elaborate methods of preparation of any Chinese cuisine
yúgān 鱼干 dried fish
yùmǐ 玉米 corn
yùmǐ bàng 玉米棒 corn cob
yútān 鱼摊 fish shop
yùtou 芋头 (EC) yam
yúxiāng 鱼香 'fragrant fish' – fish braised with either fish sauce or small dried fish

yúxiāng qiézi 鱼香茄子 (NC) shredded eggplant in a fish-flavoured sauce of vinegar, wine, garlic, ginger, pepper, spring onions & bean paste

~ Z ~

zǎo 枣 date
zǎofàn 早饭 breakfast
zhá ānchun 炸鹌鹑 fried quail
Zhècài 浙菜 Eastern (Shanghai) cuisine – the cuisine of this region is generally richer, sweeter and more oily than other Chinese cuisines; preserved vegetables & pickles, & salted meats are common ingredients

zhēng 蒸 steamed
zhēnzi 榛子 hazelnut
zhīmá jiàng 芝麻酱 sesame paste
zhōu 粥 porridge
zhǒuzi 肘子 hock (fatty pork elbow)
zhǔ 煮 boiled
zhǔjī 煮鸡 hard-boiled
zhūròu 猪肉 pork
zhǔshí 主食 staples
zhūyóu 猪油 pork lard

Dictionary

ENGLISH *to* MANDARIN
英文 – 普通话

The symbols ⓝ, ⓐ and ⓥ (noun, adjective and verb) have been added for clarity where this is not clear from the English word itself. Where necessary, sg (singular), pl (plural), inf (informal) and pol (polite) forms are also indicated.

A

abalone 鲍鱼 bàoyú
aboard 在……上 zài … shàng
abortion 堕胎 duòtāi
about 关于 guānyú
above 以上 yǐshàng
abroad 国外 guówài
accident 事故 shìgù
accommodation 住宿 zhùsù
(bank) account 账单 zhàngdān
across 对面 duìmiàn
actor 演员 yǎnyuán
acupuncture 针灸 zhēnjiǔ
adaptor 双边插座 shuāngbiān chāzuò
addiction 瘾 yǐn
address ⓝ 地址 dìzhǐ
administration 行政部门 xíngzhèng bùmén
admission price 门票钱 ménpiàoqián
admit (let in) 允许 yǔnxǔ
adult ⓝ 大人 dàrén
advertisement 广告 guǎnggào
advice 建议 jiànyì
aeroplane 飞机 fēijī
Africa 非洲 Fēizhōu
after 以后 yǐhòu

(this) afternoon (今天)下午 (jīntiān) xiàwǔ
aftershave 男用香水 nányòng xiāngshuǐ
again 再一次 zài yīcì
age ⓝ 年龄 niánlíng
(three days) ago (三天)前 (sān tiān) qián
agree 同意 tóngyì
agriculture 农业 nóngyè
ahead 前面 qiánmian
AIDS 艾滋病 àizībìng
air ⓝ 空气 kōngqì
air-conditioned 有空调的 yǒu kōngtiáo de
air-conditioning 空调 kōngtiáo
airline 航空公司 hángkōng gōngsī
airmail 航空信 hángkōng xìn
airplane 飞机 fēijī
airport 飞机场 fēijī chǎng
airport tax 机场税 jīchǎng shuì
aisle (on plane) 走廊 zǒuláng
alarm clock 闹钟 nàozhōng
alcohol 酒精 jiǔjīng
all 所有的 suǒyǒu de
allergic 过敏 guòmǐn
alleyway 胡同 hútòng
almond 杏仁 xīngrén

B

almost 差一点 chà yīdiǎn
alone 独自一个人 dúzì yīge rén
already 已经 yǐjīng
also 也 yě
altitude 海拔 hǎibá
always 每次 měicì
ambassador 大使 dàshǐ
ambulance 急救车 jíjiù chē
American football 美式橄榄球 Měishì gǎnlǎnqiú
anaemia 贫血 pínxuè
ancestors 祖先 zǔxiān
ancestral home 老家 lǎojiā
ancient 古代 gǔdài
and 和 hé
angry 生气 shēngqì
animal 动物 dòngwù
ankle 脚踝 jiǎohuái
another 再一个 zài yīge
answer 答复 dáfù
ant 蚂蚁 mǎyǐ
antibiotics 抗菌素 kàngjūnsù
antihistamines 抗组胺药 kàngzǔ'ān yào
antique ⓝ 古董 gǔdǒng
antique market 古董市场 gǔdǒng shìchǎng
antiseptic ⓝ 消毒剂 xiāodú jì
any 任何 rènhé
apartment (downmarket) 楼房 lóufáng
apartment (upmarket) 公寓 gōngyù
appendix (body part) 阑尾 lánwěi
apple 苹果 píngguǒ
appointment (to meet someone) 约会 yuēhuì
apricot 杏桃 xìngtáo
April 四月 sìyuè
archaeology 考古学 kǎogǔxué
architect 建筑师 jiànzhùshī
architecture 建筑学 jiànzhùxué
argue 吵架 chǎojià
arm 胳膊 gēbo
arrest 扣留 kòuliú
arrivals 进港口 jìngǎngkǒu
arrive 到达 dàodá

art ⓝ 艺术 yìshù
art gallery 艺术馆 yìshùguǎn
artist 艺术家 yìshùjiā
ashtray 烟灰缸 yānhuīgāng
Asia 亚洲 Yàzhōu
ask (a question) 问 wèn
ask (for something) 求 qiú
aspirin 阿斯匹林 āsīpīlín
asthma 哮喘 xiàochuǎn
at 在 zài
athletics 田径 tiánjìng
atmosphere (weather) 气候 qìhòu
August 八月 bāyuè
aunt 阿姨 āyí
Australia 澳大利亚 Àodàlìyà
Australian Rules Football 澳式橄榄球 Àoshì gǎnlǎnqiú
automated teller machine (ATM) 自动取款机 zìdòng qǔkuǎn jī
autumn 秋天 qiūtiān
avenue 大街 dàjiē
awful 可恶 kěwù

B

B&W (film) 黑白(片) hēibái (piàn)
baby ⓝ 小娃娃 xiǎo wáwa
baby food 婴儿食品 yīng'ér shípǐn
baby powder 滑石粉 huáshí fěn
babysitter 临时保姆 línshí bǎomǔ
back (body) 背 bèi
back (position) 后面 hòumian
backpack 背包 bèibāo
bacon 培根 péigēn
bad 坏 huài
bag 包 bāo
baggage 行李 xíngli
baggage allowance 免费行李 miǎnfèi xíngli
baggage claim 行李领取处 xíngli lǐngqǔ chù
balance (account) ⓝ 余额 yú'é
balcony 阳台 yángtái
ball 球 qiú
ballet 芭蕾舞 bālěi wǔ
bamboo shoots 笋 sǔn
banana 香蕉 xiāngjiāo

B

band (music) 乐队 yuè duì
bandage ⓝ 绷带 bēngdài
Band-Aid 创口贴 chuāngkǒu tiē
bank (money) 银行 yínháng
bank account 银行账户 yínháng zhànghù
banknote 纸币 zhǐbì
baptism 洗礼 xǐlǐ
bar 酒吧 jiǔbā
barbecued 烧烤 shāokǎo
barber 理发屋 lǐfàwū
baseball 棒球 bàngqiú
basin 水盆 shuǐpén
basket 篮子 lánzi
basketball 篮球 lánqiú
bath ⓝ 浴缸 yùgāng
bathing suit 游泳衣 yóuyǒngyī
bathroom 浴室 yùshì
battery 电池 diànchí
be (I want to be ...) 当 dāng
beach ⓝ 沙滩 shātān
beach volleyball 沙滩排球 shātān páiqiú
bean 豆子 dòuzi
bean noodles 豆粉 dòufěn
bean sprout 豆芽 dòuyá
beautiful 美丽 měilì
beauty salon 美容院 měiróng yuàn
because 因为 yīnwèi
bed 床 chuáng
bed linen 床单 chuángdān
bedding 被褥 bèirù
bedroom 卧室 wòshì
bee 蜜蜂 mìfēng
beef 牛肉 niúròu
beer 啤酒 píjiǔ
before 以前 yǐqián
beggar 乞丐 qǐgài
behind 背面 bèimiàn
Beijing 北京 Běijīng
Belgium 比利时 Bǐlìshí
below 下面 xiàmian
beside 旁边 pángbiān
best 最好的 zuìhǎo de
bet ⓝ 赌博 dǔbó
better 更好 gènghǎo

between 中间 zhōngjiān
bible 圣经 shèngjīng
bicycle ⓝ 自行车 zìxíngchē
big 大 dà
bigger 更大 gèngdà
biggest 最大 zuìdà
bike ⓝ 自行车 zìxíngchē
bike chain 车链 chēliàn
bike lock 车锁 chēsuǒ
bike path 自行车道 zìxíngchē dào
bike shop 修车店 xiūchē diàn
bill (restaurant etc) ⓝ 帐单 zhàngdān
binoculars 望远镜 wàngyuǎnjìng
bird 鸟 niǎo
birth certificate 出生证 chūshēngzhèng
birthday 生日 shēngrì
biscuit 饼干 bǐnggān
bite (dog) ⓝ 咬 yǎo
bite (insect) ⓝ 叮 dīng
bitter 苦 kǔ
bitter melon 苦瓜 kǔguā
black 黑色 hēisè
bladder 膀胱 pángguāng
blanket 毛毯 máotǎn
blind (unable to see) 眼瞎 yǎnxiā
blister ⓝ 起泡 qǐpào
blocked (toilet) 堵塞 dǔsè
blood 血液 xuè yè
blood group 血型 xuèxíng
blood pressure 血压 xuèyā
blood test 验血 yànxuè
blue 蓝色 lánsè
board (a plane, ship etc) 登 dēng
boarding pass 登机牌 dēngjī pái
boat 船 chuán
body 身体 shēntǐ
boil ⓥ 煮 zhǔ
bok choy 小白菜 xiǎo báicài
bone ⓝ 骨头 gǔtou
book ⓝ 书 shū
book (make a booking) ⓥ 定 dìng
book shop 书店 shūdiàn
booked out 定满 dìngmǎn
boots 靴子 xuēzi

C

border ⓝ 边界 biānjiè
bored 闷 mèn
boring 无聊 wúliáo
borrow 借 jiè
botanic garden 植物园 zhíwù yuán
both 两个都 liǎnggedōu
bottle 瓶子 píngzi
bottle opener 开瓶器 kāipíng qì
bottom (body part) 屁股 pìgǔ
bottom (position) 底 dǐ
bowl ⓝ 碗 wǎn
box ⓝ 箱子 xiāngzi
boxer shorts 小裤衩 xiǎo kùchǎ
boxing 拳击 quánjī
boy 男孩子 nán háizi
boyfriend 男朋友 nánpéngyou
(the) Boys (Beijing slang) 哥们儿 gēmenr
bra 胸罩 xiōngzhào
brakes 车闸 chēzhá
brandy 白兰地 báilándì
brave 勇敢 yǒnggǎn
bread 面包 miànbāo
break ⓥ 折断 zhéduàn
break down ⓥ 崩溃 bēngkuì
breakfast 早饭 zǎofàn
breast (body part) 乳房 rǔfáng
breathe 呼吸 hūxī
bribe ⓝ 行贿 xínghuì
bridge 桥 qiáo
briefcase 公文包 gōngwénbāo
brilliant (clever) 聪明 cōngming
bring 带 dài
broccoli 西兰花 xīlánhuā
brochure 说明书 shuōmíng shū
broken 坏了 huài le
broken down (car) 抛锚 pāomáo
bronchitis 肺炎 fèiyán
bronze medal 铜牌 tóngpái
brother 兄弟 xiōngdi
brother (elder) 哥哥 gēge
brother (younger) 弟弟 dìdi
brown 咖啡色 kāfēi sè
bruise ⓝ 青肿 qīngzhǒng
brush ⓝ 毛笔 máobǐ
bucket 水桶 shuǐtǒng

Buddha 大佛 dàfó
Buddhism 佛教 fójiào
Buddhist 佛教徒 fójiào tú
budget ⓝ 预算 yùsuàn
buffet 自助餐 zìzhùcān
bug ⓥ 虫子 chóngzi
build 建 jiàn
builder 建筑工人 jiànzhùgōngrén
building 楼 lóu
bumbag 腰包 yāobāo
burn ⓝ 烧伤 shāoshāng
burnt 烧焦 shāojiāo
bus (city) 大巴 dàbā
bus (intercity) 长途车 chángtú chē
bus station 长途车站 chángtú chēzhàn
bus stop 车站 chēzhàn
business ⓝ 生意 shēngyì
business class 商务舱 shāngwù cāng
business trip 出差 chūchāi
businessman 商人 shāngrén
businesswoman 商人 shāngrén
busy (occupied) 急急忙忙 jíjí mángmáng
busy (state of mind) 有事 yǒushì
but 但是 dànshì
butcher ⓝ 刽子手 guìzi shǒu
butcher's shop 肉店 ròudiàn
butter ⓝ 黄油 huángyóu
butterfly 蝴蝶 húdié
button ⓝ 纽扣 niǔkòu
buy ⓥ 买 mǎi

C

cabbage 白菜 báicài
cafe 咖啡屋 kāfēi wū
cake 蛋糕 dàngāo
cake shop 糕点屋 gāodiǎn wū
calculator 计算器 jìsuàn qì
calendar 日历 rìlì
call ⓥ 叫 jiào
camera 照相机 zhàoxiàng jī
camera shop 照相店 zhàoxiàng diàn
camp ⓥ 野营 yěyíng
can (be able) 能 néng
can (have permission) 可以 kěyǐ

C

can (tin) 罐头 guàntou
can opener 开罐器 kāiguàn qì
Canada 加拿大 Jiānádà
cancel 取消 qǔxiāo
cancer (illness) 癌症 áizhèng
candle 蜡烛 làzhú
candy 糖果 tángguǒ
cantaloupe 哈密瓜 hāmìguā
Cantonese (language) ⓝ 广东话 Guǎngdōng huà
capitalism 资本主义 zīběn zhǔyì
capsicum 青椒 qīngjiāo
car 轿车 jiàochē
car hire 车租赁 chē zūlìn
car park 停车场 tíngchē chǎng
car registration 车号 chēhào
cardiac arrest 心脏病 xīnzàng bìng
cards (playing) 扑克牌 pūkè pái
care (for someone) ⓥ 关心 guānxīn
Careful! 小心! Xiǎoxīn!
carp (fish) 鲤鱼 lǐyú
carpenter 木匠 mùjiàng
carrot 胡萝卜 húluóbo
carry 背 bēi
cash ⓝ 现金 xiànjīn
cash (a cheque) ⓥ 兑现 duìxiàn
cash register 收银台 shōuyín tái
cashier 出纳 chūnà
casino 赌博场 dǔbó chǎng
cassette 录音带 lùyīn dài
casual work 临时工作 línshí gōngzuò
cat 猫 māo
cathedral 大教堂 dàjiàotáng
Catholic 天主教 Tiānzhǔjiào
cave 山洞 shāndòng
CD CD CD [English pronunciation]
celebration 庆祝会 qìngzhù huì
cemetery ⓝ 坟地 féndì
cent 分 fēn
centimetre 厘米 límǐ
centre 中心 zhōngxīn
ceramics 陶瓷 táocí
certificate 证明 zhèngmíng
chain ⓝ 链子 liànzi
chair 椅子 yǐzi
Champagne 香槟 xiāngbīn

championships 竞赛 jìngsài
chance 机会 jīhuì
change 换 huàn
change (coins) 零钱 língqián
change (money) ⓥ 换钱 huànqián
changing room 更衣室 gēngyīshì
charming 有魅力 yǒu mèilì
chat ⓥ 聊天 liáotiān
chat up 调情 tiáoqíng
cheap 实惠 shíhuì
cheat ⓝ 骗子 piànzi
check ⓥ 确认 quèrèn
check (bill) 账单 zhàngdān
check-in (desk) 登记台 dēngjì tái
checkpoint 检查站 jiǎnchá zhàn
cheese 奶酪 nǎilào
chef 厨师 chúshī
chemist (pharmacist) 药剂师 yàojì shī
chemist (shop) 药房 yàofáng
cheque (banking) 支票 zhīpiào
cherry 樱桃 yīngtáo
chess (Chinese) 象棋 xiàngqí
chess (Western) 国际象棋 guójì xiàngqí
chess board 棋盘 qípán
chest (body) 胸 xiōng
chestnut 栗子 lìzi
chewing gum 口香糖 kǒuxiāngtáng
chi 气 qì
chicken 鸡 jī
chicken pox 水痘 shuǐdòu
child 孩子 háizi
child seat 婴儿座 yīng'érzuò
childminding 幼儿园 yòu'éryuán
children 孩子们 háizimen
chilli 辣椒 làjiāo
chilli sauce 辣椒酱 làjiāo jiàng
China 中国 Zhōngguó
Chinese (language) 中文 Zhōngwén
Chinese flowering cabbage 包菜 bāocài
Chinese medicine 中药 Zhōngyào
Chinese medicine doctor 中医 Zhōngyī

C

chocolate 巧克力 qiǎokèlì
cholera 霍乱 huòluàn
choose 选择 xuǎnzé
chopping board 菜板 càibǎn
chopsticks 筷子 kuàizi
Christian 基督教徒 Jīdū jiàotú
Christmas 圣诞节 shèngdànjié
Christmas Day 圣诞日 shèngdànrì
Christmas Eve 平安夜 píng'ān yè
chrysanthemum 菊花 júhuā
chrysanthemum tea 菊花茶 júhuāchá
church 教堂 jiàotáng
cigarette 香烟 xiāngyān
cigarette lighter 打火机 dǎhuǒjī
cinema 电影院 diànyǐngyuàn
cinnamon bark 桂皮 guìpí
circus 杂技 zájì
citizenship 公民 gōngmín
city 城市 chéngshì
city centre 市中心 shìzhōngxīn
civil rights 公民权 gōngmín quán
clams 蚌 bàng
class (category) 类 lèi
class system 等级制度 děngjí zhìdù
classical 古典 gǔdiǎn
clean ⓐ 干净 gānjìng
clean ⓥ 打扫 dǎsǎo
cleaning 清洁 qīngjié
client 客户 kèhù
cliff 悬崖 xuányá
climb (mountain) 爬山 páshān
cloakroom 寄存处 jìcúnchù
clock 钟表 zhōngbiǎo
close (shut) 关闭 guānbì
close (nearby) 附近 fùjìn
closed 关门 guānmén
clothesline 晾衣线 liàngyīxiàn
clothing 衣服 yīfu
clothing store 服装店 fúzhuāngdiàn
cloud 云彩 yúncǎi
cloudy 多云 duōyún
clutch (car) 换档踏板 huàndàng tàbǎn
coach (bus) 大巴 dàbā
coach (sports) 教练 jiàoliàn

coast 海边 hǎibiān
coat 大衣 dàyī
cockroach 蟑螂 zhāngláng
cocktail 鸡尾酒 jīwěi jiǔ
cocoa 可可粉 kěkě fěn
coffee 咖啡 kāfēi
coins 硬币 yìngbì
(have a) cold 伤风 shāngfēng
cold 冷 lěng
colleague 同事 tóngshì
collect call 对方付款电话 duìfāng fùkuǎndiànhuà
college (university) 大学 dàxué
colour 颜色 yánsè
comb 梳子 shūzi
come 来 lái
comedy 喜剧片 xǐjù piàn
comfortable 舒服 shūfu
commission 代理费 dàilǐ fèi
common people 老百姓 lǎobǎixìng
communications (profession) 交通 jiāotōng
communion 教会 jiàohuì
communism 共产主义 gòngchǎn zhǔyì
communist (party member) 党员 dǎngyuán
communist (party official) 干部 gànbù
companion 同伙 tónghuǒ
company (business) 公司 gōngsī
compass 指南针 zhǐnán zhēn
complain 抱怨 bàoyuàn
complaint 投诉 tóusù
complimentary (tickets) 赠(票) zèng (piào)
computer 电脑 diànnǎo
computer game 电子游戏 diànzǐ yóuxì
comrade 同志 tóngzhì
concert 音乐会 yīnyuè huì
concussion 昏迷 hūnmí
conditioner (hair) 护发素 hùfà sù
condom 避孕套 bìyùntào
conference (big) 会议 huìyì
conference (small) 会合 huìhé

confession 坦白 tǎnbái

confirm (a booking) 确定 quèdìng

congratulations 恭喜 gōngxǐ

conjunctivitis 结膜炎 jiémó yán

connection 连接 liánjiē

conservative 保守 bǎoshǒu

constipation 便秘 biànmì

consulate 领事馆 lǐngshìguǎn

contact lens solution 隐形眼镜药水 yǐnxíng yǎnjìng yàoshuǐ

contact lenses 隐形眼镜 yǐnxíng yǎnjìng

contraceptives 避孕品 bìyùnpǐn

contract 合同 hétong

convenience store 小卖部 xiǎomàibù

cook ⓝ 厨子 chúzi

cook ⓥ 炒菜 chǎocài

cooking 做菜 zuòcài

cool (temperature) 凉快 liángkuài

corkscrew 螺旋开瓶器 luóxuán kāipíng qì

corn 玉米 yùmǐ

corner 角 jiǎo

corrupt 贪污 tānwū

cost (price) 价格 jiàgé

cotton 棉花 miánhuā

cough 咳嗽 késòu

cough medicine 感冒药 gǎnmào yào

count 计算 jìsuàn

counter (at hotel) 柜台 guìtái

country (nation) 国家 guójiā

countryside 乡下 xiāngxià

coupon 票 piào

court (legal) 法庭 fǎtíng

court (tennis) (网球)场 (wǎngqiú) chǎng

cover charge 入场费 rùchǎng fèi

cow 牛 niú

crafts 手艺 shǒuyì

crash 撞车 zhuàngchē

crazy 疯了 fēngle

cream (dairy) 奶酪 nǎilào

credit 信用 xìnyòng

credit card 信用卡 xìnyòng kǎ

crop (field) 农田 nóngtián

cross (religious) 十字架 shízìjià

crowded 拥挤 yōngjǐ

cucumber 黄瓜 huángguā

cup 杯子 bēizi

cupboard 大柜 dàguì

cupping (traditional therapy) 刮痧 guāshā

currency exchange 货币兑换 huòbì duìhuàn

current (electricity) (电)流 (diàn) liú

current affairs 时事 shíshì

curry 咖喱 gālí

custom 风俗 fēngsú

customs (immigration) 海关 hǎiguān

cut ⓥ 切 qiē

cut (wound) ⓝ 疮口 chuāngkǒu

cutlery 刀叉 dāochā

CV 简历 jiǎnlì

cycle 骑自行车 qí zìxíngchē

cycling 自行车赛 zìxíngchē sài

cyclist 自行车手 zìxíngchē qíshǒu

cystitis 膀胱炎 pángguāng yán

D

dad 爸爸 bàba

daily 日常 rìcháng

dance 跳舞 tiàowǔ

dancing 舞蹈 wǔdǎo

dangerous 危险 wēixiǎn

dark 黑暗 hēiàn

dark (of colour) 深色 shēnsè

date (a person) 谈朋友 tán péngyou

date (appointment) 约会 yuēhuì

date (day) 日期 rìqī

date (fruit) 枣 zǎo

date of birth 出生日 chūshēngrì

daughter 女孩子 nǚ háizi

dawn 日出 rìchū

day 白天 báitiān

day after tomorrow 后天 hòutiān

day before yesterday 前天 qiántiān

dead 死了 sǐle

deaf 耳聋 ěrlóng

deal (cards) 发牌 fā (pái)

216

D

December 十二月 shí'èr yuè
decide 决定 juédìng
deep 深 shēn
deforestation 乱砍乱伐 luànkǎn luànfá
degrees (temperature) 度 dù
delay 延迟 yánchí
deliver 递送 dìsòng
democracy 民主主义 mínzhǔ zhǔyì
demonstration (protest) 游行 yóuxíng
Denmark 丹麦 Dānmài
dentist 牙医 yáyī
depart (leave) 离开 líkāi
department store 百货商店 bǎihuò shāngdiàn
departure 出发 chūfā
departure gate 登机口 dēngjī kǒu
deposit (bank) 存钱 cúnqián
deposit (surety) 押金 yājīn
descendant 后裔 hòuyì
desert 沙漠 shāmò
design 设计 shèjì
dessert 甜点 tiándiǎn
destination 目的地 mùdì dì
details 细节 xìjié
diabetes 糖尿病 tángniàobìng
dial tone 播音 bōyīn
diaper 尿裤 niàokù
diaphragm (anatomical) 横膈膜 héng gémó
diaphragm (contraceptive) 避孕药 bìyùn yào
diarrhoea 拉稀 lāxī
diary 日记 rìjì
dice 骰子 tóuzi
dictionary 词典 cídiǎn
die 去世 qùshì
diet 减肥 jiǎnféi
different 不同 bùtóng
difficult 困难 kùnnán
dim sum 点心 diǎnxīn
dining car 餐车 cānchē
dinner 晚饭 wǎnfàn
dipping sauce 黄酱 huángjiàng
direct 直接 zhíjiē

direct dial 直播 zhíbō
direction 方向 fāngxiàng
director (business) 董事 dǒngshì
director (film) 导演 dǎoyǎn
dirty 脏 zāng
disabled 残疾 cánjí
disco 迪斯科 dísīkē
discount 折扣 zhékòu
discrimination 歧视 qíshì
disease 疾病 jíbìng
dish (food item) 盘 pán
disk (CD-ROM) 碟子 diézi
diving (underwater) 潜水 qiánshuǐ
diving equipment 潜水设备 qiánshuǐ shèbèi
divorced 离婚 líhūn
dizzy 头晕 tóuyūn
do 做 zuò
doctor 医生 yīshēng
documentary 纪录片 jìlù piàn
dog 狗 gǒu
dole 救济 jiùjì
doll 洋娃娃 yángwáwa
(American) dollar (美)元 (měi) yuán
doona 被子 bèizi
door 门 mén
dope (drugs) 大麻 dàmá
double 双 shuāng
double bed 双人床 shuāngrén chuáng
double room 双人间 shuāngrén jiān
down 下面 xiàmian
downhill 下坡 xiàpō
dozen 打 dá
drama 戏剧 xìjù
dream ⓝ 梦 mèng
dress ⓝ 连衣裙 liányīqún
dried 干 gān
dried fruit 干果 gānguǒ
drink 喝 hē
drink (alcoholic) 酒 jiǔ
drink (nonalcoholic) 饮料 yǐnliào
drive 开车 kāichē
driver's licence 驾照 jiàzhào

drug (illicit) 毒品 dúpǐn

drug (medication) 药品 yàopǐn

drug addiction 毒品上瘾 dúpǐn shàngyǐn

drug dealer 毒贩 dúfàn

drug trafficking 贩毒 fàndú

drug user 吸毒者 xīdúzhě

drugs (illicit) 毒品 dúpǐn

drugs (medication) 药品 yàopǐn

drum (instrument) 鼓 gǔ

drunk 醉 zuì

dry ⓐ 干 gān

(blow) dry (吹)干 (chuī) gān

dry (clothes) ⓥ 晾干 liànggān

duck 鸭子 yāzi

dummy (pacifier) 奶嘴 nǎizuǐ

dumpling (boiled) 饺子 jiǎozi

dumpling (fried) 锅贴 guōtiē

dumpling (steamed) 包子 bāozi

durian 榴莲 liúlián

DVD DVD DVD [English pronunciation]

dysentery 痢疾 lìjí

E

each 每个 měige

ear 耳朵 ěrduo

early 早 zǎo

earn (money) 挣(钱) zhèng (qián)

earplugs 耳塞子 ěrsāizi

earrings 耳环 ěrhuán

Earth 地球 dìqiú

earthquake 地震 dìzhèn

east 东方 dōngfāng

Easter 复活节 fùhuójié

easy 容易 róngyì

eat 吃饭 chīfàn

economy class 经济舱 jīngjì cāng

ecstacy (drug) 摇头丸 yáotóuwán

eczema 湿疹 shīzhěn

editor 编辑 biānjí

education 教育 jiàoyù

egg (chicken) 鸡蛋 jīdàn

election 选举 xuǎnjǔ

electrical store 电子用品店 diànzǐ yòngpǐn diàn

electricity 电 diàn

elevator 电梯 diàntī

email 电子邮件 diànzǐ yóujiàn

embarrassed (slightly) 不好意思 bùhǎo yìsi

embarrassed (very) 尴尬 gāngà

embassy 大使馆 dàshǐguǎn

emergency 出事 chūshì

emotional 有情份 yǒu qíngfèn

emperor 皇帝 huángdì

employee 职员 zhíyuán

employer 老板 lǎobǎn

empress 皇后 huánghòu

empty 空 kōng

end 结束 jiéshù

endangered species 濒危动物 bīnwēi dòngwù

engaged (betrothed) 订婚 dìnghūn

engaged (occupied) 有事 yǒushì

engagement (appointment) 婚约 hūnyuē

engine 发动机 fādòngjī

engineer 工程师 gōngchéng shī

engineering 工程学 gōngchéng xué

England 英国 Yīngguó

English 英文 Yīngwén

English teacher 英文老师 Yīngwén lǎoshī

enjoy (oneself) 玩 wán

enough 足够 zúgòu

enter 入场 rùchǎng

entertainment guide 娱乐指南 yúlè zhǐnán

entry 入口 rùkǒu

envelope 信封 xìnfēng

environment 环境 huánjìng

epilepsy 癫痫 diānxián

equal opportunity 平等待遇 píngděng dàiyù

equality 平等 píngděng

equipment 设备 shèbèi

escalator 自动扶梯 zìdòng fútī

estate agency 房地产公司 fángdìchǎn gōngsī

euro 欧元 ōuyuán

Europe 欧洲 Ōuzhōu

euthanasia 安乐死 ānlè sǐ

evening 晚上 wǎnshàng
every 每次 měicì
everyone 每个人 měige rén
everything 一切 yíqiè
exactly 确切 quèqiè
example 举例 jǔlì
excellent 好极了 hǎojíle
excess (baggage) 超重(行李) chāozhòng (xíngli)
exchange ⓝ 交换 jiāohuàn
exchange ⓥ 换 huàn
exchange rate 兑换率 duìhuàn lǜ
excluded 排除 páichú
exhaust (car) 废气 fèiqì
exhibition 展览 zhǎnlǎn
exit 出口 chūkǒu
expensive 贵 guì
experience 经验 jīngyàn
exploitation 剥削 bōxuē
express 快速 kuàisù
express (mail) 快递(信) kuàidì (xìn)
express mail (by) (寄) 特快 jì tèkuài
extension (visa) (签证) 延期 (qiānzhèng) yánqī
eye(s) 眼睛 yǎnjīng
eye drops 眼药水 yǎnyàoshuǐ

F

fabric 布料 bùliào
face 脸 liǎn
face cloth 毛巾 máojīn
factory 工厂 gōngchǎng
factory worker 工人 gōngrén
fall (autumn) 秋天 qiūtiān
fall (down) 掉下 diàoxia
family 家庭 jiātíng
family name 姓 xìng
famous 出名 chūmíng
fan (hand held) 扇子 shànzi
fan (machine) 电风扇 diànfēngshàn
fan (sport etc) 球迷 qiú mí
far 远 yuǎn
fare 票价 piàojià
farm 农地 nóngdì
farmer (peasant) 农民 nóngmín
fashion 时髦 shímáo

fast 快 kuài
fat 胖 pàng
father 父亲 fùqīn
father-in-law 岳父 yuèfù
faucet 水龙头 shuǐlóngtóu
fault (someone's) 责任 zérèn
faulty 有毛病 yǒu máobìng
fax machine 传真机 chuánzhēnjī
February 二月 èryuè
feed (baby, animals) 喂 wèi
feel (touch) 触摸 chùmō
feeling (physical) 情感 qínggǎn
feelings 感情 gǎnqíng
female 女性 nǚxìng
fen (measure) 分 fēn
fence 篱笆 líba
fencing (sport) 剑术 jiànshù
feng shui 风水 fēngshuǐ
ferry 渡船 dùchuán
festival 节日 jiérì
fever 发烧 fāshāo
few 一些 yìxiē
fiancé 未婚夫 wèihūnfū
fiancée 未婚妻 wèihūnqī
fiction (novel) 虚构(小说) xūgòu (xiǎoshuō)
fight ⓥ 打架 dǎjià
fill 填满 tiánmǎn
fillet 鱼片 yúpiàn
film (cinema) 电影 diànyǐng
film (for camera) 胶卷 jiāojuǎn
film speed 感光度 gǎnguāngdù
filtered 过滤 guòlǜ
find 找到 zhǎodào
fine ⓐ 蛮好 mánhǎo
fine (penalty) 罚款 fákuǎn
finger 指头 zhǐtou
finish ⓝ 结束 jiéshù
finish ⓥ 完成 wánchéng
Finland 芬兰 Fēnlán
fire 火 huǒ
firewood 火柴 huǒchái
first 第一 dìyī
first class 头等舱 tóuděng cāng
first-aid kit 急救装备 jíjiù zhuāngbèi
first name 名字 míngzi

fish ⓝ 鱼 yú
fish shop 鱼摊 yútān
fishing 钓鱼 diàoyú
flag 国旗 guóqí
flannel 擦布 cābù
flashlight (torch) 手电筒 shǒudiàntǒng
flat (apartment) 楼房 lóufáng
flat 贬 biǎn
flea 跳蚤 tiàozǎo
flight 航班 hángbān
flood 洪水 hóngshuǐ
floor (ground) 地板 dìbǎn
floor (storey) 层 céng
florist 花店 huādiàn
flour (wheat) 面粉 miànfěn
flower 花 huā
flu 感冒 gǎnmào
fly 飞 fēi
foggy 有雾 yǒuwù
folk music 民谣 mínyáo
follow 跟随 gēnsuí
food ⓝ 食品 shípǐn
food supplies 预备食品 yùbèi shípǐn
foot 脚 jiǎo
football (soccer) 足球 zúqiú
foot massage 脚按摩 jiǎo ànmó
foreign (goods) 洋（货）yáng (huò)
foreigner 外国人 wàiguó rén
forest 森林 sēnlín
forever 永远 yǒngyuǎn
forget 忘掉 wàngdiào
forgive 原谅 yuànliàng
fork 叉子 chāzi
fortune cookies 煎饼 jiānbǐng
fortune teller 阴阳先生 yīnyáng xiānsheng
foul 犯规 fànguī
foyer 大堂 dàtáng
fragile 脆弱 cuìruò
France 法国 Fǎguó
free (available) 有空 yǒukòng
free (gratis) 免费 miǎnfèi
free (not bound) 自由 zìyóu
freeze 冻结 dòngjié

fresh 新鲜 xīnxiān
Friday 礼拜五 lǐbài wǔ
fridge 冰箱 bīngxiāng
fried (deep-fried) 炸 zhá
fried rice 炒饭 chǎofàn
friend 朋友 péngyou
Friendship Store 友谊商店 Yǒuyì Shāngdiàn
from 从 cóng
frost 霜 shuāng
frozen 冰冻 bīngdòng
fruit 水果 shuǐguǒ
fry (stir-fry) 炒 chǎo
full 满 mǎn
full-time 专职的 zhuānzhíde
fun 好玩 hǎowán
(have) fun 出去玩 chūqù wán
funeral 葬礼 zànglǐ
funny 可笑 kěxiào
furniture 家具 jiājù
future 将来 jiānglái

G

game (football) 比赛 bǐsài
game (sport) 比赛 bǐsài
garage 车库 chēkù
garbage 垃圾 lājī
garbage can 垃圾箱 lājī xiāng
garden 花园 huāyuán
gardening 养花 yǎnghuā
garlic 大蒜 dàsuàn
gas (for cooking) 煤气 méiqì
gas (petrol) 汽油 qìyóu
gastroenteritis 肠胃炎 chángwèiyán
gate (airport) 登机口 dēngjīkǒu
gate (general) 门 mén
gauze 纱布 shābù
gay (bar) 同志（吧）tóngzhì (bā)
Germany 德国 Déguó
get (fetch) 接来 jiēlái
get off (a train etc) 下（车）xià (chē)
giardiasis 鞭毛虫病 biānmáochóngbìng
gift 礼物 lǐwù
gig 节目 jiémù

H

gin 金酒 jīnjiǔ
ginger 姜 jiāng
ginseng 人参 rénshēn
girl 女孩子 nǚháizi
girlfriend 女朋友 nǚpéngyou
give 送 sòng
given name 名字 míngzi
glandular fever 腺热 xiànrè
glass (drinking) 玻璃杯 bōli bēi
glass (material) 玻璃 bōli
glasses (spectacles) 眼镜 yǎnjìng
glove 手套 shǒutào
glue 胶水 jiāoshuǐ
go 去 qù
go out 出去 chūqù
go out with 谈朋友 tán péngyou
go shopping 逛街 guàngjiē
goal 目的 mùdì
(score a) goal 进门 jìnmén
goalkeeper 守门员 shǒuményuán
goat 山羊 shānyáng
god 神 shén
goggles (swimming) 游泳镜 yóuyǒng jìng
gold 黄金 huángjīn
gold medal 金牌 jīnpái
golf ball 高尔夫球 gāo'ěrfū qiú
golf course 高尔夫场 gāo'ěrfū chǎng
good 好 hǎo
goodbye 再见 zàijiàn
goose 鹅 é
government 政府 zhèngfǔ
gram 克 kè
grandchild 孙子 sūnzi
grandfather (maternal) 外公 wàigōng
grandfather (paternal) 爷爷 yéye
grandmother (maternal) 外婆 wàipó
grandmother (paternal) 奶奶 nǎinai
grapefruit 柚子 yòuzi
grapes 葡萄 pútáo
grass 草 cǎo
grasslands 草原 cǎoyuán
grateful 感谢 gǎnxiè
grave 坟墓 fénmù

gray 灰色 huīsè
great (fantastic) 棒 bàng
Great Wall 长城 Chángchéng
green 绿色 lǜsè
green beans 扁豆 biǎndòu
green tea 绿茶 lǜchá
greengrocer 菜摊 càitān
grey 灰色 huīsè
grocery 食品 shípǐn
groundnut (peanut) 花生 huāshēng
grow 长大 zhǎngdà
guaranteed 有保证 yǒu bǎozhèng
guess 猜 cāi
guesthouse 宾馆 bīnguǎn
guide (audio) 语音导游 yǔyīn dǎoyóu
guide (person) 导游 dǎoyóu
guide dog 导盲犬 dǎománg quǎn
guidebook 旅行指南 lǚxíngzhǐnán
guided tour 团体旅行 tuántǐ lǚxíng
guilty 有罪 yǒuzuì
guitar 吉他 jítā
gum (chewing) 口香糖 kǒuxiāngtáng
gum (teeth) 齿龈 chǐyín
gun 手枪 shǒuqiāng
gut blockers (for diarrhoea) 止泻药 zhǐxiè yào
gym (place) 健美中心 jiànměi zhōngxīn
gymnastics 体操 tǐcāo
gynaecologist 妇科医生 fùkē yīshēng

H

hair 头发 tóufa
hairbrush 梳子 shūzi
haircut 理发 lǐfà
hairdresser 理发师 lǐfà shī
halal 清真 qīngzhēn
half 半个 bàngè
hallucination 幻想 huànxiǎng
ham 火腿 huǒtuǐ
hammer 锤子 chuízi
hammock 吊床 diàochuáng
hand 手 shǒu
handbag 手袋 shǒudài

handball 手球 shǒuqiú
handicrafts 手艺 shǒuyì
handkerchief 手绢 shǒujuàn
handlebars 车把 chēbǎ
handmade 手工的 shǒugōng de
handsome 英俊 yīngjùn
happy 快乐 kuàilè
harassment 骚扰 sāorǎo
harbour 港口 gǎngkǒu
hard (difficult) 困难 kùnnán
hard (not soft) 很硬 hěn yìng
hard seat 硬座 yìngzuò
hard sleeper 硬卧 yìngwò
hard-boiled egg (tea egg) 茶叶蛋 cháyè dàn
hardware store 五金店 wǔjīn diàn
hash 麻精 májīng
hat 帽子 màozi
have 有 yǒu
hay fever 花粉热 huāfěn rè
he 他 tā
head 头 tóu
head massage 头按摩 tóu ànmó
headache 头疼 tóuténg
headlights 车灯 chēdēng
health 身体 shēntǐ
hear 听到 tīngdào
hearing aid 助听器 zhùtīng qì
heart 心脏 xīnzàng
heart attack 心脏病突发 xīnzàngbìng tūfā
heart condition 心脏病 xīnzàngbìng
heat 热气 rèqì
heated 有暖气 yǒu nuǎnqì
heater 暖气管 nuǎnqì guǎn
heating 暖气 nuǎnqì
heavy 重 zhòng
Hello. (general greeting) 你好。 Nǐhǎo.
Hello. (Beijing) pol 您好。 Nínhǎo.
Hello. (answering telephone) 喂。 Wèi.
helmet 头盔 tóukuī
help 帮助 bāngzhù
Help! 救人! Jiùrén!
hepatitis 肝炎 gānyán

her 她的 tāde
herb (culinary) 香料 xiāngliào
herb (medicinal) 药材 yàocái
herbalist 中医 zhōng yī
here 这里 zhèlǐ
heroin 海洛因 hǎiluòyīn
herring (canned salted fish) 咸鱼罐头 xiányú guàntou
high 高 gāo
high school 中学 zhōngxué
highchair 高凳 gāodèng
highway 高速公路gāosù gōnglù
hike ⓥ 步行 bùxíng
hiking 徒步旅行 túbù lǚxíng
hiking boots 步行靴子 bùxíng xuēzi
hiking route 步行路线 bùxíng lùxiàn
hill 山丘 shānqiū
Hindu 印度 Yìndù
hire 租赁 zūlìn
his 他的 tāde
historical (site) 名胜古迹 míngshèng gǔjì
history 历史 lìshǐ
hitchhike 搭便车 dā biànchē
HIV 艾滋病毒 àizī bìngdú
hockey 曲棍球 qūgùn qiú
holiday 度假 dùjià
holidays 假期 jiàqī
home 家 jiā
homeless 无家可归 wújiā kěguī
homemaker 管家 guǎnjiā
homosexual 同性恋 tóngxìng liàn
honey 蜂蜜 fēngmì
honeymoon 蜜月 mìyuè
Hong Kong 香港 Xiānggǎng
horoscope 星象 xīngxiàng
horse 马 mǎ
horse riding 骑马 qímǎ
hospital 医院 yīyuàn
hospitality 好客 hàokè
hot 热 rè
hot water 热水 rèshuǐ
hotel 酒店 jiǔdiàn
hour 小时 xiǎoshí
house 房子 fángzi
housework 家务 jiāwù

I

how 怎么 zěnme
how much 多少 duōshǎo
hug 抱住 bàozhù
huge 巨大 jùdà
human resources 人事 rénshì
human rights 人权 rénquán
humanities 文科 wénkē
hundred 百 bǎi
hungry (to be) 饿 è
hunting 打猎 dǎliè
(to be in a) hurry 忙得 mángde
hurt 疼 téng
husband 丈夫 zhàngfu

I

I 我 wǒ
ice 冰 bīng
ice axe 冰镐 bīnggǎo
ice cream 冰激凌 bīngjīlíng
ice hockey 冰球 bīngqiú
ice skating 溜冰 liúbīng
identification 证件 zhèngjiàn
identification card (ID) 身份证 shēnfèn zhèng
idiot 白痴 báichī
if 如果 rúguǒ
ill 有病 yǒubìng
immigration 移民 yímín
important 重要 zhòngyào
impossible 不可能 bù kěnéng
in 在……里面 zài ... lǐmian
in front of ... 在……前面 zài ... qiánmian
included 包括 bāokuò
income tax 所得税 sǔodé shuì
India 印度 Yìndù
indicator 指标 zhǐbiāo
indigestion 肚子疼 dùzi téng
indoor 室内 shìnèi
industry 行业 hángyè
infection 感染 gǎnrǎn
inflammation 发炎 fāyán
influenza 感冒 gǎnmào
information 信息 xìnxī
ingredient 原料 yuánliào
inhaler 吸入器 xīrù qì

inject 注射 zhùshè
injection 打针 dǎzhēn
injured 受伤 shòushāng
injury 伤害 shānghài
inner tube 内胎 nèitāi
innocent 无辜 wúgū
insect repellent 防虫剂 fángchóngjì
inside 里面 lǐmian
instructor 培训员 péixùn yuán
insurance 保险 bǎoxiǎn
interesting 有趣 yǒuqù
intermission 休息 xiūxi
international 国际 guójì
internet 因特网 yīntèwǎng
internet cafe 网吧 wǎngbā
interpreter 翻译 fānyì
interview 采访 cǎifǎng
invite 请客 qǐngkè
iodine 碘水 diǎnshuǐ
Ireland 爱尔兰 Ài'ěrlán
iron (for clothes) 熨斗 yùndǒu
island 岛 dǎo
Israel 以色列 Yǐsèliè
it 它 tā
IT 信息技术 xìnxī jìshù
Italy 意大利 Yìdàlì
itch 痒 yǎng
itemised 分项的 fēnxiàng de
itinerary 日程表 rìchéng biǎo
IUD 宫内节育器 gōngnèi jiéyù qì

J

jacket 外套 wàitào
jail 监狱 jiānyù
jam 果酱 guǒjiàng
January 一月 yīyuè
Japan 日本 Rìběn
jar 玻璃罐头 bōli guàntou
jasmine tea 花茶 huāchá
jaw 下巴 xiàba
jealous 嫉妒 jídù
jeans 牛仔裤 niúzǎi kù
jeep 吉普车 jípǔ chē
jellyfish 海蜇 hǎizhé
jet lag 时差反应 shíchà fǎnyìng
jewellery 首饰 shǒushì

K

Jewish 犹太 Yóutài
jin (measure) 斤 jīn
job 工作 gōngzuò
jogging 慢跑 mànpǎo
joke ⓝ 开玩笑 kāi wánxiào
journalist 记者 jìzhě
journey 旅程 lǚchéng
judge 法官 fǎguān
juice 果汁 guǒzhī
July 七月 qīyuè
jump 跳 tiào
jumper (sweater) 毛衣 máoyī
June 六月 liùyuè

K

kelp 海带 hǎidài
ketchup 番茄酱 fānqié jiàng
key 钥匙 yàoshi
keyboard 键盘 jiànpán
kick ⓥ 踢 tī
kidney 肾 shèn
kilogram 公斤 gōngjīn
kilometre 公里 gōnglǐ
kind (nice) 善良 shànliáng
kindergarten 幼儿园 yòu'éryuán
king 国王 guówáng
kiosk 小卖部 xiǎo màibù
kiss ⓝ 亲吻 qīnwěn
kiss ⓥ 亲 qīn
kitchen 厨房 chúfáng
kiwi fruit 猕猴桃 míhóu táo
knee 膝盖 xīgài
knife 刀 dāo
know 知道 zhīdào
Korea (North) 朝鲜 Cháoxiǎn
Korea (South) 韩国 Hánguó
Korean 朝鲜话 Cháoxiǎn huà
kosher 洁净 jiéjìng
kuai (currency) 块 kuài

L

Labour Day 劳动节 láodòngjié
labourer 劳工 láogōng
labyrinth 迷宫 mígōng
lace 花边 huābiān

lake 湖 hú
lamb 羊肉 yángròu
land 土地 tǔdì
landlady 房东 fángdōng
language 语言 yǔyán
laptop 手提电脑 shǒutí diànnǎo
large 很大 hěndà
last (final) 最后的 zuìhòude
last (previous) 前一个 qián yīge
last (week) 上个 shàngge
late 迟到 chídào
later 以后 yǐhòu
laugh ⓥ 笑 xiào
launderette 洗衣店 xǐyīdiàn
laundry (clothes) 洗 xǐ
law (study, professsion) 法律 fǎlù
lawyer 律师 lǜshī
laxative 止泻药 zhǐxiè yào
lazy 懒惰 lǎnduò
leader 领导 lǐngdǎo
leaf 叶子 yèzi
leafy vegetables 青菜 qīngcài
learn 学习 xuéxí
leather 皮革 pígé
lecturer 教师 jiàoshī
ledge 边 biān
left (direction) 左边 zuǒbian
left luggage 行李寄存 xínglì jìcún
left-luggage office 寄存处 jìcún chù
left-wing 左派 zuǒpài
leg 腿 tuǐ
legal 法律 fǎlù
legislation 法规 fǎguī
legume 豆类 dòulèi
leisure 消遣 xiāoqiǎn
lemon 柠檬 níngméng
lemonade 柠檬汁 níngméng zhī
lens 透镜 tòujìng
lentil 小扁豆 xiǎobiǎndòu
lesbian 女同性恋 nǚ tóngxìng liàn
less 少 shǎo
letter (mail) 信 xìn
lettuce 生菜 shēngcài
liar 骗子 piànzi
library 图书馆 túshū guǎn
lice 头虱 tóushī

M

licence 执照 zhízhào
license plate number 车号 chēhào
lie (not stand) 躺下 tǎngxià
life 生命 shēngming
life jacket 救生衣 jiùshēng yī
lift (elevator) 电梯 diàntī
light 光 guāng
light (not heavy) 轻 qīng
light (of colour) 浅色 qiǎnsè
light bulb 灯泡 dēngpào
light meter 测光表 cèguāng biǎo
lighter (cigarette) 打火机 dǎhuǒ jī
like ... 同……一样 tóng ... yīyàng
lime (chemical) 石灰 shíhuī
linen (material) 亚麻布 yàmá bù
linen (sheets etc) 床单 chuángdān
lip balm 唇膏 chúngāo
lips 嘴唇 zuǐchún
lipstick 口红 kǒuhóng
liquor store 啤酒摊 píjiǔ tān
listen (to) 听 tīng
litre 公升 gōngshēng
little 小 xiǎo
(a) little 一点 yīdiǎn
live (inhabit) 住 zhù
liver 肝 gān
lizard (gecko) 壁虎 bìhǔ
local 地方 dì fāng
lock ⑩ 锁 suǒ
lock ⑨ 锁上 suǒshàng
locked (door etc) 锁上了 suǒshàng le
lollies 糖果 tángguǒ
long 长 cháng
look 看 kàn
look after 照顾 zhàogù
look for 找 zhǎo
lookout 了望台 liàowàng tái
loose 很松 hěnsōng
loose change 零钱 língqián
lose 丢 diū
lost (one's way) 迷路 mílù
lost property 遗失物 yíshī wù
(a) lot 好多 hǎoduō
loud 吵 chǎo
love ⑩ 爱情 àiqíng
love ⑨ 爱 ài

lover 爱人 àirén
low 低 dī
lubricant 润滑油 rùnhuá yóu
luck 运气 yùnqì
lucky 有福气 yǒu fúqi
luggage 行李 xíngli
luggage lockers 行李寄存 xíngli jìcún
luggage tag 行李标签 xíngli biāoqiān
lump 疙瘩 gēda
lunch 午饭 wǔfàn
lung 肺 fèi
luxury 奢侈 shēchǐ
lychee 荔枝 lìzhī
lychee-flavoured soft drink
荔枝汁 lìzhī zhī

M

machine 机器 jīqì
magazine 杂志 zázhi
mah-jong 麻将 májiàng
mail (letters) 来信 láixìn
mail (postal system) 邮电 yóudiàn
mailbox 信箱 xìnxiāng
main 主要 zhǔyào
main road 干道 gàndào
make 制作 zhìzuò
make-up 打扮 dǎbàn
malaria 疟疾 nüèji
mammogram 肉眼 ròuyǎn
man (male person) 男人 nánrén
man (mankind) 人 rén
manager 经理 jīnglǐ
mandarin 橘子 júzi
Mandarin 普通话 pǔtōnghuà
mango 芒果 mángguǒ
manual worker 手工 shǒugōng
many 好多 hǎoduō
mao-tai (Chinese vodka) 茅台酒
máotái jiǔ
map 地图 dìtú
March 三月 sānyuè
marijuana 大麻 dàmá
marital status 婚姻状况 hūnyīn
zhuàngkuàng
market 市场 shìchǎng
marriage 婚姻 hūnyīn

M

married 已婚 yǐ hūn

marry 结婚 jiéhūn

martial arts (Chinese kung fu) 武术 (中国功夫) wǔshù (Zhōngguó gōngfu)

mass (Catholic) 礼拜 lǐbài

massage 按摩 ànmó

masseur/masseuse 按摩师 ànmó shī

mat 地毯 dìtǎn

match (sports) 比赛 bǐsài

matches (for lighting) 火柴 huǒchái

mattress 垫子 diànzi

May 五月 wǔyuè

maybe 可能 kěnéng

mayor 市长 shìzhǎng

me 我 wǒ

meal 一顿饭 yídùn fàn

measles 麻疹 mázhěn

meat 肉 ròu

mechanic 机修工 jīxiūgōng

medal tally 奖牌数 jiǎngpái shù

media 媒体 méitǐ

medicine (study, profession) 医学 yīxué

medicine (medication) 医药 yīyào

meditation 静坐 jìngzuò

meet 会见 huìjiàn

melon 瓜 guā

member 成员 chéngyuán

menstruation 月经 yuèjīng

menu 菜单 càidān

message 信息 xìnxī

metal 金属 jīnshǔ

metre 米 mǐ

meter (taxi) 表 biǎo

metro (train) 地铁 dìtiě

metro station 地铁站 dìtiě zhàn

microwave (oven) 微波炉 wēibō lú

midday/noon 中午 zhōngwǔ

midnight 午夜 wǔyè

migraine 偏头疼 piān tóuténg

military 国防 guófáng

military service 兵役 bīngyì

milk 牛奶 niúnǎi

millet 小米 xiǎomǐ

millimetre 毫米 háomǐ

million 百万 bǎiwàn

mince 肉馅 ròuxiàn

mineral water 矿泉水 kuàngquán shuǐ

minute 分钟 fēnzhōng

mirror 镜子 jìngzi

miscarriage 流产 liúchǎn

miss (feel absence of) 想念 xiǎngniàn

mistake 过失 guòshī

mix 调拌 tiáobàn

mobile phone 手机 shǒujī

modem 猫 māo

modern 现代 xiàndài

moisturiser 护肤膏 hùfū gāo

monastery (Buddhist) 佛寺 fósì

Monday 星期一 xīngqī yī

money 钱 qián

Mongolia 蒙古 Ménggǔ

monk 和尚 héshang

month 月 yuè

monument 纪念碑 jìniàn bēi

moon 月亮 yuèliang

more 多 duō

morning (after breakfast) 早上 zǎoshàng

morning (before lunch) 上午 shàngwǔ

morning sickness 晨吐症 chéntùzhèng

mosque 清真寺 qīngzhēn sì

mosquito 蚊子 wénzi

mosquito coil 蚊香 wénxiāng

mosquito net 蚊帐 wénzhàng

mother 母亲 mǔqin

mother-in-law 岳母 yuèmǔ

motorbike 摩托车 mótuō chē

motorboat 摩托艇 mótuō tǐng

motorcycle 摩托车 mótuō chē

motorway (tollway) 收费公路 shōufèi gōnglù

mountain 山 shān

mountain bike 山地车 shāndì chē

mountain climbing 爬山 páshān

mountain path 山路 shānlù

N

mountain range 山脉 shānmài
mouse 耗子 hàozi
mouth 口 kǒu
movie 电影 diànyǐng
Mr 先生 xiānsheng
Mrs 女士 nǚshì
Ms/Miss 小姐 xiǎojiě
MSG 味精 wèijīng
mud 泥巴 níba
mum 妈妈 māma
mumps 麻疹 mázhěn
mung beans (red) 红豆 hóngdòu
murder ⓝ 谋杀罪杀人犯 móushā zuì shārén fàn
murder ⓥ 谋杀杀 móushā shā
muscle 瘦肉 shòuròu
museum 博物馆 bówù guǎn
mushroom 蘑菇 mógu
music 音乐 yīnyuè
music shop 音像店 yīnxiàng diàn
musician 音乐家 yīnyuè jiā
Muslim 穆斯林 Mùsīlín
mussel 蚌 bàng
mustard 芥末 jièmo
mustard greens 油菜 yóucài
mute 哑巴 yǎba
my 我的 wǒde

N

nail clippers 指甲刀 zhǐjiadāo
name 名字 míngzi
napkin 餐巾 cānjīn
nappy 尿裤 niàokù
nappy rash 尿裤疹 niàokùzhěn
national park 自然保护区 zìrán bǎohù qū
nationality 国籍 guójí
nature 大自然 dà zìrán
nausea 恶心 èxīn
near 近 jìn
nearby 附近 fùjìn
nearest 最近 zuìjìn
necessary 必要的 bìyào de
necklace 项链 xiàngliàn
nectarine 油桃 yóutáo
need ⓥ 需要 xūyào

needle (sewing) 针线 zhēnxiàn
needle (syringe) 注射针 zhùshè zhēn
negative 消极 xiāojí
neither 两个都不 liǎngge dōu bù
net 网 wǎng
Netherlands 荷兰 Hélán
never 从来不 cónglái bù
new 新 xīn
New Year's Day 元旦 yuándàn
New Year's Eve 除夕 chúxī
New Zealand 新西兰 Xīnxīlán
news 新闻 xīnwén
newsstand 报刊亭 bàokāntíng
newspaper 报纸 bàozhǐ
next (month) 下个 xiàge
next to 旁边 pángbiān
nice 善良 shànliáng
nickname 昵称 nìchēng
night 晚上 wǎnshàng
night out 晚上活动 wǎnshàng huódòng
nightclub 夜总会 yèzǒnghuì
no 不对 búduì
no vacancy 没空 méikòng
noisy 吵 chǎo
none 一个也没有 yīge yě méiyǒu
nonsmoking 不吸烟 bù xīyān
noodle house 面馆 miànguǎn
noodles 面条 miàntiáo
noon 中午 zhōngwǔ
north 北边 běibiān
Norway 挪威 Nuówēi
nose 鼻子 bízi
not 不是 bùshì
notebook 笔记本 bǐjì běn
nothing 一无所有 yīwú suǒyǒu
November 十一月 shíyī yuè
now 现在 xiànzài
nuclear energy 核能 hé néng
nuclear testing 核试验 hé shìyàn
nuclear waste 核废物 hé fèiwù
number 号码 hàomǎ
number plate 车牌 chēpái
nun 尼姑 nígū
nurse 护士 hùshi
nut 果仁 guǒrén

O

oats 燕麦片 yànmài piàn
occupation 工作 gōngzuò
occupied 有事 yǒushì
ocean 大海 dàhǎi
October 十月 shíyuè
off (spoiled) 过时 guòshí
office 办公室 bàngōng shì
office worker 白领 báilíng
often 经常 jīngcháng
oil (food) 石油 shíyóu
oil (petroleum) 汽油 qìyóu
old 老 lǎo
old man (derogatory) 老头 lǎotóu
old man (respectful) 大爷 dàyé
old woman (derogatory) 老太太 lǎotàitai
old woman (respectful) 大妈 dàmā
Olympic Games 奥运会 Àoyùn huì
Olympic record 奥运会纪录 Àoyùn huì jìlù
omelette 炒鸡蛋 chǎo jīdàn
on 以上 yǐshàng
on time 准时 zhǔnshí
once 一次 yīcì
one 一个 yīge
one-way (ticket) 单程 dānchéng
onion 洋葱 yángcōng
only 只有 zhǐyǒu
oolong tea 乌龙茶 wūlóng chá
open ⓐ 开放 kāifàng
open ⓥ 打开 dǎkāi
opening hours 营业时间 yíngyè shíjiān
opera (Chinese) 京剧 jīngjù
opera (Western) 歌剧 gējù
opera house 剧场 jùchǎng
operation (medical) 手术 shǒushù
operator 操作工 cāozuògōng
opinion 看法 kànfǎ
opposite 对面 duìmiàn
optometrist 眼科医生 yǎnkē yīshēng
or 或者 huòzhě
orange (fruit) 橙子 chéngzi
orange (colour) 橙色 chéngsè

orange juice 橙汁 chéngzhī
orchestra 交响乐队 jiāoxiǎng yuèduì
order (arrangement) 顺序 shùnxù
order (food) 点菜 diǎncài
ordinary 普通 pǔtōng
orgasm 高潮 gāocháo
original 开拓性 kāituò xìng
other 其他 qítā
our 我们的 wǒmende
out of order 坏了 huàile
outside 外面 wàimian
ovarian cyst 卵巢脓包 luǎncáo nóngbāo
ovary 卵巢 luǎncáo
oven 烤箱 kàoxiāng
overcoat 大衣 dàyī
overdose 过量 guòliàng
overnight 过夜 guòyè
overseas 海外 hǎiwài
owe 欠 qiàn
owner 主人 zhǔrén
oxygen 氧气 yǎngqì
oyster 蚝 háo
oyster sauce 蚝油 háoyóu
ozone layer 臭氧层 chòu yǎng céng

P

pacemaker 心律调节器 xīnlù tiáojié qì
pacifier (dummy) 奶嘴 nǎizuǐ
package 包裹 bāoguǒ
packet (general) 包 bāo
padlock 锁 suǒ
page 页 yè
pagoda 八角塔 bājiǎotǎ
pain 疼 téng
painful 很疼 hěnténg
painkiller 止痛药 zhǐtòngyào
painter 画家 huàjiā
painting (a work) 画 huà
painting (the art) 画画 huàhuà
pair 对 duì
Pakistan 巴基斯坦 Bājīsītǎn
palace 宫殿 gōngdiàn
pan 小锅 xiǎoguō
panda 熊猫 xióngmāo

pants (trousers) 长裤 chángkù
panty liners 卫生巾 wèishēngjīn
pantyhose 长袜 chángwà
pap smear 擦片检查 cāpiàn jiǎnchá
papaya 木瓜 mùguā
paper 纸 zhǐ
papers (official documents) 证件 zhèngjiàn
paperwork 手续 shǒuxù
paraplegic 双肢障 shuāngzhīzhàng
parcel 包裹 bāoguǒ
parents 父母 fùmǔ
park 公园 gōngyuán
park (a car) 停(车) tíng (chē)
parliament 议会 yìhuì
part (component) 部分 bùfen
part-time 临时工 línshígōng
party (night out) 连酒吧 guàng jiǔbā
party (politics) 党 dǎng
pass (mountain) 关口 guānkǒu
pass (permit) 许可证 xǔkézhèng
pass 通过 tōngguò
passenger 乘客 chéngkè
passionfruit 鸡蛋果 jīdàn guǒ
passport 护照 hùzhào
passport number 护照号码 hùzhào hàomǎ
past 过去 guòqù
pasta 意大利面 yìdàlì miàn
pastry 法式面包 fǎshì miànbāo
path 小路 xiǎolù
pavillion 亭子 tíngzi
pawpaw 木瓜 mùguā
pay ⊙ 付 fù
payment 付款 fùkuǎn
pea shoots 豆苗 dòumiáo
peace 和平 hépíng
peach 桃子 táozi
peak (mountain) 山顶 shāndǐng
peanut 花生 huāshēng
pear 梨 lí
peasant 农民 nóngmín
pedal 脚蹬 jiǎodēng
pedestrian 行人 xíngrén
pedicab 三轮车 sānlúnchē

Peking duck 北京烤鸭 Běijīng kǎoyā
Peking opera 京剧 jīngjù
pen (ballpoint) 钢笔 gāngbǐ
pencil 铅笔 qiānbǐ
penis 阳具 yángjù
penknife 小刀 xiǎodāo
pensioner 退休职工 tuìxiū zhígōng
people 人 rén
pepper (vegetable) 青椒 qīngjiāo
pepper (spice) 辣椒 làjiāo
per (day) 每(天) měi(tiān)
per cent 百分比 bǎifēnbǐ
perfect 完美 wánměi
performance 演出 yǎnchū
perfume 香水 xiāngshuǐ
period pain 痛经 tòngjīng
permission 许可 xǔkě
permit 许可证 xǔkě zhèng
persimmon 柿子 shìzi
person 人 rén
petition 投诉 tóusù
petrol 汽油 qìyóu
petrol station 加油站 jiāyóu zhàn
pharmacy 西药房 xīyào fáng
phone box 公用电话 gōngyòng diànhuà
phonecard 电话卡 diànhuà kǎ
photo 照片 zhàopiàn
photographer 摄影家 shèyíng jiā
photography 摄影 shèyǐng
phrasebook 短语集 duǎnyǔ jí
pickles 咸菜 xiáncài
picnic 野餐 yěcān
pie 馅饼 xiànbǐng
piece 块 kuài
pig 猪 zhū
pigeon 鸽子 gēzi
pill 药片 yàopiàn
Pill (the) 避孕药 bìyùn yào
pillow 枕头 zhěntou
pineapple 菠萝 bōluó
pink 粉色 fěnsè
pistachio 开心果 kāixīnguǒ
PLA (People's Liberation Army) 解放军 jiěfàng jūn

PRC (People's Republic of China)
中华人民共和国 Zhōnghuá rénmín
gònghé guó
PSB (Public Security Bureau) 公安
局 gōng'ān jú
place 地方 dìfang
place of birth 出生地 chūshēng dì
plane 飞机 fēijī
planet 星球 xīngqiú
plant 植物 zhíwù
plastic 塑料 sùliào
plate 盘子 pánzi
plateau 高原 gāoyuán
platform 站台 zhàntái
play (cards) 打 dǎ
play (guitar) 弹 tán
play (theatre) 剧 jù
plug (bath) 塞子 sāizi
plug (electricity) 插头 chātóu
plum 梅子 méizi
pocket 口袋 kóudài
pocket knife 小刀 xiǎodāo
poetry 诗歌 shīgē
point ⓝ 点 diǎn
point ⓥ 指 zhǐ
poisonous 有毒 yǒudú
police 警察局 jǐngchájú
police officer 警察 jǐngchá
public security officer 公安 gōng'ān
police station 派出所 pàichū suǒ
policy 政策 zhèngcè
politician 政治家 zhèngzhì jiā
politics 政治 zhèngzhì
pollen 花粉 huāfěn
pollution 污染 wūrǎn
pool (game) 台球 táiqiú
pool (swimming) 游泳池 yóuyǒng
chí
poor 穷 qióng
popular 流行 liúxíng
pork 猪肉 zhūròu
pork sausage 香肠 xiāng cháng
port (sea) 港口 gǎngkǒu
portrait sketcher 画像师 huàxiàng
shī
positive 正 zhèng

possible 有可能 yǒukénéng
post code 邮政编码 yóuzhèng
biānmǎ
post office 邮局 yóujú
postage 邮电 yóudiàn
postcard 明信片 míngxinpiàn
poster 画报 huàbào
pot (ceramics) 瓶 píng
pot (dope) 大麻 dàmá
potato 土豆 tǔdòu
pottery 陶器 táoqì
pound (money, weight) 镑 bàng
poverty 贫穷 pínqióng
powder 粉 fěn
power 权利 quánlì
prawn 虾子 xiāzi
prayer 祈祷 qídǎo
prayer book 祈祷书 qídǎo shú
prefer 更喜欢 gèng xǐhuān
pregnancy test kit 妊娠试验
rènshēn shìyàn
pregnant 怀孕 huáiyùn
prehistoric art 原始艺术 yuánshǐ
yìshù
premenstrual tension 经前紧张
jīngqián jǐnzhāng
prepare 准备 zhǔnbèi
prescription 药方 yàofāng
present (gift) 礼物 lǐwù
present (time) 现在 xiànzài
president 总统 zǒngtǒng
pressure 压力 yālì
pressure point massage 经络按摩
jīngluò ànmó
pretty 漂亮 piàoliang
price 价格 jiàgé
priest 牧师 mùshī
prime minister 首相 shǒuxiàng
printer (computer) 打印机 dǎyìnjī
prison 监狱 jiānyù
prisoner 罪犯 zuìfàn
private 私人 sīrén
produce ⓥ 生产 shēngchǎn
profit 利润 lìrùn
program 节目 jiémù
projector 投影机 tóuyǐngjī

Q

promise 发誓 fāshì
prostitute 妓女 jìnǚ
protect 保护 bǎohù
protected (animal etc) 受保护动物 shòu bǎohù dòngwù
protest ⓝ 游行 yóuxíng
protest ⓥ 抗议 kàngyì
provisions 预备品 yùbèipǐn
pub (bar) 酒吧 jiǔbā
public gardens 公园 gōngyuán
public relations 公共关系 gōnggòng guānxì
public telephone 公用电话 gōngyòng diànhuà
public toilet 公厕 gōngcè
pull 拉 lā
pump ⓝ 打气筒 dǎqìtóng
pumpkin 南瓜 nánguā
pumpkin seeds 瓜子 guāzi
puncture 穿孔 chuānkǒng
pure 纯 chún
purple 紫色 zǐsè
purse 钱包 qiánbāo
push 推 tuī
put 放 fàng

Q

quadriplegic 四肢瘫 sìzhīzhuàng
qualifications 学历 xuélì
quality 质量 zhìliàng
quarantine 免疫站 miǎnyìzhàn
quarter 四分之一 sìfēn zhī yī
queen 女王 nǚwáng
question 问题 wèntí
queue 排队 páiduì
quick 快 kuài
quiet 安静 ānjìng
quit 辞职 cízhí

R

rabbit 兔子 tùzi
race (sport) 比赛 bǐsài
racetrack 赛场 sàichǎng
racing bike 赛车 sàichē
racism 种族歧视 zhǒngzú qíshì

racquet 拍子 pāizi
radiator 暖气管 nuǎnqìguǎn
radio 收音机 shōuyīnjī
radish 萝卜 luóbo
railway station 火车站 huǒchēzhàn
rain ⓝ 下雨 xiàyǔ
raincoat 雨衣 yǔyī
raisin 葡萄干 pútáogān
rape ⓝ 强奸 qiángjiān
rare (uncommon) 罕见 hǎnjiàn
rare (about food) 半生 bànshēng
rash 疹子 zhěnzi
raspberry 山莓 shānméi
rat 老鼠 lǎoshǔ
rave 电子舞会 diànzǐ wǔhuì
raw 生 shēng
razor 剃刀 tìdāo
razor blade 剃刀片 tìdāo piàn
read 读 dú
reading 看书 kànshū
ready 做好了 zuòhǎole
real-estate agent 房产代理 fángchǎn dàilǐ
realistic 现实 xiànshí
rear (seat etc) 后 hòu
reason 原因 yuányīn
receipt 发票 fāpiào
recently 最近 zuìjìn
recommend 推荐 tuījiàn
record ⓥ 录 lù
recording 录音 lùyīn
recyclable 可回收 kě huíshōu
recycle 回收 huíshōu
red 红色 hóngsè
referee 裁判 cáipàn
reference (letter) 推荐(信) tuījiàn (xìn)
reflexology 反射疗法 fǎnshè liáofǎ
refrigerator 冰箱 bīngxiāng
refugee 难民 nànmín
refund ⓝ 退钱 tuìqián
refuse 拒绝 jùjué
regional 地方性 dìfāng xìng
registered mail/post 挂号 guàhào
rehydration salts 补液盐 bǔyèyán

reiki 灵气按摩 língqì ànmó
relationship 关系 guānxi
relax 放松 fàngsōng
relic 活恐龙 huókǒnglóng
religion 宗教 zōngjiào
religious 宗教性的 zōngjiào xìngde
remote 偏僻 piānpì
remote control 遥控 yáokòng
rent 租赁 zūlìn
repair 修理 xiūlǐ
republic 共和国 gònghéguó
reservation (booking) 预定 yùdìng
rest 休息 xiūxi
restaurant 饭馆 fànguǎn
resumé (CV) 简历 jiǎnlì
retired 退休 tuìxiū
return (come back) 回来 huílái
return (ticket) 双程(票)
shuāngchéng (piào)
review ⓝ 复查 fùchá
rhythm 节奏 jiézòu
ribs (beef) 排骨 páigǔ
rice (raw) 大米 dàmǐ
rice (cooked) 米饭 mǐfàn
rice cake 年糕 niángāo
rice vinegar (white) 白醋 báicù
rich (wealthy) 有钱 yǒuqián
ride (horse) ⓥ 骑 qí
right (correct) 对 duì
right (direction) 右边 yòubiān
right-wing 右派 yòupài
ring (on finger) 戒指 jièzhǐ
ring (phone) 打(电话) dǎ (diànhuà)
rip-off 贼人 zéirén
risk ⓝ 风险 fēngxiǎn
river 川 chuān
road 道路 dàolù
road map 交通地图 jiāotōng dìtú
rob 偷 tōu
rock (stone) 石头 shítou
rock (music) 摇滚 yáogǔn
rock climbing 攀岩 pānyán
rock group 摇滚乐队 yáogǔn yuèduì
roll (bread) 小面包 xiǎo miànbāo
rollerblading 旱冰 hànbīng
romantic 浪漫 làngmàn

room 房间 fángjiān
room number 房间号 fángjiān hào
rope 绳子 shéngzi
round 圆 yuán
roundabout 圆环岛 yuánhuándǎo
route 路线 lùxiàn
rowing 划船 huáchuán
rubbish 垃圾 lājī
rubella 德国麻疹 déguó mázhěn
rug 地毯 dìtǎn
rugby 英式橄榄球 yīngshì gǎnlǎn qiú
ruins 废墟 fèixū
rule ⓝ 规定 guīdìng
run 跑 pǎo
running (sport) 跑步 pǎobù
runny nose 流鼻涕 liú bítì

S

sad 郁闷 yùmèn
saddle 马鞍 mǎ'ān
safe 安全 ānquán
safe sex 安全性交 ānquán xìngjiāo
safebox 保险箱 bǎoxiǎn xiāng
saint 圣人 shèngrén
salad 沙拉 shālā
salami 香肠 xiāngcháng
salary 薪水 xīnshuǐ
sale 大甩卖 dà shuǎimài
sales tax 销售税 xiāoshòu shuì
salmon 三文鱼 sānwén yú
salt 盐 yán
same 一样 yīyàng
sand 沙子 shāzi
sandal 凉鞋 liángxié
sanitary napkin 卫生巾 wèishēngjīn
sardine 咸鱼 xiányú
SARS 非典 fēidiǎn
Saturday 星期六 xīngqī liù
sauce 酱 jiàng
sauna 桑拿 sāngná
sausage 香肠 xiāngcháng
say 说 shuō
scarf 头巾 tóujīn
scenic area 风景区 fēngjǐngqū
school 学校 xuéxiào
science 科学 kēxué

scientist 科学家 kēxué jiā
scissors 剪刀 jiǎndāo
score (goal) 进球 jìnqiú
Scotland 苏格兰 Sūgélán
scrambled (stir-fried) 炒炒 chǎo chǎo
sculpture 塑像 sùxiàng
sea 海 hǎi
sea cucumber 海参 hǎishēn
seafood 海鲜 hǎixiān
seasick 晕船 yùnchuán
seaside 海边 hǎibiān
season 季节 jìjié
seat (place) 座位 zuòwèi
seatbelt 安全带 ānquándài
second ⓝ 秒 miǎo
second ⓐ 第二 dì'èr
second-class 二等 èrděng
secondhand 二手 èrshǒu
secondhand shop 二手店 èrshòu diàn
secretary 秘书 mìshū
see 看见 kànjiàn
self service 自助 zìzhù
self-employed 个体户 gètǐ hù
selfish 自私 zìsī
sell 卖 mài
send 寄送 jìsòng
sensible 有理的 yǒulǐde
sensual 肉体的 ròutǐde
separate 分开的 fēnkāide
September 九月 jiǔyuè
serious 严肃 yànsù
service 服务 fúwù
service charge 服务费 fúwù fèi
service station 加油站 jiāyóu zhàn
serviette 纸巾 zhǐjīn
sesame paste 芝麻酱 zhīma jiàng
several 好几个 hǎo jǐge
sew (mend) 补 bǔ
sew (not mend) 缝纫 féngrèn
sex 男女事 nánnǚ shì
sexism 重男轻女 zhòngnán qīngnǚ
sexy 性感 xìnggǎn
shade ⓝ 树荫 shùyīn
shadow 影子 yǐngzi
shallots 小葱 xiǎocōng

shampoo 洗发膏 xǐfàgāo
Shanghai 上海 Shànghǎi
shape ⓝ 形状 xíngzhuàng
share 公用 gōngyòng
shave 刮脸 guāliǎn
shaving cream 剃须膏 tìxūgāo
she 她 tā
sheep 绵羊 miányáng
sheet (bed) 床单 chuángdān
shelf 架子 jiàzi
shiatsu 指压按摩 zhǐyā ànmó
shingles (illness) 带状泡疹 dàizhuàng pàozhěn
ship 船 chuán
shirt 衬衫 chénshān
shoe 鞋 xié
shoe shop 鞋店 xiédiàn
shoes 鞋子 xiézi
shoot 打枪 dǎqiāng
shop ⓝ 店 diàn
shop ⓥ 买东西 mǎi dōngxi
shopping 逛街 guàngjiē
shopping centre 商场 shāngchǎng
short (height) 矮 ǎi
short (length) 短 duǎn
shortage 紧缺 jǐnquē
shorts 短裤 duǎnkù
shoulder 肩膀 jiānbǎng
shout 喊 hǎn
show 表演 biǎoyǎn
shower 浴室 yùshì
shrine 庙 miào
shut 关 guān
shy 害羞 hàixiū
sick 病 bìng
side 旁边 pángbiān
sign 牌子 páizi
signature 签名 qiānmíng
silk 丝绸 sīchóu
silver 银子 yínzi
silver medal 银牌 yínpái
similar 同样 tóngyàng
simple 简单 jiǎndān
since (May) 从(五月) 以来 cóng (wǔ yuè) yǐlái
sing 唱歌 chànggē

Singapore 新加坡 Xīnjiāpō

singer 歌手 gēshǒu

single (person) 单人 dānrén

single room 单人间 dānrén jiān

singlet 背心 bèixīn

sister (elder) 姐姐 jiějie

sister (younger) 妹妹 mèimei

sisters 姐妹 jiěmèi

sit 坐下 zuòxià

size (general) 大小 dàxiǎo

skateboarding 滑板 huábǎn

ski ⓥ 滑雪 huáxuě

skiing 滑雪 huáxuě

skin 皮肤 pífū

skirt 裙子 qúnzi

skull 窟窿 kūlong

sky 天 tiān

sleep 睡觉 shuìjiào

sleeping bag 睡袋 shuìdài

sleeping berth 卧铺 wòpù

sleeping car 卧铺车厢 wòpù chēxiāng

sleeping pills 安眠药 ānmián yào

sleepy 犯困 fànkùn

slice (cake) 蛋糕 dàngāo

slide (film) 幻灯片 huàndēng piàn

slippers 拖鞋 tuōxié

slow 慢 màn

slowly 慢慢地 mànmande

small 小 xiǎo

smaller 更小 gèngxiǎo

smallest 最小 zuìxiǎo

smell 味道 wèidào

smile 微笑 wēixiào

smoke 抽烟 chōuyān

snack 小吃 xiǎochī

snail 蜗牛 wōniú

snake 蛇 shé

snorkelling 潜水 qiánshuǐ

snow 雪 xuě

snow pea 荷兰豆 hélán dòu

snowboarding 滑雪 huáxuě

soap 肥皂 féizào

soap opera 肥皂剧 féizào jù

soccer 足球 zúqiú

social welfare 社会福利 shèhuì fúlì

socialism 社会主义 shèhuì zhǔyì

socialist 社会主义战士 shèhuì zhǔyì zhànshì

sock 袜子 wàzi

soft drink 汽水 qìshuǐ

soft seat 软座 ruǎnzuò

soft sleeper 软卧 ruǎnwò

soldier 军人 jūnrén

some 一些 yìxiē

someone 某人 mǒurén

something 一个什么的 yīge shénme de

sometimes 偶尔 ǒu'ěr

son 儿子 érzi

song 歌曲 gēqǔ

soon 快 kuài

sore 疮口 chuāngkǒu

sore throat 喉咙疼 hóulóngténg

soup 汤 tāng

sour plum drink 酸梅汤 suānméitāng

south 南 nán

souvenir 纪念品 jìniàn pǐn

souvenir shop 纪念品店 jìniànpǐn diàn

soybean 黄豆 huángdòu

soy milk (fresh) 豆浆 dòujiāng

soy milk (powdered) 豆奶粉 dòunǎi fěn

soy sauce 酱油 jiàngyóu

space 空间 kōngjiān

Spain 西班牙 Xībānyá

sparkling wine 香槟 xiāngbīn

speak 说话 shuōhuà

special 特别 tèbié

specialist 专家 zhuānjiā

speed 速度 sùdù

speed limit 最高车速 zuìgāo chēsù

speedometer 速度表 sùdù biǎo

spider 蜘蛛 zhīzhū

spinach 菠菜 bócài

spirits (Chinese alcohol) 白酒 báijiǔ

spoiled 烂掉了 làndiàole

spoon 勺 sháo

sport 体育 tǐyù

S

sports store 体育用品店 tǐyù yòngpǐn diàn
sportsperson 运动员 yùndòng yuán
sprain 扭伤 niǔshāng
spring (coil) 弹簧 tánhuáng
spring (season) 春天 chūntiān
Spring Festival 春节 chūnjié
square (town) 广场 guǎngchǎng
stadium 体育场 tǐyù chǎng
stairway 台阶 táijiē
stale 过时 guòshí
stamp 邮票 yóupiào
standby ticket 站台票 zhàntái piào
star 星星 xīngxing
(four-)star (四) 星级 (sì) xīngjí
star anise 八角 bājiǎo
start ⓝ 开头 kāitóu
start ⓥ 开始 kāishǐ
station 车站 chēzhàn
stationer's (shop) 文具店 wénjù diàn
statue 塑像 sùxiàng
stay (at a hotel) 住 zhù
stay (in one place) 留在 liúzài
steak (beef) 排骨 páigǔ
steal 偷 tōu
steamed bun 馒头 mántou
steep 陡 dǒu
step 台阶 táijiē
stereo 音响 yīnxiǎng
sticking plaster 创口贴 chuāngkǒu tiē
still water 净水 jìngshuǐ
stock (broth) 鸡汤 jītāng
stockings 长袜 chángwà
stolen 盗窃的 dàoqiède
stomach 肚子 dùzi
stomach ache (to have a) 肚子疼 dùzi téng
stone 石头 shítou
stoned (drugged) 吃毒晕晕的 chīdú yūnyunde
stop (bus, tram etc) 停 tíng
stop (cease) 停止 tíngzhǐ
stop (prevent) 防止 fángzhǐ
Stop! 救人！Jiùrén!
storm 风暴 fēngbào

story 故事 gùshi
stove 炉子 lúzi
straight 直接 zhíjiē
strange 奇怪 qíguài
stranger 陌生人 mòshēngrén
strawberry 草莓 cǎoméi
stream 山泉 shānquán
street 街头 jiētóu
street market 街市 jiēshì
strike 罢工 bàgōng
string 绳子 shéngzi
stroke (medical) 中风 zhòngfēng
stroll 散步 sànbù
stroller 婴儿推车 yīng'ér tuīchē
strong 有劲 yǒujìn
stubborn 固执 gùzhí
student 学生 xuéshēng
studio 工作室 gōngzuò shì
stupid 愚蠢 yúchǔn
style 风格 fēnggé
subtitles 字幕 zìmù
suburb 郊区 jiāoqū
subway 地铁 dìtiě
suffer 吃苦 chīkǔ
sugar 砂糖 shātáng
sugar cane 甘蔗 gānzhè
suitcase 旅行箱 lǚxíng xiāng
summer 夏天 xiàtiān
sun 太阳 tàiyáng
sunblock 防晒油 fángshài yóu
sunburn 晒伤 shàishāng
Sunday 星期天 xīngqītiān
sunflower seeds 瓜子 guāzǐ
sunglasses 墨镜 mòjìng
sunny 很晒 hěnshài
sunrise 日出 rìchū
sunset 日落 rìluò
sunstroke 中暑 zhòngshǔ
supermarket 超市 chāoshì
superstition 迷信 míxìn
supporter (politics) 支持者 zhīchí zhě
supporter (sport) 球迷 qiúmí
surf (waves) 海浪 hǎilàng
surface mail (land) (陆运)平信 (lùyùn) píngxìn

surface mail (sea) (海运) 平信 (hǎiyùn) píngxìn
surfboard 冲浪板 chōnglàng bǎn
surfing 冲浪 chōnglàng
surname 姓 xìng
surprise 惊讶 jīngyà
sweater 上衣 shàngyī
Sweden 瑞典 Ruìdiǎn
sweet 甜 tián
sweet potato 地瓜 dìguā
sweets 甜点 tiándiǎn
swim 游泳 yóuyǒng
swimming (sport) 游泳 yóuyǒng
swimming pool 游泳池 yóuyǒng chí
swimsuit 游泳衣 yóuyǒng yī
Switzerland 瑞士 Ruìshì
swollen 肿了起来 zhǒngle qǐlái
synagogue 犹太教堂 yóutài jiàotáng
synthetic 人为的 rénwéide
syringe 注射针 zhùshè zhēn

T

table 桌子 zhuōzi
table tennis 乒乓球 pīngpāng qiú
tablecloth 桌布 zhuōbù
tail 尾巴 wěiba
tailor 裁缝 cáiféng
Taiwan 台湾 Táiwān
take 拿走 názǒu
take a photo 照相 zhàoxiàng
talk 谈话 tánhuà
tall 高 gāo
tampon 棉条 miántiáo
Taoism 道教 Dàojiào
tap 水龙头 shuǐlóngtóu
tap water 自来水 zìlái shuǐ
tape (recording) 磁带 cídài
tasty 好香 hǎoxiāng
tax 税 shuì
taxi 出租车 chūzū chē
taxi stand 出租车站 chūzū chē zhàn
tea 茶 chá
teapot 茶壶 cháhú
teacher 老师 lǎoshī
teahouse 茶馆 cháguǎn
team 运动队 yùndòng duì

technique 做法 zuòfǎ
teeth 牙齿 yáchǐ
telegram 电报 diànbào
telephone ⓝ 电话 diànhuà
telephone ⓥ 打电话 dǎ diànhuà
telescope 望远镜 wàngyuǎn jìng
television 电视 diànshì
tell 告诉 gàosu
temperature (fever) 发烧 fāshāo
temperature (weather) 温度 wēndù
temple 寺庙 sìmiào
tennis 网球 wǎngqiú
tennis court 网球场 wǎngqiú chǎng
tent 帐篷 zhàngpeng
terrible 可怕的 kěpà de
test 考试 kǎoshì
thank 道谢 dàoxiè
thank you 谢谢 xièxie
that (one) 那个 nàge
theatre 剧场 jùchǎng
their 他们的 tāmen de
there 那边 nàbian
thermometer 体温计 tǐwēn jì
thermos 热水瓶 rèshuǐpíng
they 他们 tāmen
thick 厚 hòu
thief 小偷 xiǎotōu
thin 薄 báo
think 想 xiǎng
third 第三 dìsān
thirsty (to be) 渴 kě
this (month) 这个 (月) zhège (yuè)
this (one) 这个 zhège
thread 棉线 miánxiàn
throat 脖子 bózi
thrush (health) 鹅口疮 ékǒuchuāng
thunderstorm 雷雨 léiyǔ
Thursday 星期四 xīngqī sì
Tibet 西藏 Xīzàng
ticket 票 piào
ticket collector 售票员 shòupiào yuán
ticket office 票房 piàofáng
tide 潮流 cháoliú
tight 很紧 hěnjǐn
time 时间 shíjiān

U

time difference 时差 shíchā
timetable 时刻表 shíkè biǎo
tin (can) 罐头 guàntou
tin opener 开罐器 kāiguànqì
tiny 微小 wēixiǎo
tip (gratuity) 消费 xiāofèi
tired 累 lèi
tissues 纸巾 zhǐjīn
to (go to, come to) 到 dào
toast 烤面包 kǎo miànbāo
tobacco 烟丝 yānsī
tobacco kiosk 烟摊 yāntān
today 今天 jīntiān
toe 脚指头 jiǎo zhǐtou
tofu 豆腐 dòufu
together 一起 yìqǐ
toilet 厕所 cèsuǒ
toilet paper 手纸 shǒuzhǐ
tomato 西红柿 xīhóngshì
tomato sauce 番茄酱 fānqié jiàng
tomb 坟墓 fénmù
tomorrow 明天 míngtiān
tonight 今天晚上 jīntiān wǎnshàng
too (expensive etc) 太 tài
tooth 牙齿 yáchǐ
toothache 牙齿疼 yáchǐ téng
toothbrush 牙刷 yáshuā
toothpaste 牙膏 yágāo
toothpick 牙签 yáqiān
torch (flashlight) 手电筒 shǒudiàntǒng
touch 触摸 chùmō
tour 向导游 xiàngdǎo yóu
tourist 旅客 lǚkè
tourist hotel 旅店 lǚdiàn
tourist office 旅行店 lǚxíng diàn
towards 向 xiàng
towel 毛巾 máojīn
tower (telecoms) (电视)塔 (diànshì) tǎ
toxic waste 有毒废物 yǒudú fèiwù
toy shop 玩具店 wánjù diàn
track (path) 山路 shānlù
track (sport) 田径 tiánjìng
trade 行业 hángyè
tradesperson 工匠 gōngjiàng

traffic 交通 jiāotōng
traffic light 红绿灯 hónglǜdēng
trail 步行 bùxíng
train 火车 huǒchē
train station 火车站 huǒchē zhàn
tram 电车 diànchē
transit lounge 转机室 zhuǎnjī shì
translate 翻译 fānyì
transport 运输 yùnshū
travel 旅游 lǚyóu
travel agency 旅行社 lǚxíng shè
travel sickness 晕车 yùnchē
travellers cheque 旅行支票 lǚxíng zhīpiào
tree 树 shù
trip (journey) 旅程 lǚchéng
trolley 车子 chēzi
trousers 休闲裤 xiūxián kù
truck 卡车 kǎchē
trust 信用 xìnyòng
try ⊙ 尝试 chángshì
try ⊙ 试图 shìtú
T-shirt T恤 tìxù
tube (tyre) 内胎 nèitāi
Tuesday 星期二 xīngqī èr
tumour 肿瘤 zhǒngliú
tuna 金枪鱼 jīnqiāngyú
tune 曲调 qúdiào
turkey 火鸡 huǒjī
turn 转身 zhuǎnshēn
TV 电视 diànshì
tweezers 镊子 nièzi
twice 两次 liǎngcì
twin room 双人房 shuāngrén fáng
twins 双胞胎 shuāngbāo tāi
two 两个 liǎngge
type 类型 lèixíng
typical 通常 tōngcháng
tyre 轮胎 lúntāi

U

ultrasound 超声检查 chāoshēng jiǎnchá
umbrella 雨伞 yǔsǎn
uncle 叔叔 shūshu
uncomfortable 不舒服 bù shūfu

understand 懂 dǒng
underwear 内衣 nèiyī
unemployed 事业 shìyè
unfair 不公平 bù gōngping
uniform 工作服 gōngzuò fú
universe 宇宙 yǔzhòu
university 大学 dàxué
unleaded 无铅 wúqiān
unsafe 不安全 bù ānquán
until (Friday etc) 一直到 yīzhí dào
unusual 反常 fǎncháng
up 上 shàng
uphill 上坡 shàngpō
urgent 要紧 yàojǐn
urinary infection 尿道感染 niàodào gǎnrǎn
USA 美国 Měiguó
useful 有用的 yǒuyòng de

V

vacancy 空房 kōngfáng
vacant 有空 yǒukòng
vacation 度假 dùjià
vaccination 免疫针 miǎnyì zhēn
vagina 阴道 yīndào
validate 确认 quèrèn
valley 山谷 shāngǔ
valuable 贵重 guìzhòng
value (price) 实价 shíjià
van 面的 miàndī
veal (beef) 牛肉 niúròu
vegetable 蔬菜 shūcài
vegetarian 吃素的 chīsù de
vein 血脉 xuèmài
venereal disease 性病 xìngbìng
venue 地点 dìdiǎn
vermicelli 粉丝 fěnsī
very 很 hěn
video recorder 录像机 lùxiàng jī
Vietnam 越南 Yuènán
view 视野 shìyě
villa 别墅 biéshù
village 村庄 cūnzhuāng
vine (creeper) 攀藤 pānténg
vinegar 醋 cù
vineyard 葡萄园 pútáo yuán

virus 病毒 bìngdú
visa 签证 qiānzhèng
visit 拜访 bàifǎng
vitamins 维生素 wéishēngsù
vodka 伏特加 fútèjiā
voice 声音 shēngyīn
volleyball (sport) 排球 páiqiú
volume 声音大小 shēngyīn dàxiǎo
vote 投票 tóupiào

W

wage 工资 gōngzī
wait (for) 等 děng
waiter 服务员 fúwù yuán
waiting room 等候室 děnghòu shì
wake (someone) up 叫醒 jiàoxǐng
walk 走路 zǒulù
wall (outer) 墙壁 qiángbì
want 想要 xiǎngyào
war 战争 zhànzhēng
wardrobe 衣柜 yīguì
warehouse 仓库 cāngkù
warm 暖和 nuǎnhuo
warn 警告 jǐnggào
wash 洗 xǐ
wash cloth (flannel) 毛巾 máojīn
washing machine 洗衣机 xǐyī jī
watch ⋒ 手表 shǒubiǎo
watch ⊙ 观望 guānwàng
water 水 shuǐ
water bottle (hot) 热水袋 rèshuǐ dài
waterfall 瀑布 pùbù
watermelon 西瓜 xīguā
waterproof 防水 fángshuǐ
water purification tablets 清水药 qīngshuǐyào
waterskiing 滑水 huáshuǐ
wave 海浪 hǎilàng
way 道 dào
we 我们 wǒmen
weak 弱 ruò
wealthy 富裕 fùyù
wear 穿 chuān
weather 气候 qìhòu
wedding 婚礼 hūnlǐ

wedding cake 喜糖 xǐtáng
wedding present 红包 hóngbāo
Wednesday 星期三 xīngqī sān
week 星期 xīngqī
(this) week (这个)礼拜 (zhège) lǐbài
weekend 周末 zhōumò
weigh 称 chēng
weight 重量 zhòngliàng
weights (lift) 健身 jiànshēn
welcome 欢迎 huānyíng
welfare 福利 fúlì
well 很好 hěnhǎo
west 西 xī
wet 湿透 shītòu
what 什么 shénme
wheel 车轮 chēlún
wheelchair 轮椅 lúnyǐ
when 什么时候 shénme shíhòu
where 哪里 nǎlǐ
which 哪个 nǎge
whisky 威士忌 wēishìjì
white 白色 báisè
who 谁 shéi
wholemeal bread 粗谷面包 cūgǔ miànbāo
why 为什么 wèi shénme
wide 宽 kuān
wife 太太 tàitai
wild rice root 茭白 jiāobái
win 胜利 shènglì
wind 风 fēng
window 窗 chuāng
windscreen 车窗防风屏 chēchuāng fángfēng píng
windsurfing 滑浪风帆 huálàng fēngfān
wine 葡萄酒 pútáo jiǔ
wings 翅膀 chìbǎng
winner 胜利者 shènglìzhě
winter 冬天 dōngtiān
wire 金属丝 jīnshǔ sī
wish ⊙ 祝愿 zhùyuàn
with 跟 gēn
within (an hour) (一个小时)以内 (yīge xiǎoshí) yǐnèi
without 以外 yǐwài
wok 锅 guō

woman 女人 nǚrén
wonderful 奇妙 qímiào
wonton soup 馄饨 húntun
wonton stall 馄饨摊 húntun tān
wood 木柴 mùchái
wool 羊毛 yángmáo
word 单词 dāncí
work ⊙ 工作 gōngzuò
work ⊙ 打工 dǎgōng
work experience 实习 shíxí
work permit 工作证 gōngzuò zhèng
workout 锻炼 duànliàn
workshop 工作室 gōngzuòshì
world 世界 shìjiè
world record 世界纪录 shìjiè jìlù
worm 蚯蚓 qiūyǐn
worried 着急 zháojí
worship 崇拜 chóngbài
wrist 手腕 shǒuwàn
write 写 xiě
writer 作家 zuòjiā
wrong 错 cuò

Y

year 年 nián
(this) year (今)年 (jīn) nián
yellow 黄色 huángsè
yes 是 shì
yesterday 昨天 zuótiān
(not) yet 还(没有) hái (méiyǒu)
yoga 瑜伽 yújiā
yoghurt 酸奶 suānnǎi
you sg inf 你 nǐ
you (Beijing) pol 您 nín
you pl 你们 nǐmen
young 年轻 niánqīng
your 你的 nǐde
youth hostel 青年旅栈 qīngnián lǚzhàn

Z

zip/zipper 拉链 lāliàn
zodiac 星象 xīngxiàng
zoo 动物园 dòngwù yuán
zucchini 西葫芦 xī húlu

一画

Dictionary

MANDARIN *to* ENGLISH
普通话 – 英文

The Mandarin–English dictionary is arranged according to the number of strokes in the first character of the Chinese word. Thus, the dictionary starts with 一个 yīge 'one' (the character 一 yī has one stroke), and ends with 罐头 guàntou (罐 guàn has 23 strokes). As there are many first characters with the same number of strokes, the characters within this number-of-strokes classification system are then ordered according to radical – the element of a character which conveys the meaning of a word.

The symbols ⓝ, ⓐ and ⓥ (noun, adjective and verb) have been added for clarity where this is not clear from the English word itself. Where necessary, inf (informal) and pol (polite) forms are also indicated.

一画 **1 stroke**

一个 yīge one
一无所有 yīwú suǒyǒu nothing
一切 yīqiè everything
一月 yīyuè January
一直到 yīzhí dào until (Friday etc)
一起 yīqǐ together
一顿饭 yīdùn fàn meal

二画 **2 strokes**

二月 èryuè February
二等 èrděng second class ⓝ
十一月 shíyī yuè November
十二月 shí'èr yuè December
十月 shíyuè October
T-恤 tìxù T-shirt
七月 qīyuè July
人 rén mankind

人参 rénshēn ginseng
入口 rùkǒu entry
入场费 rùchǎng fèi cover charge
八月 bāyuè August
儿子 érzi son
九月 jiǔyuè September
刀 dāo knife

三画 **3 strokes**

三月 sānyuè March
干 gān dry
干净 gānjìng clean ⓥ
干部 gànbù communist party official
上 shàng up
上衣 shàngyī sweater
工人 gōngrén factory worker
工作 gōngzuò job
工程师 gōngchéng shī engineer
工程学 gōngchéng xué engineering

四画

下 (车) xiàchē get off (a train etc)
下个 xiàge next (month)
(今天) 下午 (jīntiān) xiàwǔ (this) afternoon
下雨 xiàyǔ rain ⓝ
下面 xiàmian down
大 dà big
大小 dàxiǎo size ⓝ
大夫 dàifu doctor
大巴 dàbā bus (city)
大米 dàmǐ rice (raw)
大衣 dàyī coat ⓝ
大佛 dàfó Buddha
大使 dàshǐ ambassador
大使馆 dàshǐguǎn embassy
大学 dàxué university
大麻 dàmá dope (drugs) ⓝ
川 chuān river
小 xiǎo small
小刀 xiǎodāo penknife
小心! Xiǎoxīn! Careful!
小吃 xiǎochī snack ⓝ
小时 xiǎoshí hour
小卖部 xiǎo màibù convenience store • kiosk
小姐 xiǎojiě Ms/Miss
小娃娃 xiǎo wáwa baby
小路 xiǎolù path
口 kǒu mouth
口红 kǒuhóng lipstick
山 shān mountain
门票钱 ménpiàoqián admission price • fare
勺 sháo spoon ⓝ
广东话 Guǎngdōng huà Cantonese (language) ⓝ
女人 nǚrén woman
女士 nǚshì Mrs
女同性恋 nǚ tóngxìng liàn lesbian ⓝ
女性 nǚxìng female
女朋友 nǚpéngyou girlfriend
女孩子 nǚháizi daughter • girl
已婚 yǐ hūn married
卫生巾 wèishēngjīn panty liners • sanitary napkins
叉子 chāzi fork
广场 guǎngchǎng square (town)

飞 fēi fly ⓥ
飞机 fēijī aeroplane
飞机场 fēijī chǎng airport
乡下 xiāngxià countryside

四画 4 strokes

开车 kāichē drive ⓥ
开放 kāifàng open ⓥ
开罐器 kāiguàn qì can/tin opener
无聊 wúliáo boring
元旦 yuándàn New Year's Day
艺术 yìshù art
艺术馆 yìshùguǎn art gallery
艺术家 yìshùjiā artist
不可能 bù kěnéng impossible
不对 búduì no
不同 bùtóng different
不吸烟 bù xīyān nonsmoking
不舒服 bù shūfu uncomfortable
长 cháng long
长城 Chángchéng Great Wall
长途车 chángtú chē bus (intercity)
长途车站 chángtú chēzhàn bus station
长袜 chángwà pantyhose
长裤 chángkù pants (trousers)
木柴 mùchái wood
支票 zhīpiào cheque/check
太阳 tàiyáng sun
比赛 bǐsài match (sports) ⓝ
五月 wǔyuè May
车子 chēzi trolley
车号 chēhào car registration
车灯 chēdēng headlights
车闸 chēzhá brakes
车站 chēzhàn bus stop/station ⓝ
车租赁 chē zūlìn car hire
牙痛 yáchǐ téng toothache
牙医 yáyī dentist
牙刷 yáshuā toothbrush
牙膏 yágāo toothpaste
切 qiē cut ⓥ
止痛药 zhǐtòngyào painkiller
少 shǎo less
中午 zhōngwǔ midday
中文 Zhōngwén Chinese (language)
中心 zhōngxīn centre ⓝ

中国 Zhōngguó China
中华人民共和国 Zhōnghuá rénmín gònghé guó People's Republic of China (PRC)
中医 Zhōngyī Chinese medicine doctor
中药 Zhōngyào Chinese medicine
日本 Rìběn Japan
日出 rìchū dawn ⓝ
日常 rìcháng daily
日期 rìqī date (day)
日程表 rìchéng biǎo itinerary
日出 rìchū sunrise
日落 rìluò sunset
月 yuè month
水 shuǐ water ⓝ
水龙头 shuǐlóngtóu faucet/tap
水果 shuǐguǒ fruit ⓝ
内衣 nèiyī underwear
牛仔裤 niúzǎi kù jeans
牛奶 niúnǎi milk
牛肉 niúròu beef
午饭 wǔfàn lunch ⓝ
午夜 wǔyè midnight
气 qì chi
手 shǒu hand
手工艺 shǒugōngyì handicrafts
手工的 shǒugōng de handmade
手电筒 shǒudiàntǒng flashlight/torch
手袋 shǒudài handbag
手提包 shǒutíbāo briefcase
手机 shǒujī mobile/cell phone
手套 shǒutào glove
手纸 shǒuzhǐ toilet paper
手续 shǒuxù paperwork
手表 shǒubiǎo watch ⓝ
毛巾 máojīn towel
毛衣 máoyī jumper/sweater
毛毯 máotǎn blanket
斤 jīn jin (measure)
什么时候 shénme shíhòu when
反胃 fǎnwèi nausea
父亲 fùqin father
从 cóng from
父母 fùmǔ parents
火车 huǒchē train ⓝ
火车站 huǒchēzhàn railway station

火柴 huǒchái matches (for lighting)
今天 jīntiān today
今天晚上 jīntiān wǎnshàng tonight
分 fēn fen (measure)
分钟 fēnzhōng minute ⓝ
公斤 gōngjīn kilogram
公司 gōngsī company (business)
公用 gōngyòng share ⓥ
公用电话 gōngyòng diànhuà public telephone
公园 gōngyuán park ⓝ
公安 gōng'ān police officer (in country)
公安局 gōng'ān jú Public Security Bureau (PSB)
公里 gōnglǐ kilometre
公厕 gōngcè public toilet
公寓 gōngyù apartment (upmarket)
风俗 fēngsú custom
风水 fēngshuǐ feng shui
方向 fāngxiàng direction
六月 liùyuè June
文具店 wénjù diàn stationer's (shop)
计算器 jìsuànqì calculator
计算机 jìsuànjī computer
心脏 xīnzàng heart
心脏病 xīnzàngbìng heart condition
为什么 wèi shénme why
双边插座 shuāngbiān chāzuò adaptor
双人床 shuāngrén chuáng double bed
双人间 shuāngrén jiān double room
双人房 shuāngrén fáng twin room
双程(票) shuāngchéng (piào) return (ticket)
书 shū book ⓝ
幻灯片 huàndēng piàn slide (film)

五画 5 strokes

未婚夫 wèihūnfū fiancé
未婚妻 wèihūnqī fiancée
去 qù go
玉米 yùmǐ corn
打开 dǎkāi open ⓥ
打火机 dǎhuǒjī cigarette lighter
打电话 dǎ diànhuà telephone ⓥ
打印机 dǎyìnjī printer (computer)
打扫 dǎsǎo clean ⓐ
打扮 dǎbàn make-up ⓝ

五画

打针 dǎzhēn injection
古代 gǔdài ancient
古典 gǔdiǎn classical
古董 gǔdǒng antique ⓝ
古董市场 gǔdǒng shìchǎng antique market
艾滋病 àizībìng AIDS
节日 jiérì festival
左边 zuǒbian left (direction)
右边 yòubian right (direction)
石油 shíyóu oil (food) ⓝ
头 tóu head ⓝ
头巾 tóujīn scarf
头疼 tóuténg headache
头等舱 tóuděng cāng first class
商务舱 shāngwù cāng business class
东方 dōngfāng east
北边 běibian north
北京烤鸭 Běijīng kǎoyā Peking duck
以上 yǐshàng on
以外 yǐwài without
以后 yǐhòu after • later
目的地 mùdì dì destination
兄弟 xiōngdi brother
叫 jiào call ⓥ
叫醒 jiàoxǐng wake (someone) up
(美)元 (Měi) yuán (American) dollar
号码 hàomǎ number ⓝ
电子用品店 diànzǐ yòngpǐn diàn electrical store
电子邮件 diànzǐ yóujiàn email ⓝ
电子舞会 diànzǐ wǔhuì rave ⓝ
电风扇 diànfēngshàn fan (machine)
电池 diànchí battery
电报 diànbào telegram
电视 diànshì television
电话 diànhuà telephone
电话卡 diànhuà kǎ phonecard
电梯 diàntī elevator/lift
电影 diànyǐng movie
电影院 diànyǐngyuàn cinema
四月 sìyuè April
生日 shēngrì birthday
生意 shēngyì business ⓝ
皮革 pígé leather ⓝ
付款 fùkuǎn payment

代理费 dàilǐ fèi commission
他 tā he
他的 tāde his
乐队 yuèduì band (music)
冬天 dōngtiān winter
外套 wàitào jacket
外国人 wàiguó rén foreigner
外面 wàimian outside
包 bāo bag • packet
包子 bāozi dumpling (steamed)
包括 bāokuò included
包裹 bāoguǒ package • parcel ⓝ
写 xiě write
市中心 shìzhōngxīn city centre
市场 shìchǎng market ⓝ
白天 báitiān day
白色 báisè white
半个 bàngè half
礼物 lǐwù present ⓝ
记者 jìzhě journalist
民主主义 mínzhǔ zhǔyì democracy
出口 chūkǒu exit ⓝ
出去 chūqù go out
出发 chūfā departure
出生日 chūshēngrì date of birth
出生证 chūshēngzhèng birth certificate
出纳 chūnà cashier
出事 chūshì emergency ⓝ
出差 chūchāi business trip
出租车 chūzū chē taxi
出租车站 chūzū chē zhàn taxi stand
奶奶 nǎinai grandmother (paternal)
奶酪 nǎilào cream (dairy)
加油站 jiāyóu zhàn service station
加拿大 Jiānádà Canada
加油站 jiāyóu zhàn petrol station
发动机 fādòngjī engine
发烧 fāshāo fever
发票 fāpiào receipt
边界 biānjiè border ⓝ
圣诞节 shèngdànjié Christmas
对方付款电话 duìfāng fùkuǎn diànhuà collect call
台阶 táijiē stairway
台湾 Táiwān Taiwan
母亲 mǔqīn mother ⓝ

幼儿园 yòu'éryuán childminding ⓝ
丝绸 sīchóu silk ⓝ

六画 6 strokes

买 mǎi buy ⓥ
买东西 mǎi dōngxi shop ⓥ
亚麻布 yàmá bù linen (material)
交换 jiāohuàn exchange ⓝ
价格 jiàgé cost • price ⓝ
休闲裤 xiūxián kù track pants
休息 xiūxi intermission ⓝ
会议 huìyì conference (big)
会合 huìhé conference (small)
传真机 chuánzhēnjī fax machine
伤害 shānghài injury
先生 xiānsheng Mr
光 guāng light ⓝ
光盘 (CD) CD [English pronunciation] CD
共产主义 gòngchǎn zhǔyì communism
关 guān shut
关口 guānkǒu pass (mountain)
关门 guānmén closed
关闭 guānbì close ⓐ
再一个 zài yīge another
再见 zàijiàn goodbye
军人 jūnrén soldier
农民 nóngmín farmer (peasant)
冰 bīng ice ⓝ
冰冻 bīngdòng frozen
冰箱 bīngxiāng refrigerator
动物 dòngwù animal ⓝ
动物园 dòngwù yuán zoo
危险 wēixiǎn dangerous
吃饭 chīfàn eat
吃的 chīde food
吃素的 chīsù de vegetarian ⓐ
同……一样 tóng ... yīyàng like
同伙 tónghuǒ companion
同志 (吧) tóngzhì (bā) gay (bar)
同事 tóngshì colleague
同性恋 tóngxìng liàn homosexual ⓝ
名字 míngzi given name • name
后 hòu rear (seat etc)
后天 hòutiān day after tomorrow

团体旅行 tuántǐ lǚxíng guided tour
因特网 yīntèwǎng internet
回来 huílái return (come back)
在……上 zài ... shàng aboard
在……里面 zài ... lǐmiàn in
地方 dìfang local
地址 dìzhǐ address ⓝ
地图 dìtú map ⓝ
地铁 dìtiě subway
地铁站 dìtiě zhàn subway station
地震 dìzhèn earthquake
(网球)场 (wǎngqiú) chǎng court (tennis)
多 duō more
她的 tāde her
好 hǎo good
好香 hǎoxiāng tasty
字幕 zìmù subtitles
存钱 cúnqián deposit (bank)
孙女 sūnnǚ granddaughter
孙子 sūnzi grandson
安全 ānquán safe ⓐ
安全性交 ānquán xìngjiāo safe sex
安全带 ānquándài seatbelt
安静 ānjìng quiet
导游 dǎoyóu guide (person) ⓝ
年 nián year
年龄 niánlíng age ⓝ
忙得 mángde in a hurry
收费公路 shōufèi gōnglù motorway (tollway)
收音机 shōuyīnjī radio ⓝ
收银台 shōuyín tái cash register
早 zǎo early
早上 zǎoshàng morning ⓝ
早饭 zǎofàn breakfast ⓝ
约会 yuēhuì appointment
有事 yǒushì engaged (occupied)
有空 yǒukòng free (available) • vacant
有空调的 yǒu kōngtiáo de air-conditioned
有保证 yǒu bǎozhèng guaranteed
有病 yǒubìng ill
有暖气 yǒu nuǎnqì heated
机场税 jīchǎng shuì airport tax
杂技 zájì circus

灰色 huīsè grey
爷爷 yéye grandfather (paternal)
百货商店 bǎihuò shāngdiàn department store
米 mǐ metre
米饭 mǐfàn rice (cooked)
红色 hóngsè red
纪念品 jìniàn pǐn souvenir
纪念品店 jìniànpǐn diàn souvenir shop
网吧 wǎngbā internet cafe
网球 wǎngqiú tennis
网球场 wǎngqiú chǎng tennis court
羊毛 yángmáo wool
羊肉 yángròu lamb
耳朵 ěrduo ear
老 lǎo old
老公 lǎogōng husband
老师 lǎoshī teacher
老百姓 lǎobǎixìng common people
老婆 lǎopo wife
肉 ròu meat
肉店 ròudiàn butcher's shop
自动取款机 zìdòng qǔkuǎn jī automated teller machine (ATM)
自行车 zìxíngchē bicycle ⑩
自行车骑手 zìxíngchē qíshǒu cyclist
自助 zìzhù self service
血型 xuèxíng blood group
血液 xuè yè blood
行李 xínglǐ luggage
行李寄存 xínglǐ jìcún luggage lockers
行李领取处 xínglǐ lǐngqǔ qù baggage claim
衣服 yīfu clothing
西 xī west
西药房 xīyào fáng pharmacy
西班牙 Xībānyá Spain
西藏 Xīzàng Tibet
许可证 xǔkězhèng pass (permit)
过时 guòshí off (spoiled)
过夜 guòyè overnight
超重(行李) chāozhòng xínglǐ excess (baggage)
那个 nàge that (one)
那边 nàbian there
防晒油 fángshài yóu sunblock

七画 7 strokes

两个 liǎnggè two
两个都 liǎnggèdōu both
住宿 zhùsù accommodation
体育用品店 tǐyù yòngpǐn diàn sports store/shop
体育场 tǐyù chǎng stadium
运动员 yùndòng yuán sportsperson
佛寺 fósì monastery (Buddhist)
佛教 Fójiào Buddhism
佛教徒 Fójiào tú Buddhist
你 nǐ you inf
克 kè gram
免疫针 miǎnyì zhēn vaccination
免费 miǎnfèi free (gratis)
免费行李 miǎnfèi xínglǐ baggage allowance
兑现 duìxiàn cash (a cheque)
兑换率 duìhuàn lǜ exchange rate
冷 lěng cold
医学 yīxué medicine (study, profession)
医药 yīyào medicine (medication)
医院 yīyuàn hospital
吵 chǎo loud
帐单 zhàngdān bill (restaurant etc)
听 tīng listen (to)
坏了 huàile out of order
坟地 féndì cemetery
妓女 jìnǚ prostitute
尿裤 niàokù diaper/nappy
层 céng floor (storey)
岛 dǎo island
床 chuáng bed
床单 chuángdān bed linen
弟弟 dìdi brother (younger)
快 kuài fast • soon
快乐 kuàilè happy
快递(信) kuàidì xìn express (mail)
怀孕 huáiyùn pregnant
我 wǒ I • me
我们的 wǒmende our
我的 wǒde my
戒指 jièzhǐ ring (on finger)
扶梯 fútī escalator
投诉 tóusù complaint

折扣 zhékòu discount ⓝ
抗菌素 kàngjùnsù antibiotics
护士 hùshì nurse ⓝ
护照 hùzhào passport
护照号码 hùzhào hàomǎ passport number
扭伤 niǔshāng sprain ⓝ
报纸 bàozhǐ newspaper
抛锚 pāomáo broken down (car)
时刻表 shíkè biǎo timetable ⓝ
时差反应 shíchà fǎnyìng jet lag
更大 gèngdà bigger
更小 gèngxiǎo smaller
更好 gènghǎo better
更衣室 gēngyīshì changing room
来信 láixìn mail (letters)
步行 bùxíng hike ⓥ
每（天）měi(tiān) per (day)
每个 měige each
每个人 měige rén everyone
每次 měicì every
沙滩 shātān beach
沙漠 shāmò desert
汽油 qìyóu oil (petroleum) • petrol
没空 méikòng no vacancy
男人 nánrén man (male person)
男女事 nánnǚ shì sex
男朋友 nánpéngyou boyfriend
男孩子 nán háizi boy
社会主义战士 shèhuì zhǔyì zhànshì socialist
私人 sīrén private
纸巾 zhǐjīn tissues
纸币 zhǐbì banknote
罕见 hǎnjiàn rare (uncommon)
肚子 dùzi stomach
肚子疼 dùzi téng indigestion • stomach ache
肠胃炎 chángwèiyán gastroenteritis
花园 huāyuán garden ⓝ
花粉热 huāfěn rè hay fever
苏格兰 Sūgélán Scotland
证件 zhèngjiàn identification • papers (official documents)
词典 cídiǎn dictionary
豆浆 dòujiāng soy milk (fresh)
豆腐 dòufu tofu

走廊 zǒuláng aisle (on plane)
走路 zǒulù walk ⓥ
足够 zúgòu enough
足球 zúqiú football (soccer)
身份证 shēnfèn zhèng identification card (ID)
近 jìn near
这个 zhège this (one)
这里 zhèlǐ here
进港口 jìngǎngkǒu arrivals
远 yuǎn far
连衣裙 liányīqún dress ⓝ
连接 liánjiē connection
迟到 chídào late
邮电 yóudiàn mail (postal system)
邮政编码 yóuzhèng biānmǎ post code
邮局 yóujú post office
邮票 yóupiào stamp ⓝ
针灸 zhēnjiǔ acupuncture
针线 zhēnxiàn needle (sewing)
阿姨 āyí aunt
阿斯匹林 āsīpǐlín aspirin
附近 fùjìn nearby
（陆运）平信 (lùyùn) píngxìn surface mail (land)
饭馆 fànguǎn restaurant
饮料 yǐnliào drink ⓝ
鸡 jī chicken
鸡蛋 jīdàn egg (chicken)

八画 **8 strokes**

现代 xiàndài modern
现在 xiànzài now
现金 xiànjīn cash ⓝ
表演 biǎoyǎn show ⓝ & ⓥ
武术（中国功夫）wǔshù (Zhōngguó gōngfu) martial arts (Chinese kung fu)
其他 qítā other
取消 qǔxiāo cancel
抽烟 chōuyān smoke ⓥ
拉稀 lāxī diarrhoea
拉链 lāliàn zip/zipper
事故 shìgù accident
卧室 wòshì bedroom
卧铺车厢 wòpù chēxiāng sleeping car
直接 zhíjiē direct

八画

直播 zhíbō direct dial
苦 kǔ bitter
英文 Yīngwén English
英文老师 Yīngwén lǎoshī English teacher
英国 Yīngguó England
英俊 yīngjùn handsome
雨伞 yǔsǎn umbrella
雨衣 yǔyī raincoat
杯子 bēizi cup ⓝ
枕头 zhěntou pillow
画 huà painting (a work)
画儿 huàhuàr painting (the art)
画家 huàjiā painter
厕所 cèsuǒ toilet
矿泉水 kuàngquán shuǐ mineral water
转机室 zhuǎnjī shì transit lounge
软卧 ruǎnwò soft sleeper
软座 ruǎnzuò soft seat
软盘 ruǎnpán disk (floppy)
轮椅 lúnyǐ wheelchair
轮胎 lúntāi tyre
欧元 Ōuyuán euro
欧洲 Ōuzhōu Europe
到 dào to (go to, come to)
垃圾 lājī garbage
垃圾箱 lājī xiāng garbage can
周末 zhōumò weekend
味道 wèidao smell ⓝ
咖啡 kāfēi coffee
咖啡色 kāfēi sè brown
咖啡屋 kāfēi wū cafe
国际象棋 guójì xiàngqí chess (international)
国家 guójiā country (nation)
明天 míngtiān tomorrow
明天下午 míngtiān xiàwǔ tomorrow afternoon
明天早上 míngtiān zǎoshàng tomorrow morning
明天晚上 míngtiān wǎnshàng tomorrow evening
明信片 míngxìnpiàn postcard
朋友 péngyou friend
服务 fúwù service ⓝ
服务员 fúwù yuán waiter
服务费 fúwù fèi service charge

服装店 fúzhuāngdiàn clothing store
肥皂 féizào soap
图书馆 túshū guǎn library
账单 zhàngdān (bank) account
账单 zhàngdān check (bill)
钓鱼 diàoyú fishing
刮脸 guāliǎn shave
刮痧 guāshā cupping (therapy)
季节 jìjié season ⓝ
岳父 yuèfù father-in-law
岳母 yuèmǔ mother-in-law
昏迷 hūnmí unconscious
货币兑换 huòbì duìhuàn currency exchange
往后退 wǎnghòutuì delay ⓝ
炸 zhá fry (stir-fry)
炒菜 chǎocài cook ⓥ
贪污 tānwū corrupt
鱼 yú fish ⓝ
鱼摊 yútān fish shop
狗 gǒu dog
京剧 jīngjù classical theatre
京剧 jīngjù opera (Chinese)
夜总会 yèzǒnghuì nightclub
店 diàn shop ⓝ
废墟 fèixū ruins
闹钟 nàozhōng alarm clock
定 dìng book (make a booking)
定满 dìngmǎn booked out
宝贝 bǎobèi child
实惠 shíhuì cheap
空 kōng empty
空房 kòngfáng vacancy
法国 Fǎguó France
法律 fǎlǜ law (study, professsion)
注射针 zhùshè zhēn needle (syringe)
浅色 qiǎnsè light (of colour)
单人 dānrén single (person)
单人间 dānrén jiān single room
单程 dānchéng one-way (ticket)
学生 xuéshēng student
房东 fángdōng landlord
房地产公司 fángdìchǎn gōngsī estate agency
房间 fángjiān room
房间号 fángjiān hào room number

九画

肩膀 jiānbǎng shoulder
衬衫 chènshān shirt
视野 shìyě view ⓝ
建筑师 jiànzhùshī architect
建筑学 jiànzhùxué architecture
录像机 lùxiàng jī video recorder
妹妹 mèimei sister (younger)
姐姐 jiějie sister (elder)
姓 xìng family name
驾照 jiàzhào driver's licence
纸 zhǐ paper
经络按摩 jīngluò ànmó pressure point massage
经济舱 jīngjì cāng economy class

九画 **9 strokes**

春天 chūntiān spring (season)
毒品 dúpǐn drug (illicit)
玻璃杯 bōli bēi glass (drinking)
玻璃 bōli glass (material)
帮助 bāngzhù help ⓝ
帮 bāng help ⓥ
城市 chéngshì city
项链 xiàngliàn necklace
挂号 guàhào registered mail/post ⓝ
指 zhǐ point ⓥ
指头 zhǐtou finger
指南书 zhǐnán shū guidebook
按摩 ànmó massage ⓝ
按摩师 ànmó shī masseur • masseuse
垫子 diànzi mattress
政治 zhèngzhì politics
胡同 hútòng alleyway
点心 diǎnxīn dim sum
药片 yàopiàn pill
药方 yàofāng prescription
药剂师 yàojì shī chemist/pharmacist
药房 yàofáng chemist (shop)
药品 yàopǐn drug (medication)
茶馆 cháguǎn teahouse
南 nán south ⓝ
要紧 yàojǐn urgent
树荫 shùyīn shade ⓝ
迷路 mílù lost (one's way)
厘米 límǐ centimetre
残疾 cánjí disabled
面包 miànbāo bread

面馆 miànguǎn noodle house
面条 miàntiáo noodles
止泻药 zhǐxiè yào laxative
轻 qīng light (not heavy)
背 bèi back (body)
背包 bèibāo backpack
背面 bèimiàn behind
尝试 chángshì try ⓥ
新加坡 Xīnjiāpō Singapore
星期 xīngqī week
星期一 xīngqī yī Monday
星期二 xīngqī èr Tuesday
星期三 xīngqī sān Wednesday
星期四 xīngqī sì Thursday
星期五 xīngqī wǔ Friday
星期六 xīngqī liù Saturday
星期天 xīngqī tiān Sunday
哪里 nǎli where
哪个 nǎge which
是 shì yes
昨天 zuótiān yesterday
贵 guì expensive
罚款 fákuǎn fine (penalty)
贵重 guìzhòng valuable
钥匙 yàoshi key ⓝ
钢笔 gāngbǐ pen (ballpoint)
重 zhòng heavy ⓐ
重要 zhòngyào important
香烟 xiāngyān cigarette
香港 Xiānggǎng Hong Kong
秋天 qiūtiān autumn/fall
科学 kēxué science
科学家 kēxué jiā scientist
复活节 fùhuójié Easter
饺子 jiǎozi dumpling (boiled)
便秘 biànmì constipation
保险 bǎoxiǎn insurance
修理 xiūlǐ repair ⓥ
信 xìn letter (mail)
信用 xìnyòng credit
信用卡 xìnyòng kǎ credit card
信息 xìnxī message
信息 xìnxī information
信息技术 xìnxī jìshù IT
信箱 xìnxiāng mailbox
徒步旅行 túbù lǚxíng hiking
很硬 hěn yìng hard (not soft)

十画

律师 lǜshī lawyer
很疼 hěnténg painful
食品 shípǐn grocery
受伤 shòushāng injured
独自一个人 dú zì yīge rén alone
急救车 jíjiù chē ambulance
急急忙忙 jíjí mángmang busy (occupied)
急救装备 jíjiù zhuāngbèi first-aid kit
临时保姆 línshí bǎomǔ babysitter
亭子 tíngzi pavillion
疮口 chuāngkǒu cut (wound)
度假 dùjià vacation
音乐会 yīnyuè huì concert
音乐 yīnyuè music
音像店 yīnxiàng diàn music shop
皇帝 huángdì emperor
皇后 huánghòu empress
美丽 měilì beautiful
姜 jiāng ginger
美国 Měiguó USA
首饰 shǒushì jewellery
前一个 qián yīge last (previous) ⓐ
前天 qiántiān day before yesterday
宫殿 gōngdiàn palace
客户 kèhù client
洪水 hóngshuǐ flood
洋(货) yáng (huò) foreign (goods)
洗 xǐ wash (something)
洗衣店 xǐyī diàn launderette
洗衣服 xǐyīfu laundry (clothes)
洗衣机 xǐyī jī washing machine
测光表 cèguāng biǎo light meter
派出所 pàichū suǒ police station
剃刀 tìdāo razor
剃刀片 tìdāo piàn razor blade
语言 yǔyán language
祖先 zǔxiān ancestors
说明书 shuōmíng shū brochure
退休职工 tuìxiū zhígōng pensioner
退钱 tuìqián refund ⓝ
孩子们 háizimen children
除夕 chúxī New Year's Eve

十画 10 strokes

换 huàn change • exchange
换钱 huànqián change (money)

热 rè hot ⓐ
热气 rèqì heat ⓝ
热水瓶 rèshuǐpíng thermos
热水袋 rèshuǐ dài hot water bottle
哥哥 gēge brother (elder)
恭喜 gōngxǐ congratulations
荷兰 Hélán Netherlands
桥 qiáo bridge
粉色 fěnsè pink
夏天 xiàtiān summer
党员 dǎngyuán communist (party member)
轿车 jiàochē car
晒伤 shàishāng sunburn
晕车 yùnchē travel sickness
晚上 wǎnshàng evening • night
晚上活动 wǎnshàng huódòng night out
晚饭 wǎnfàn dinner
胳膊 gēbo arm ⓝ
胶卷 jiāojuǎn film (for camera)
胸 xiōng chest (body)
脆弱 cuìruò fragile
脏 zāng dirty
钱 qián money
钱包 qiánbāo purse
铅笔 qiānbǐ pencil
乘客 chéngkè passenger
租赁 zūlìn rent ⓥ
透镜 tòujìng lens
预定 yùdìng reservation (booking)
饿 è hungry (to be)
笔记本 bǐjì běn notebook
健美中心 jiànměi zhōngxīn gym (place)
烟丝 yānsī tobacco
烤面包 kǎo miànbāo toast
烧伤 shāoshāng burn ⓝ
烧焦 shāojiāo burnt
爱 ài love ⓥ
爱尔兰 Ài'ěrlán Ireland
爱情 àiqíng love ⓝ
逛酒吧 guàng jiǔbā party (night out)
酱油 jiàngyóu soy sauce
离开 líkāi depart (leave)
离婚 líhūn divorced
高 gāo high ⓐ

高尔夫场 gāo'ěrfū chǎng golf course
高速公路 gāosù gōnglù highway
准时 zhǔnshí on time
座位 zuòwèi seat (place) ⓝ
病 bìng sick
疼 téng pain
旁边 pángbian beside
站台 zhàntái platform
站台票 zhàntái piào standby ticket
资本主义 zīběn zhǔyì capitalism
旅行支票 lǚxíng zhīpiào travellers cheque
旅行店 lǚxíng diàn tourist office
旅行社 lǚxíng shè travel agency
旅行箱 lǚxíngxiāng suitcase
旅店 lǚdiàn tourist hotel
旅栈 lǚzhàn youth hostel
旅程 lǚchéng journey
航空信 hángkōng xìn airmail
航空公司 hángkōng gōngsī airline
航班 hángbān flight
家 jiā home
家具 jiājù furniture
家庭 jiātíng family
宾馆 bīnguǎn guesthouse
酒吧 jiǔbā bar ⓝ
酒店 jiǔdiàn hotel
酒 jiǔ drink (alcoholic)
酒精 jiǔjīng alcohol
消毒剂 xiāodújì antiseptic
消费 xiāofèi tip (gratuity) ⓝ
海 hǎi sea
海外 hǎiwài overseas
海关 hǎiguān custom (immigration)
(海运)平信 (hǎiyùn) píngxìn surface mail (sea)
浴室 yùshì bathroom • shower ⓝ
浴缸 yùgāng bath
润滑油 rùnhuá yóu lubricant
(电)流 (diàn) liú current (electricity)
递送 dìsòng deliver
浪漫 làngmàn romantic
瓶子 píngzi bottle ⓝ
逛街 guàngjiē go shopping
谁 shéi who
袜子 wàzi sock
剧 jù play (theatre)

剧场 jùchǎng theatre
展览 zhǎnlǎn exhibition
陶瓷 táocí ceramics
娱乐指南 yúlè zhǐnán entertainment guide
预备食品 yùbèi shípǐn food supplies

十一画

十一画 11 strokes

理发 lǐfà haircut
理发屋 lǐfà wū hairdresser
推荐 tuījiàn recommend
博物馆 bówù guǎn museum
搭便车 dā biànchē hitchhike
票 piào ticket ⓝ
票房 piàofáng ticket office
黄色 huángsè yellow
黄金 huángjīn gold ⓝ
剪刀 jiǎndāo scissors
剪指刀 jiǎnzhǐ dāo nail clippers
菊花 júhuā chrysanthemum
菜单 càidān menu
营业时间 yíngyè shíjiān opening hours
非典 fēidiǎn SARS
雪 xuě snow ⓝ
救人！jiùrén! Help!
厨子 chúzi cook ⓝ
厨房 chúfáng kitchen
奢侈 shēchǐ luxury
插头 chātóu plug (electricity)
帽子 màozi hat
喝 hē drink
啤酒 píjiǔ beer
啤酒摊 píjiǔ tān liquor store
眼睛 yǎnjīng eye(s)
眼镜 yǎnjìng glasses (spectacles)
累 lèi tired
脖子 bózi throat
脚 jiǎo foot
脚踝 jiǎohuái ankle
脸 liǎn face
野餐 yěcān picnic ⓝ
银子 yínzi silver
银行 yínháng bank (money)
银行账户 yínháng zhànghù bank account
甜 tián sweet

蒙古 Ménggǔ Mongolia
蓝色 lánsè blue
零钱 língqián change (coins)
楼 lóu building
楼房 lóufáng apartment (downmarket)
感光度 gǎnguāngdù film speed
感冒 gǎnmào influenza
感冒药 gǎnmào yào cough medicine
感染 gǎnrǎn infection
感谢 gǎnxiè grateful
碗 wǎn bowl ⓝ
暖气管 nuǎnqì guǎn heater
照片 zhàopiàn photo
暖和 nuǎnhuo warm
照相 zhàoxiàng take a photo
照相机 zhàoxiàng jī camera
睡觉 shuìjiào sleep ⓥ
睡袋 shuìdài sleeping bag
腿 tuǐ leg
跳舞 tiàowǔ dance
矮 ǎi short (height)
筷子 kuàizi chopsticks
签证 qiānzhèng visa
车锁 chēsuǒ lock
微波炉 wēibō lú microwave (oven) ⓝ
解放军 jiěfàng jūn People's Liberation Army (PLA)
煤气 méiqì gas (for cooking)
遥控 yáokòng remote control
新 xīn new
新西兰 Xīnxīlán New Zealand
新闻 xīnwén news
新鲜 xīnxiān fresh
塑像 sùxiàng sculpture
塞子 sāizi plug (bath)
满 mǎn full

十四画 **14 strokes**

碟子 diézi disk (CD-ROM)
磁带 cídài tape (recording) ⓝ

十四画

棒 bàng great (fantastic)
慢慢地 mànmande slowly
墨镜 mòjìng sunglasses
舞蹈 wǔdǎo dancing
辣椒 làjiāo chilli
辣椒酱 làjiāo jiàng chilli sauce
鼻子 bízi nose
演出 yǎnchū performance
演员 yǎnyuán actor
蜜月 mìyuè honeymoon
熊猫 xióngmāo panda

十五画 **15 strokes**

蔬菜 shūcài vegetable
醉 zuì drunk
鞋 xié shoe
鞋店 xiédiàn shoe shop
膝盖 xīgài knee
镊子 nièzi tweezers
镑 bàng pound (money, weight)
箱子 xiāngzi box ⓝ
德国 Déguó Germany
摩托车 mótuō chē motorcycle ⓝ
颜色 yánsè colour
澳大利亚 Àodàlìyà Australia

十六至二十三画 **16 to 23 strokes**

橙色 chéngsè orange (colour)
糖尿病 tángniàobìng diabetes
赠(票) zèng (piào) complimentary (tickets)
穆斯林 Mùsīlín Muslim
避孕套 bìyùntào condom
餐巾 cānjīn napkin
餐车 cānchē dining car
翻译 fānyì interpreter • translator
警察 jǐngchá police • police officer (in city)
罐头 guàntou can/tin

Index

For topics that are covered in several sections of this book, we've indicated the most relevant page number in bold.

10 Ways to Start a Sentence

When does (the next bus) leave?	(下一趟车) 几点走?	(Xià yītàng chē) jǐdiǎn zǒu?
Where's (the tourist office)?	(旅行社) 在哪儿?	(Lǚxíng shè) zài nǎr?
How much is (the deposit)?	(押金) 多少?	(Yājīn) duōshǎo?
Do you have (a room)?	有没有 (房)?	Yǒuméiyǒu (fáng)?
Is there (heating)?	有(暖气)吗?	Yóu (nuǎnqì) ma?
I'd like (that one).	我要(那个)。	Wǒ yào (nàge).
Please give me (the menu).	请给我 (菜单)。	Qǐng gěiwǒ (càidān).
Can I (sit here)?	我能 (坐这儿)吗?	Wǒ néng (zuòzhèr) ma?
I need (a can opener).	我想要 (一个开罐器)。	Wǒ xiǎngyào (yīge kāiguàn qì).
Do we need (a guide)?	需要 (向导)吗?	Xūyào (xiàngdǎo) ma?